TRIBES AND GOVERNMENT POLICIES

TRIBES AND GOVERNMENT POLICIES

Edited by
J.S. Bhandari
And
Subhadra Mitra Channa
Department of Anthropology
Delhi University, Delhi.

COSMO PUBLICATIONS
1997 India

ISBN : 81-7020-696-0

First Published : **1997**

Manufactured in India

Published By :
MRS. RANI KAPOOR
COSMO PUBLICATIONS
***For* GENESIS PUBLISHING (P) LTD.**
24-B, Ansari Road,
Darya Ganj,
New Delhi-110002

Lasertypeset by:
HYLITE GRAFIX

Dedicated to
The Memory of
Prof. K.S. Mathur
and
Prof. L.P. Vidhyarthi

Whose contribution to the discipline of Social Anthropology in teaching, research and its development in India remain unmatched.

Dedicated to
The Memory of
Prof. K.S. Mathur
and
Prof. L.P. Vidyarthi

Whose contribution to the discipline of Social Anthropology in teaching, research and its development in India remain unmatched.

Preface

A great deal of interest was generated about the so called tribal people of the world in the past several years, mostly because of their own emergence onto the political scene of the world as assertive pressure groups. Slowly and steadily, the tribal people everywhere have found their voice and it has been raised loud and clear, again and again, in their search for an identity.

The self-assertion of the tribes and their changing political role has forced the rulers, administrators and academicians to sit up and take a fresh look at them, giving rise to much debate and discussion regarding their changing politico-economic status in today's world.

A seminar was held in the Department of Anthropology, Delhi University, in the year 1992, which was in keeping with the renewed interest in the tribal people of the world and the changing perspective on them. This Seminar was organized around the theme of government policies with respect to tribes and the various planned projects directed towards them. However, the seminar, which was attended by many administrators and social-workers,aswell as scholars and students from several disciplines, raised many issues and led to debates on many points.

A point at which questions were raised, right at the beginning, in fact during the inaugural session itself, was in regard to the use of the term 'tribe', in preference to the term indigenous- which was viewed by many, including scholars and academicians, to be the politically correct usage. It is this very political usage of this term to which we as anthropologists, disagree inspite of its current popularity and status of being 'in vogue'. The term 'tribe' as used here is in a cultural sense and hence neutral in a political historical context. The term 'indigenous was in this perspective understood to be value laden, implying certain anomalies in the political positioning of groups not commensurate with their historical positioning. In other words, it simply meant that those who were new comers to certain lands had usurped all the resources of those who were 'indigenous', and therefore the rightful owners. The problem of 'new comer' and 'late comer' becomes a matter of debate when we have no standard measure of time scale on which this criterion is to be applied. It then becomes a matter of political interpretation and the use of time becomes a strategic tool for manipulating political opinions.

A second approach is to assess the situation more objectively, seeing the actual distribution of resources, the historicity of the situation and the game of power between the various groups, without presupposing any prior opinion,-which was the general framework adopted by most scholars to the seminar.

Apart from the terminological debate there is little difference of opinion among scholars as to the political status of tribes. They have definitely been on the losing side and in the distribution of resources, definitely been robbed rather than rewarded.

Administrators, government officials, academicians and the tribals themselves (who were both academicians and administrators) were invited to speak and discuss various dimensions of the problem, presenting different points of view. The book encompasses much of those discussions, containing in addition, invited papers from a number of specialists.

The editors are indeed greatful to the Ministry of Welfare, Tribal division, Government of India; to the Jt. Sec. Mr. P.K. Mohanty, Deputy Director, Mr P.K. Mohanty and the Senior Research Officer Mr R.K. Mohapatra. We are also indebted to a number of young and enthusiastic colleagues whose efforts went into making the seminar a success, of whom we must mention Mr. Sukant Choudhury, Dr. Soumendra Patnaik and a number of research scholars who put in tremendous efforts.This volume is a testimony to the interest created by the seminar and the valuable material it generated.

We are also extremely thankful to all the contributors, both the participants to the seminar and those who responded to our invitation to contribute papers, even though they coulld not be present for the seminar.

We are also thankful to all our friends and well wishers whose number is too large to mention individually but whose good wishes and moral support have provided encouragement and motivation.

(Dept. of Anthropology, University of Delhi:) **Prof. J.S. Bhandari**
Dr. Subhadra Mitra Channa

Contents

About the Contributors

1.	Prof. J.S. Bhandari	: Prof. of Social Anthropology, Delhi University.
2.	Dr. S. M. Channa	: Reader in Social Anthropology, Delhi University.
3.	Prof. B.K. Roy Burman	: Senior Fellow, Centre for the Study of Developing societies, New Delhi.
4.	Prof. A.P. Sinha	: Retd. Prof. and Head, Dept. of Sociology, N.E.H.U. Shillong.
5.	Prof. Sachchidananda	: Director (Retd) A.N. Sinha Institute of Social Sciences. Patna.
6.	Dr. Bhupinder Singh	: Director : Council for Social Development. 53, Lodi Estate, New Delhi-110003.
7.	Prof. B. Pakem	: Vice-Chancellor, North Eastern Hill University Shillong.
8.	Dr. C.B. Tripathi	: Commission for Schedul Castes and Scheduled Tribes, Govt. of India, New Delhi.
9.	Prof. B. Chaudhuri	: Prof. Dept. of South and S.E. Asian Studies, Calcutta University.

10. Dr. Walter Fernandes	:	Editor, 'Social Action' Indian Social Institute. Lodi Estate, New Delhi.
11. Prof. Jagannath Pathy	:	Prof. of Sociology, South Gujarat University.
12. Dr. Lancy Lobo	:	Fellow, Centre for Social Studies, South Gujarat University Campus, Gujarat.
13. Prof. M.L. Patel	:	Director, Research, Bhartiya Adim Jati Sevak Sangh. Thakkar Bapa Smarak Sadan. New Delhi.
14. Prof. A.C. Sinha	:	Prof. of Sociology, Dept. of Sociology, N.E.H.U.
15. Prof. A.R.N. Srivastava	:	Prof. and Head of the Dept. Anthropology & Biology University of Allahabad, Allahabad.
16. Dr. Gangwar	:	Centre for Environment Education, Nehru Foundation for Development, Thaltj Tekra, Ahmedabad.
17. Dr. Tiplut Nongbri	:	Associate, Institute of Development Studies, University of Sussex, England.
18. Mr. S. K. Chaudhury	:	Lecturer, Department of Sociology, Lucknow University Lucknow.

Introduction

Tribal Policy

Issues And Themes

Subhadra Mitra Channa

The very phrase, 'Tribal Policy in India' involves a host of questions. Why specifically a Tribal Policy ? Who are the tribes ? What is the need for a policy for them ? Who makes the policy ? These questions are rooted in both conceptual and practical discourse. They become relevant in the context of an ideological evolution and the practical actions which the ideas inform.

Without much debate we can contextualize the origin of the concept to the colonization by the west and the theoretical discourse regarding the nature of civilized society and the State. The early western thinkers developed a dialectical mode of thinking in which they always tried to understand something by that which it was not.

The word tribe arises as an anti-thesis of the word nontribe. In order to understand themselves and their own society which they labelled as a civilization, western thinkers looked to an opposed category which would reflect back their own characters by default. It did not matter, as Kuper (1988) has aptly described that this opposite was only an illusion. Before a theory of civilization there were no tribes.

It is not of relevance for us to go into the entire gamut of the formation of the concept tribe and its various connotations, as much has already been written on this. In discussing Tribal Policy, the one aspect with which we should be concerned is the place of the 'tribe' in the formation of a Nation-State and the relations of power and hierarchy that inform this position.

By and large the post-World War formation of large Nation-States of the world has been a historical process to which the early part of the twentieth century has been witness. It is another matter that the later part of this very century has seen the disintegration of some of them. In fact it is this process that has rekindled interest in what really constitutes a Nation-State ?

From the point of view of the centralized power structure of the Nation-State which is always ideological as well as hegemonical, the Nation is an ongoing constructive process, it is always projected in terms of a mythical', a common identity, expressed through a powerful set of symbols, the National flag, the National anthem, the National institutions, etc. However, this process of construction is at the expense of individual identities, the Nation constructs itself by a process of deconstruction, a breakdown of identities, to be merged into one. This, however, is at the ideological level only. At the action level the process is not smooth, it is not voluntary, it is necessarily a process inherently violent both physically and psychologically. It is also essentially one which involves elements of racism.

Race is not merely understood as a biological construct but as an abstraction involving the basic element of separatism on the basis of gradation. "Race" is a concept that basically arose from the misplaced concept of "progress" and is thus value laden, values which go into the conceptualization of 'ethnic groups', tribes, etc.

As Wallerstein puts it, "A race is supposed to be a genetic category which has a physical form...A 'nation' is supposed to be a socio-political category, to actual or potential boundaries of a state. An 'ethnic group' is supposed to be a cultural category, of which there are said to be certain continuing behaviour that are passed on from generation to generation and that are not usually linked in theory to state boundaries". (1991 : 77)

In reality, however, there is very little definitional clarity of these terms. All that exists is an interpretative understanding, both relativistic and subjective.

Recently the focus has been on the power equation and the exploitative activities resultant from certain types of labelling rather than on the theoretical conceptualization among scholars who are becoming more aware of what is actually happening to people under certain labels rather than going into hairsplitting discourses over names. In this context, it makes sense to simply accept the label as it is applied to a group or people, by those who have the power to take decisions which affect them. In this sense, the terms Government and 'tribes' become meaningful.

A Nation-State, by its very size and complexity is never composed of a uniform category of people. There are numerous modes of classification and division but the most primary is an ethnic division, because this is supposedly an immutable division. All other categories are based on achievable criterion, only ethnicity is putatively ascribed. It is believed to be inherent. It is based on blood and common ancestory.

A democratic Nation-State based on capitalist ideology is ideally one in which people's position should be defined only by an economic criteria. All are uniformly placed within the capitalist free market system. But this does not or cannot happen because there are pre-existing systems of differences. These differences are prior to the formation of the Nation-State and continue into them. In spite of best efforts they refuse to dissolve, their resurgence as ethnicity has created serious fissions in the structures of contemporary Nation-States, leading sometimes to their collapse, as witnessed in Russia.

A Nation-State, in order to defend its identity, evolves a set of policies. These are directed towards preservation of its own identity but disguised as the welfare and preservance of ethnic groups, especially those whose identities are strongly individualistic. It is here I think that one may define a tribe as an entity which is incompletely integrated within a Nation-State. These are those social formations that have their own strong and individualistic identities, they are those who can think of themselves as a 'people'. Their view of their 'past' is independent of the 'past' of the Nation-State. Hence, quite often their view of their present and their future is also independent of the present and future of the Nation-State. Essentially this identity evolves from real or imaginary beliefs of common ancestory, a common 'pastness' as Wallerstein would like to call it and a strong faith in the efficacy of their independent existance.

It is the disruptive possibilities of the assertive independence that has led to the formation of the successive tribal policies. It is the manifestation of a process of continuous struggle between the identity of the Nation-State and the independent identities of the tribes. It is a different matter that differing ideological stances may emphasize one at the expense of the other. The nature of the policies vary from being paternalistic, racist, democratic or discriminative, but the effects have more or less been the same. Whatever intentions have been, good or bad, the outcomes have largely been discriminatory because the power equation behind the policies has always been lop-sided. In a country like India, the overt constitution is non-discriminatory but at the actual level of operations, the ground level realities of power relations and values interfere with the ideal.

All the assertions and protests of the tribals in various movements and upsurge against the hegemony of the Nation-State has been, as well defined by two of the well known policy-makers, Bhupinder Singh and C.B. Tripathi (this volume) been a result of the ethnocentric stand of the policy makers.

Even though a democratic Nation-State like India or the U.S.A. may profess equality for all its constituent ethnic groups, this is only at best an illusion, the very structure of the Nation-State demands a fusion, a common identification or at least a symbolic unity. There must be something that has to be identified as Indian, American, French or Japanese. Given the historically evolved power structure of the Nation-States, both formed by a process of colonization or by long drawn processes of migrations and conquests like India and Russia, it is essential to understand that in defining a common identity, it is the identity of one single dominant group that manifests itself. By implicit reasoning the 'others' are expected to merge their identities into this so called 'mainstream'. (Channa : 1995) In spite of all the ideological assertions of the power holders, there is always a hiatus between professed democracy and the true conditions. Octavio Inanni (1972 : 252) puts its well "the myth of racial democracy is an ideological expression in a society which does not and cannot allow democracy to make advances. The myth reverses the real conditions of existence and the standards of organization of relationships between men". A Nation-State prides its existence, its unity and continuity on such myths.

Nongbri (this volume) takes a critical look at the historical reconstruction of the fusion of the tribes with the so called mainstream population in India. The claims of scholars such as Vidyarthi, Majumdar, N.K. Bose, D.D. Kosambi and Niharranjan Roy has been towards a past unity of the tribes with the mainstream (dominant) Hindu population in the sub-continent. These scholars have gone to painstaking lengths to provide authentic data base to substantiate their arguments. The *'jana'* (Castes) were one, and they later divided into two separate categories. The *"jana"* and the *"jati"*, the latter forming the Hindu Castes and the former, the tribes. Such a claim, pointing to an original unity is directed towards a specific goal, future unity, with its deeply extended roots in the past. It is significant to note that all claims of present unity become authenticated only with reference to a 'past' unity. Without a claim to deep rooted, ancestral kinship, such claims sound superficial and hollow. The line of action for the present is that if we were united in the past, let us unite in the present. But what does this amalgamation mean ? Unity involves a dissolution of differences but there is a definite power hierarchy involved in the process. The tendency is always of the dominant cultures to absorb the marginal ones. However, in spite of their politically weak positions, most ethnic groups exhibit a remarkable resistance to change. Instead of a "melting pot" most Nation-States have emerged as hot beds of revitalized ethnic conflicts. Interesting here is the concept of 'Indigenous people' as opposed to the term 'tribe'. The inherent distinction between these two terms is in the political ideology involved. 'Tribe' is seen essentially as a product of the colonial and capitalist ideology, an entity defined in terms of its progressive and evolutionary characteristics which essentially places it at a scale lower than the more advanced forms of 'the state' and 'the Nation-State'. The colonial anthropology considered the incorporation of the tribal entities with the larger Nation-State as a natural process of progress or evolution, for e.g., Juian Steward's theory of levels of socio-cultural integration. The term 'indigenous people' seeks to reverse the equation, they see the process of smooth incorporation as 'usurping', the Nation-State not as constructive but destructive.

The term indigenous people is related to the notion of social justice. It seeks to return power to the primordial inhabitants of particular land masses. However, the crucial *'catche'* in this process is where and to what point do we turn back the clock ? The past is not as Wallerstein (1991) would put it 'inscribed in stone' the 'past' that is invoked in any political discourse is a construction, its relevance lies in the present political relations which are sought to be justified or upgraded. It is to this end that the Indian delegate at the Geneva conference denied the use of the concept 'indigenous people' as being relevant to the Indian situation (Roy Burman : this volume).

The use of these terms are closely linked to the policy of the Nation-State. In the weakly constructed Nation-States where the relationship between the power holders and the 'independent' entities are still competitive, there is a strong tendency to stick to the concept of Tribe. The ideological significance is that 'they' should become like 'us'. In strongly formed Nation-States like the U.S.A., where the hegemony of the State is already fully established, the competition from the 'ethnic groups' is nearly eliminated. The relationship has now become 'paternalistic'. For such Nations to talk of 'indigenous peoples' is not a threat to the Nations' identity. However, a comparatively newly formed Nation like India cannot afford to indulge in such a political usage. The construction of ethnicity in the sub-continent is far too divisive and yet individualistic and largely independent. Such conceptualization would be a definite threat to the Nations' integrity.

Now where does the anthropologist take a stand ? Can we wish away the ethnic realities as if they did not exist ? Can we afford to give them the kind of independent recognition that they want without threatening the very existence of the Nation ? Pathy, (this volume) pleads strongly for 'self-determination' which he insists is not secessionistic. He refers to the "internal colonial situation" of the Nation-State. He pleads for greater control by tribals of their own resources, greater participation in decision making processes. However, the practicalities of the federal type of structure envisaged by Pathy seems frought with danger, seeing the collapse of some of the Nation-States.

Largely without exception the writers to this volume are critical of the policies framed for the tribals by a succession of governments, starting from the British. Prior to the establishment of colonial rule there is no evidence of an explicitly tribal policy. The tribals were treated as 'people', albeit different but then difference has always been on established feature of the Indian sub-continent.

Sachchidananda (this volume) has given a rather comprehensive picture of the evolution of tribal policy in India. From the British times to modern days one sees a definite change of direction in the policies towards the tribes. From a paternalistic indulgent stand, the so called development plans of the modern Indian government are a direct attack on the identity of the tribals.

Bhupinder Singh (this volume) however turns to the basic issue involved in the formulation of tribal policies. They are invariably formed by those in power and those who are non-tribals. The total assimilationist *vs.* integrative debate falls flat because both are the views of the non-tribals.

The entire crux of the debate revolves around, as mentioned by author after author in this volume, the question of National development *Vs.* individual interests/identities. All policies are implicity directed towards national development. The explicit goals being development of the ethnic groups in their 'own interests'. The truth, as its emerges is that there is a big gap between what the planners peddle as "interest" and what the people percieve as their "own interests".

Several papers in this volume devolve around Nehru's formulation of the *Panchsheel.* While all agree on the honest intentions of the *Panchsheel,* especially the emphasis on letting the tribals develop according to their own genius, there is also a general agreement that the results unfortunately have been quite contrary to the ideals expressed in the charter. As Buddhadeb Choudhary and Walter Fernandes (this volume) have pointed out, there has been increasing commercialization and commodification of natural resources lying in tribal areas. With the connivance of the World Bank, large tracks of natural forests have been converted to commercial forests, causing severe ecological imbalance. As Fernandes correctly observes, planned development approach has treated poverty alievation as a technological problem, whereas the reality of all development policies directed towards the tribals is that they are ideological products of the Nation-State; there remains an inherent contradiction between tribe and industrialization, between equality and productivity.

Another important dimension of development projects undertaken in tribal areas is the displacement suffered by the tribes. As Lobo (this volume) mentions, there is no National Policy for the relocation and rehabilitation of the oustees. Whatever has been mentioned in the policies at the ideological level is totally negated at the implementation level. What actually takes place is rampant corruption, a fact also mentioned by Bhandari. There is a nexus between the capitalists, profiteer and the government agents.

The academicians and social workers have also not come clear in their approach to the tribals. A.C. Sinha and C.B. Tripathy, one academician and the other an administrator himself, have criticized the lackadaisical stand taken by the academicians. According to Tripathy, the academics are only concerned about tribals as subject matters of study. Their approach is impersonal and unconcerned about the human dimension, Sinha especially criticises the anthropologists in India for shying away from any radical politico-economic stand and hence failing to make any impact on government policies. Tripathy has also criticized Gandhian workers like Thakkar Bapa for imposing alien values on the tribals. This moral up-manship is demonstrated by most social workers.

M.L. Patel has highlighted the role of voluntary agencies in promoting awareness and providing feed-back to Government programmes. In fact the voluntary agencies are credited with a broader outlook and more rational approach to tribes than the Government agents.

Two problems remain glaringly visible. One, the outsider/insider dilemma in the formulation of tribal policies and second, the uniform categorization of the term tribe.

As for the second problem, it has been comprehensibly dealt with by J.S. Bhandari and mentioned by a number of authors. Some like Nangbri have mentioned the internal class division among tribes, others have emphasized on the ecological, economic and cultural differences. Buddhadeb Choudhary points to the effect of postive discrimination policies in creating a class division among tribes.

It is probably difficult, given the wide range of socio-economic conditions under which tribes exist, to fully agree with the characterization of tribal people as sharing common features of marginal lives, characterized by poverty and dependence, economic subjugation, socio-cultural stigmatization and lack of political power. One is more inclined to agree with Nongbri in visualizing tribes as having common characteristics of shared principles of cooperation, egalatarianism and value based behaviour. Culture and history seem definitely two more substantive ways of defining what a tribe is, than socio-economic characters, which are both variant and not confined to the tribes alone. Like, if we talk of poverty and exploitation, then they are shared by millions of non-tribals as well. It makes sense to talk of the tribals as entities in term of their history of incorporation into the Nation-State, a history different from subjugated sections of the 'mainstream' population in India, such as the depressed caste's assertions of an identity in terms of cultural and psychological characteristics away from the high castes. Only then such an exercise as formulation and implementation of tribal policy makes sense.

Secondly, having become clear as to for whom the policies are to be made, we come to the second aspect, that is the necessity for a tribal policy. In interesting papers on the views of Gandhi and Nehru on tribal policy, we get a picture of what the framers of the Indian constitution had in mind, while formulating a tribal policy. The most immediate concern of Nehru was a recognition of the independent identity and cultural freedom of the tribals. Gandhi was of a more conservative view to treat them at par culturally but to view them as socially and economically deprived. The policy of positive discrimination was put in at the insistance of Gandhi. The papers in this volume critically analyse both views. Alternative, remedial views have been put forward. From the radical self-determination view of Pathy, to the more data based, practical solutions as offered by scholars such as Gangwar and L.R.N. Srivastava, who have critically analyzed particular problems in particular regions, there are a spectra of opinions and solutions.

However, what emerges as almost a unanimous opinion is the condemnation of the institutional approach and the need for greater 'empowerment' of the tribes themselves, an approach which is oriented to 'their' needs 'not' ours !

At a broader level, the paper by Bhandari and Channa (this volume) looks at the problem of tribals in a global perspective. The problem faced by so called tribes or 'ethnic groups' within various types of Nation-States is examined. This broad based view is a direct correlation of the fundamental theoretical premise accepted in this volume that the tribe is a creation of, and is to be understood only as a phenomenon of the Nation-State.

The Nation-States have been largely formed over a historical period by a process of incorporation by conquest, colonization, migration or a simple redefining of political boundaries. The latter process being significant in the latter part of the twentieth century. This inevitably leads to a multi ethnic character of the Nation State. However, the Nation-State must also present an unified identity, hence some dominant cultural symbols have to be upheld which belongs most to that particular ethnic stream that forms the central power structure of the Nation-State due to historical circumstances. This then becomes the so-called mainstream culture (Channa : 1995). No amount of ideological stress on democracy and equal rights can over ride this reality. Not only does the powerholding centre exert ideological hegemony and cultural domination, these have to be built upon an edifice of resource monopolization. There is a concerted effort at the centre to mobilize resources for the welfare of the politically dominant group, whether in a minority or in a majority.

When the dominant group is a minority ethnic group its legitimacy is definitely questionable as was with the minority government in South Africa, but where it is in a majority as in U.S.A., China, India, Australia, etc., its legitimacy to complete monopolization can still be questioned. It is in the latter context that the concept of indigenous peoples comes up.

The indigenous are those, who within the Nation-State have had control over certain parts of the environment and resources in terms of a primordial system of inheritance. The dispossesian of these people from what is believed to be their original habitats and resources raises questions of ethics and morality. It also brings into focus the concept of legitimacy of the Nation-State. It brings into focus the notion of social justice. How far is it justified to sacrifice the interests of some for the welfare of others ? The question is not really of the past.

The question is of the present and the future. The power hierarchies have been steadily easing out some identities at the expense of the others. The most poignant indicator to this is that in India, 'Tribal Policy' is actually nothing but a rename for 'Tribal Development Plan'. The ethno-centricism of the term 'development' is self-evident. The 'lip service' paid by academicians to this term is also worth noting'.

REFERENCES

1. Channa, Subhadra M. 1995 : "Evolution of Mainstream Concept" in *Mainstream* Jan. 29, 1995 PP 27-31.
2. Kuper, Adam, 1988 : *The Invention of Primitive Society* London, Routledge.
3. Innani, Octavio, 1972 : "Race and Class in Latin America" in *Readings in Race and Ethnic Relations* (Ed). Anthony. H. Richards Oxford, Pergamon Press.
4. Wallerstein, Immanuel, 1991 : "The Construction of Peoplehood: Racism, Nationalism, Ethnicity". In Etienne Balibar and Immannuel Wallerstein (Ed). *Race, Nation, Class : Ambiguous Identities,* London, Verso.

1

Tribal And Analogous Social Entities In Different Countries Of The World And Relevance Of Gandhi-Nehru Framework Of Socialist Humanism.

B.K. Roy Burman

An independent commission on the indigenous peoples of the world has brought out its first report "Indigenous Peoples : Global Quest for Justice". The Commission includes such eminent personalities as I.P. Blishchenko, Chairman of the International Law Department of Patrice Lumumba University Moscow, Sadruddin Aga Khan, U.N. High Commissioner for Refugees, S.S. Ramphal, Secretary General of the Commonwealth, Justice Hidayatullah, Ex-Vice President of India, L.S. Senghor, Ex- President of Senegal, Desmond Tutu, Archbishop of Cape Town and Winner of the Nobel Peace Prize and others.

In the editorial note of the report it has been mentioned that there is no universally accepted description or definiton of indigenous peoples. One cannot accept the contention in its totality. Whether they are called indigenous, autochonous, tribal, Fourth World or First Nations, there is a growing consensus about them and their continuing plight.

It is however difficult to say that there is a growing consensus all over the world as to who the indigenous people are. On 6th August, 1987, in the meeting of the United Nations Working Group on Indigenous population, held at Geneva, Sri Jayanta Prasad stated on behalf the official delegation of India, that it would be a difficult task to say which section of India's population was indigenous and which was not. The position he had taken can be termed as historical nominalism. But it is very different from critical realism. Irrespective of the place and time of their origin or their occupation of the present habitats in India, there are certainly communities which until recently maintained practically autogenous sources of legitimation of cultural and social processes; were activated by the ideology of a self-regulated economy and had only marginal articulation with external political structures. Their indigenous identity cannot be brushed away by justaposition of non-meaningful occurrances in space and time in systemic terms.

From this perspective a question arises whether the term 'indigenous people' can be equated with the term tribe. Beteille has examined the concept of tribe with special reference to India. As he points out, an important issue in the study of tribes today is how we understand the relationship between tribes and civilization. In his words " I would like to make a distinction between two approaches, which I will describe as the 'evolutionary' and the 'historical'. The evolutionary appoach takes long-range view of the passage of time and stresses the co-existence of different social formations within that framework. What is regarded as anachronism in the evolutionary perspective may appear as a necessary component in the historical framework. Among attempts to provide a general definition of tribe, those by Ellman Service and by Marshall Sahlins have received some attention. "Underlying the classification is the dichotomy between 'State' and 'non-state' societies, but non-state societies are not viewed as being all of the same kind; they ae divided into bands, tribes and chiefdoms" For Godelier the tribe is at one and the same time a type of society and a stage of evolution.

When tribe is looked upon as a type of society, coexisting with our social formation, it is the inner dynamics of each, which matters; the question of superiority or inferiority of either does not arise. And yet in the contemporary world the crisis in the drift of the social formations, which claim to be the hallmark of civilization cannot be ignored. As observed by the Co-chairman of the Independent Commission on indigenous people in his foreword to the report mentioned earlier "Our technological and social achievements seem precarious in a world which edges ever closer to nuclear armageddon, whose environment is collapsing, where individuals feel increasingly alienated and governments ever less tolerant of diversity and non-conformity" "As we survey the social, environmental and humanitarian fall-out of industrial development, it is occurring to more of us—indigenous and itinerant alike, that we may have some urgent practical lessons to learn, if it is not already too late, from societies which have succeeded in managing a sustainable environment for millennia".

This perspective imparts an element of permanence embedded in the social formations described as tribals in some contexts and indigenous in other contexts. It is to be examined whether by refusing to recognise the existence of indigenous populations of specific 'identities' as repository of values of crucial importance for the survival of mankind, the opportunity of learning the lessons alluded to in the foreword, are not being fritted away.

"Indigenous peoples have custodial attitudes toward

land and life, which respects inter-generational rights. During this century, an ever growing demand, particularly from industrial nations, for natural resources has spurred a global search for untapped reserves. Once thought of as barren wastelands of little economic value, the unexploited territories of indigenous peoples have been identified as areas of rich timber, minerals and river valleys. In the name of development, forests are being removed, mining projects started and dams built, forcing indigenous people out of their traditional habitat—it is a tragedy not only for the indigenous people but for mandkind".

On the other hand, as pointed out in the report

"even in countries where the indigenous still constitute a majority they remain powerless, by and large unheard, misunderstood, or simply ignored by their 'civilised' patrons. Their past history is disdained; their way of life scorned; their situation of subjugation unrecognised; their social and economic system unvalued" (p.XVII)

Colonial Underpinnings

The present situation of indigenous peoples is rooted in their colonial past. It is because of the relationship of the conqueror and conquered which was established during the early years of colonial contact that a higher proportion of indigenous peoples, in all countries today remain unemployed, than in society as a whole. Even when employed, they are concentrated in unskilled and low paid jobs. In the USA, half the Indians living on reservations have no work. In Australia the aboriginal unemployment rate is more than seven times that for the country as a whole. In New Zealand one in seven Maoris is unemployed, while the figure is only one in 30 for the rest of the population. In the Brazilian and Peruvian Amazon, in Eastern Bolivia and in Paraguay, there are cases of Indians working as virtual slaves and debt-bonded labourer. They are pressurised by local landowners and entrepreneurs into taking a loan and are charged high interest. They pay the debt with labour.

Indigenous people also suffer comparatively poor health. In the rich countries the differences are marked. In the USA., for example, malnutrition as well as obesity are higher among Indians than any other group. Native Americans are eight times more likely to contact tuberculosis than other U.S. citizens. In Australia, the average life span of an aboriginal is about 20 years less than that of a White. High infant mortality largely accounts for the disparity. In Brazil, it is estimated that 87 Indian Groups have become extinct in this century as a consequence of epidemic diseases. The perpetuation of the underprivileged position of most indigenous peoples has been ensured by the low priority accorded to their education by governments. This is reflected in the low investment in rural, and particularly indigenous, education (pp. 16-18).

As a result, while the laws and constitution of most countries provide for the protection of the indigenous peoples located in their territories, these have not improved the overall political and legal position of majority of indigenous peoples. The police often abuse the indigenous. The courts with their overwhelmingly non-indigenous judges and juries are not free of prejudice. In Victoria, Australia, the aboriginal peoples are 45 times more likely to go to prison than Whites. In the U.S.A, in Alaska, Arizona and South Dakota, the indigenous Indians, less than 10 per cent of the population, account for 60 per cent of the prison population (p.20). Afte taking note of such facts, the Commission observes that :

> the Governments, international agencies, non-governmental organisations and corporations, as well as individuals, all have a role in changing this situ-

ation by reversing the course of history which continues to subject indigenous peoples to such injustice...1992 the 500 year anniversary of Columbus reaching America, should be declared International Year for indigenous peoples. National histories throughout the world must be revised, not only for the benefit of the indigenous, but also for the general population, who presently learn false history, thereby perpetuating racism, intolerance and support for inhuman policies."

This suggestion of the Commission is in contrast with the proposal of the Western countries that 1992 be celebrated as the fifth centenary of the "discovery" of America. This was opposed by indigenous peoples as it would have legitimised their colonisation, enslavement and in many cases, extermination during the last five centuries. The Western nations revived their proposal once again in 1988.

Control of Natural Resources

However, mere decolonisation and opposition to this western demand cannot change the situation of the indigenous peoples. Both the histories in vogue even today and the struggle for the control of the natural resources ensure their continued exploitation. Hence many suggestions and observations of the Commission hold good for India.

To begin with, the first tribal histories presented by colonial historians and still in vogue today, project colonial armed encroachments on tribal territories as quests for peace and the reprisals of the indigenous peoples as barbarian resistance to the entry of civilisation. The task of revising these histories has to be taken up on an intellectual moral war footing.

As for the latter, in a large number of countries, this process of what the first report describes as colonial invasion has not ended but is being continued by the national governments, because minerals and other natural resources are in these territories. In India, for example, about 45 per cent of the mineral products of the country and a third of its known reserves are on indigenous lands in the State of Bihar. Similar is the situation in USA and elsewhere.

As the competition for the control and extraction of resources has intensified, the search has extended to areas of low population density. And much of the resources are obtained from the 'frontier' lands occupied by indigenous peoples. The surge in industrialisation and urbanisation on indigenous people's traditional land has also, oftener than not, affected them adversely. Since the 1960's many poor countries, mainly in response to industrial needs and encouraged by the availability of financial support from the multilateral development banks, have invested in hydro-power. The territories of indigenous peoples, consisting of river valleys of comparatively low population density are generally physically suited to dam constructions. But as indigenous people are politically marginal, they are unable to protest effectively.

Most importantly, they often do not have clear ownership rights in the modern sense, to the land designated for hydro-electric development. So governments are not obliged to provide expensive compensation. On the other hand, most indigenous peoples do not benefit in any way from the massive investments made for dam constructions; at the same time increasingly, dams affecting indigenous peoples are being recognised as damaging to the wider environment.

Another point made in the report is that East-West confrontation has brought indigenous peoples into the international arena and led to further incursions into their land. One wonders whether this is an adequate description of the world situation. Jackson Dachi reported in the Hindustan Times of Delhi on 6th July,

1988, that Romania has planned to tear down about 7000 of the country's 16000 villages, many of which are inhabited by ethnic Hungarians and when a massive public demonstration took place against this in Hungary's capital, Romania reacted by closing down the consulate in the Transylvanian city of Cluj.

Ambiguity of Land Rights

Two other lacunae in the report deserve mention. While there is a passing reference to the ambiguity about land rights, the source of the ambiguity has not been analysed. It centres round two conflicting orientations to law, namely legal positivism and legal pluralism. At the operational level the concept of *resnullius* or non-existence of a right which has not been assigned by the sovereign, is tied up with the former and the concept of *res loci sitae* or right effective in a place, is tied up with the latter. Going deeper, these two legal orientations are rooted in two world views, two meaning systems informing one's negotiation with one's own 'self', with other 'self' and with his existential conditions.

While the Commission has by-passed these issues of social philosophy, it has made its position vulnerable, when it is claimed on its authority that the indigenous peoples had 'a glorious past and a future which is slowly but surely beginning to look bright'. Such sweeping assertions are not contested here on empirical grounds. But unless one analytically goes into the heart of the matter these are of little help in the urgent tasks of human reconstruction.

When one looks into other sources, one finds that where the Commission has failed, the indigenous peoples themselves are trying to step in. The Interntional Work Group For Indigenous Affairs (IWGIA) in its Year Book for 1986, has published excerpts from the intervention of its Vice-President in a meeting of I.L.O. experts. In his words:

> For indigenous peoples, life and earth are synonymous...The earth is the rejuvenative power of life to indigenous peoples; she is our means to economic independence; social and cultural development, which will in turn lead to return of a sense of dignity and pride indigenous peoples can feel in themselves...If one can appreciate this importance of the earth to indigenous peoples, one then can understand why we cannot treat the earth as a commodity that can merely be equated with an economic value.

In the contemporary era of ecological crisis this is a message of hope. Another dimension of the meaning of being rooted in the soil has been highlighted by a tribal leader of India, Samar Brahma Chaudhury, in his intervention in the U.N. Working Group, earlier referred to.

"The concept of self-determination is inbuilt in our relationship with nature and with one another, both as individuals and as groups. It is fundamental, related and consequential, just as we find a relationship with the Sun, the Moon, the Universe, the change of season and its reflections in nature and in relationship with human beings. So also the concept of self-determination has in itself a rhythm, a balance, an excellence and conscience...It means to achieve harmony, cohesion with other groups in the country so that in a peaceful atmosphere even the ethnic minorities and weaker sections of the population can preserve their geographical boundry or territory and maintain their distributive ethnic identity and that way help attaining dignity and self respect, attaining the highest standard of civilisation. Self determination also imposes a sense of self-discipline. It is a principle of live and let live." Though the Commission has eschewed the philosophical dimension, it has highlighted the struggle of the indigenous peoples for survival in the face of involuntary displacement and relocation, militarisation and bland genocide in several countries, including the Chakmas of Bangladesh. It has also reported some of the actions of the national governments, corporations and international community in the face of growing consciousness and new challenges.

Integration and Identity

Here, it is to be noted that in stimulating international action, The World Council of Indigenous People (WCIP) has played the most significant role. It was set up in 1975 at Port Alberny, near Vancouver on the initiative of the National Brotherhood of (Red) Indians (NBI) of Canada which was earlier granted the status of an N.G.O. by the Economic and Social Council of U.N. After the establishment of the WCIP the N.G.O. status was transferred to it. In 1987 an Indian Council of Indigenous and Tribal Peoples was constituted and was granted the status of an affiliate of WCIP. Without going into the history of the formation of WCIP, the present report gives details of some of the actions of the U.N. bodies. In 1957 I.L.O. convention No. 107 was adopted as an International instrument dealing exclusively with the problems of the indigenous peoples. One of its highlights is that, it is the only international instrument which recognises the right to collective ownership of land. Another high-light is its original orientation towards the 'integration' of the indigenous peoples into the dominant society and towards 'development' in the Western sense. But later many among the indigenous peoples strongly objected to the convention's paternalism. This is to be understood in the context of the statement made in the report that government officials, executives of transnational corporations and officers of development banks have often only a limited knowledge of indigenous societies. Yet the projects these officials authorise—dams, roads, relocations of population—affect irrevocably the people who lie in their paths. It is not just a case of ignorance; a basic change of attitude is required.

A more fortright indictment of the concept of 'integration' is found in the report of a seminar on the Future of Pastoral Peoples which was co-sponsored by the International Development Research Centre of Canada. Dan R. Aronson of McGill University, Montreal, stated in this seminar.

"Development is process at the aggregate national level, that whatever may be defined by the national leaders as the public benefit overrides sectional or sectoral interests. Because those who define public good also hold crucial power, this belief justifies their working, their will upon society and their decrying anti-state any seriously competing visions of the integration of a given population into national participation by means of the elaboration of bureaucratic mechanisms of control, and it seeks the specialisation of the economic function of the group within the national organism."

It, however, appears that while some amount of reservation against excessive emphasis on integration in the ILO convention No. 107 of 1957 is justified, there is a danger of moving unawares into a trap of a different type. A compilation of working papers of the All India Consultation on Indigenous and Tribal Peoples Affairs available with the Department of Tribal and Regional Languages, Ranchi University includes the report of the Pacific-Asia Empowerment Conference held in Hawai in 1987. This Conference led to the formation of a council for this region including India. One of the resolutions of this conference runs as follows :

> That the World Bank requires an investigation into any project financed, of the social, economic and cultural implications upon the indigenous peoples of concerned territory and the surrouning areas. It

adversely affects the indigenous people, the World Bank must refuse approval of financing such projects until the adverse effect is overcome.

This pitiable dependence on the World Bank bureaucracy, rather than the long-term political processes of the community of nations, certainly sounds odd. Here it is to be noted that the Copenhagen based International Work Group for Indigenous Affairs, in their Year Book referred to, has stated that the World Bank has a publicly stated tribal policy and a secret tribal policy (p. 143). From the document furnished in this source, it appears that the World Bank has taken an intermediate position between those of the indigenous peoples and the independent states. It is, however, not the nature of the World Bank's position which is under scrutiny now. What is more important is the readiness of a section of the indigenous people to pass on the *veto* right to the World Bank. The incongruity of such a move would be obvious from the Report of the Independent Commission which has highlighted some of the negative features of the World Bank's approach and has asked for a review (p. 113).

The future of the indigenous people depends on their vigorous action to protect their own heritage, which in fact is the core of common heritage of mankind. In this the Gandhi-Nehru frame work of socialist humanism provides a strong intellectual moral support.

Nehru, who in the early 50's enthusiastically observed "can there be anything more exciting than the idea that the welfare state of our dream will raise hundreds of millions of people to a fuller way of life ?" stated in 1959 "the welfare state is a worth while ideal, but it may well be a drab". Earlier in December 1958 Nehru observed "we labour to bring about a welfare state in India. In countries where such a state has been established, in so far as the material things of life are concerned, we see patterns of behaviour which shock the older generation". "The question for us to consider is whether we can retain in this process some of the basic values to which humanity has attached great importance in the past and whether spiritual element in life-using the word in the widest sense, can be retained or augmented or whether it will fade away. Without that spiritual element probably the disintegration of society will proceed in spite of all material advance". In September 1963, Nehru described himself as one the relics of Gandhian days. "He was looking all the time at the villages of India, at the most backward people of India". Obviously, he was moving towards people's power, rather than state power. As mentioned earlier, recent trend in anthropology is to differentiate tribal and non-tribal societies by the emergence or not of state structures. When one speaks of people's power it is in the same wavelength with the positive humanist core of tribal social formations. More important is the relevance of Gandhiji's concept of trusteeship as revised in 1945, with the assistance of Prof. Dantwala, the doyen of the Indian economists. The salient points of the trusteeship concept as in the draft finalised by Gandhiji are as follows: (1) Trusteeship provides means of transforming the present capitalist order of society into an egalitarian one; (2) It does not recognise any right of private ownership of property except so far as it may be permitted by society for its own welfare; (3) It does not exclude legislative regulation of the ownership and use of wealth; (4) Thus under state regulted trusteeship, an individual will not be free to hold or use his wealth for selfish satisfaction or in disregard of the interest of the society; (5) Just as it is proposed to fix a decent minimum living wage, even so a limit should be fixed for the maximum income that could be allowed to any person in society; (6) Under the Gandhian economic order the character of production will be determined by social necessity and not by personal whim or greed. When one compares the cardinal principles of Gandhiji's revised version of trusteeship with Nehru's *Panchsheel* for the tribals, one immediately feels the kinship of spirit, if not of full identity of content of both. Again one finds that both sets of cardinal principles are in the same wavelength as the concept of 'custodial attitude' mentioned in the Forword of the Co-Chairman of the Independent Commission on Indigenous People, alluded to earlier. One thus finds a global convergence; and the future course of action is to be sought in this direction.

2

Tribal Policy—Issues and Themes

A.P. Sinha

The Preface

Tribal policy (here, abbreviation for Tribal Development in India) is a subject which is now nearly forty years old. Within this period, TD has been a subject which has drawn widespread and pronounced attentions, ranging from the platforms of the political parties to the syllabi of academics, with the committee rooms of the development planners and programme administrators providing material for both. By today, TD is a well definable subject with the politics in power, with the planners and, with the academics, receiving pronounced attention with each of them, all these forty years.

The Constitution of India (1950) defines the broad considerations that should guide the efforts and attentions towards Tribal Development. From the First Five-Year Plan (1952) till the Seventh Five-Year Plan (1990), sustained specialized attention of the planners have been invested, and these have guided the investment of financial and material resources towards Tribal Development, in increasing, prominent sizes, intending to reach every family of the tribal community, in whatever part of the community it may be located.

With every serious and sustained attentions, with uninterrupted investments of money and materials, in prominent sizes, if there is still an unease in regard to the achievements from tribal development, obviously there is something which eludes us in our efforts towards tribal development. The questions to ask, thus are : What eludes us and Why ? The paper attempts an exercise to find answers to such questions.

The Perspective

In an analytical discussion, 'the perspective' refers to introductory statements on (a) the dependent and the independent variables in terms of which the analysis is presented, and preceeding this, (b) statement on the understanding with which the relevance of the variables and their interaction has been perceived, when organising the discussion. TD is an action-programme, and hence it represents a system of complex processes. In the full scenario, TD involves the interplay of (a) *Ideology* (objectives and goals), *Action* (planning and implementation), *Evaluation* (feed back), and (b) the political leadership (ideology), the development planners and the development administrators, and the academics.

Tribal Policy In India
(Paradigm I)

	Ideology	*Action*	*Evaluation*
Political Leadership			
Planners and administrators			
Academics			

Between the academics in India, the involvement of the anthropologists with TD stands out prominent. It has been substantial, and progressively deep. The beginning of such involvement can be traced to the very early years of TD in India (Circa, 1954-1956). Any discussion on TD, when initiated by anthropologists, as a result, carries overshadowing arguments on the role of anthropology and the anthropologists. In terms of Paradigm I, it will confine discussion to only one cell (anthropology, evaluation), or at the most two cells (anthropology and evaluation as well as planning), out of the nine cells. With all the contributions anthropology and the anthropologists in India have made towards TD, this far, I feel they can improve significantly in their roles by extending beyond the ethnocentric concerns, and formulate critical, comprehensive system-analysis of TD. In such an exercise each of the nine cells of Paradigm I may be taken to represent the system-components. Such an exercise, initiated in a forum of anthropologists will go a long way in reinforcing the role of anthropology in TD. It will help the anthropologists in India to take a realistic view of their role in the total scenario as represented by Paradigm I.

Paradigm I represents one of the facets of TD. Interlocked with this are some other facets of TD.

(i) TD is an action-programme, and therefore, there is the *objective*, the *action*, and the *achievements* component of TD.

(ii) TD is an action programme, and therefore, it represents the involvement of the *action-groups* and the *client-groups* in TD.

The components of TD from each of these two sets, namely, objectives, action, achievements, the action-group, the client-group represent a complex range of sub-components.

(a) *Objectives*—We know, and as mentioned earlier,

the Constitution of India (1950) defines the broad considerations that should guide the efforts and attentions towards tribal development. These have been prescribed broadly as (a) protection from exploitation and (b) promotion of their socio-economic interests. Formal attention towards these were formulated from the First Five-Year Plan (1952) onwards. With the progress of each of the Five Years Plan, the operational aspects of the objectives of TD were refined, through redefined formulations. It was realized that the social-economic conditions of the tribal communities will need to be enhanced to bring it to levels comparable with the level of social economic development of other communities. With reference to this, it was realized that there will be a need to develop 'inner-strength' among the tribal communities (cf. Shivraman Committee, 1950).

To achieve the broad objectives of tribal development, specific programmes through a wide range of sectors were formulated. In 1954 formal approaches to rural development were formulated. The Community Development Programme (CD) marks the beginning of this. From the very early years of CD, it was realized that to achieve the objectives of tribal welfare and the promotion of their economic interests, specialized strategy will have to be designed. Within the frame work of CD, (programmes for rural development) additional inputs of finance and material were provided for the development of tribal areas. Concurrent with the formal, systematized approaches to rural development, the CD approach onwards, formal systematized approaches to tribal development and welfare were also designed. It started with the TD Block approach, and evolving through the SMPT and the TDA approach, it has reached the TSP approach.

Forty years of TD in India is rich with a wide variety of experiences. One branch of this relates to the story of evolution of definition of objectives of TD, feedback and re-definition of the objectives. In view of the directions from the constitution, and for other reasons as well, protection from exploitation and promotion of social economic interests have remained the objective all through. Refinement in the definition of the objectives, from the First-Five-Year plan to the Seventh Five-Year Plan, reveal a characteristic shift in the thrust and over-all orientation, from welfare oriented approach there is greater emphasis now on social-economic development.

Welfare approach .... Social Economic Development Approach

When objectives of welfare/development are formulated as action programmes, two exercises become incumbent—one, to translate the broad objectives into specific goals, and two, formulate action-programmes in the appropriate sectors.

One of the critical aspect of TD in India has been the evolution-requirements in the definition of its 'objectives'. The evolution requirement has been in two directions—(1) in terms of the shift from welfare orientation, to social-economic development orientation, and (ii) to reflect such orientation through order of priority between programmes from different sectors. The sectors of developments have been placed into three categories : (a) Sectors of economic development, (b) Sectors of infra-structural development, and (c) Sectors of social welfare/service development. Each of these broad categories, again comprise a number of specific sectors, such as, Agriculture, Horticulture, Soil Conservation, Roads and Communication, Energy, Irrigation, Forest, Institutional Finance, Cooperatives, Health, Education, Child and Women's programmes, and a host of many others.

A realistic understanding, a pragmatic approach to understand the evolution of the definition of objectives of TD can come through a systematic analysis of how through the successive Plan periods, the definition of priority sectors have shifted from the welfare emphasis to social-economic development emphasis.

We can discuss the evolution of objectives, from the TD Block approach to the TSP approach, in terms of two sets of disaggregation:—

(a) at the level of the 'broad considerations', and

(b) at the level of specific Sectors.

Tribal Policy In India
(Paradigm II)

Sector/Broad considerations	*Protection from Exploitation*	*Improved standard of living*	*Lift to comparable level of Development*	*Build inner strength for Development*
Economic Development Sectors				
Infra-Structural Development Sectors				
Social Service Sectors				

One approach to present an account of forty-years of TD in India, between the many other possible approaches, is to divide the account in forms of the pre-TSP phase and the TSP phase of TD. The pre-TSP phase of account will have to be divided into the TD Block phase and the SMPT phase, the TDA phase (for a short duration), and then the TSP phase.

(b) *Action*—A number of issues of vital importance are involved with this. According to one explanation : "Before discussing the question of effective coordination and implemention of plan and programmes it will be appropriate to consider three important aspects of development planning process, namely, plan formulation, monitoring and evolution. These aspects have a direct bearing of implementations and coordination"...

These three exercises are inter-related. It is necessary to device guidance for one based on the achievement in the other".

Elaborating on this, there is mentioned "This involves five steps—(a) analysis of existing situation, (b) translating objectives into specific targets, (c) arrangement of priorities, (d) identification of constraints operating from within and/or outside the system, and (e) suggestion for removal of constraints. A look at the present status in regard to these three aspects as obtained in the N.E. Region will be relevant. The first question that calls for an answer is whether in this region the planning set-up at the State/District/Block level has the required data base. Unless programmes are drawn up keeping in view the current status and problem of the progress area, successful implementation of the programme can not be expected. Thus the analysis of the existing situation is the foundation that has to be carefully and skillfully laid in order to build programme-planning target. Data in the North-East Region are either not available or not accessible or not collected at the required level of disaggregation or not collected regularly or collected with a considerable time lag". (Report of the Working Group for the Development of the North-Eastern Region during the Seventh Plan period).

The success of development programme, more correctly, the performance of such programmes depends on two vital components, i.e. planning and implementation. Each of these planning as well as implementation, imply a series of complex exercises. Before proceeding any further with our analysis, there is one clarification which needs to be made. This relates to the notion 'development'. In a way, this clarification could have been made in the outset, in the opening part of the paper.

The notion of 'development' has to be perceived at

two levels of 'reality', at the level of theoretical-conceptual-reality, and at the level of operational-reality. It will be better to refer to the distinction between the two 'reality' in terms of the 'order of perception' rather than 'level of reality'. (i) Development when perceived in the theoretical conceptual order, is a subject of discussion by the academics. On such occasions, the notion of development appears in the company of terms like, modernization, change, transformation, political development, economic development. Characteristically distinct from this, (ii) when Development is perceived in the operational order, it is subject for discussion by those involved with planning and implementation of development programmes. The notion of development refers to specific sectors of development, such as Tribal Development, Community Development, Urban Development, Industrial Development, Hill Development, Social Welfare, Child Development, Women Development, and quite many others of similar level of reference. (iii) Discussions initiated and organized by the academics refer to the theoretical-conceptual order of perception, through their 'research'. In sharp contrast to this, discussions on the operational dimension of development are initiated, for all practical purposes, from the documents of the Five-Year Plans, and the subsequent operational exercises involved with it. When refering to this dimension of the notion, initial attention is on the visibles, on the ground, the array of development programmes.

In any analytical discussion on 'development' it is advisable to bring out clear, in the very outset, the order of perception with reference to which the discussion on 'development' is being made. The need to obey such caution becomes all the more important when the academics initiate a discussion on a subject like 'Tribal Policy-Issues and Themes". In view of this, in the present writing when refering to the operational order, the first letter will be written capital, thus Development. When refering to the theoretical-conceptual motion, as common with the academic, the word will start with small letter 'd'.

The Constitution (1950) lays down the 'direction principles' on the educational and the economic interests of the tribal communites, and the need to present them from social injustice and exploitation. The first Five-Year Plan was introduced in 1952, and by 1954, programmes for rural development were formalized through Community-Development. By 1956, concurrent to CD (Community Development) programmes for Tribal Development were formalized and initiated. This mark is the beginning of policy of Tribal Development in India. The main substance for the discussions in the present paper comes from the forty years of Tribal Development, the Constitution of India, 1950, till date.

We may recall, the title of the Seminar is 'Tribal Policy-Issues and Themes'. We may explain, the academics can present meaningful and realistic analytical discussion on 'Issues and themes' by initiating the discussion through focus on the operational dimension of TD. In any discussion of this nature, namely, one in which the discussion is initiated, and for the most part, is organized through focus on the operational dimension of TD, and later the issues and themes thus formulated, are re-examined in the theoretical-conceptual frame of social science, the academics will need to maintain careful distinction between the two orders of perception. To facilitate this, a somewhat expanded discussion on the operational components of TD and a synoptic history of TD have been presented. This will help ready reference and facilitate to appreciate the destinations.

We may return now to discussion on the planning, implementation and associated dimensions of TD. As mentioned earlier, the success and performance of any development programme depends, for the most part, on their planning, implementation and evaluation. Each of these three represent a set of complex systematically elaborate and formalized exercises. These exercises appear in their visible form, at different levels, from the centre to the ITDP, the Block and the grassroot level. The procedures and objectives of exercises at different points of levels are codified. The Reports of the Working Groups on Tribal Development, as constituted for the 6th Plan Period by the Planning Commission, and for the 7th Plan Period by the Ministry of Home Affairs, present most inclusive account of such exercises. By the end of the 4th Plan period, the Ministry of Welfare and the Planning Commission, each individually, constituted Expert Group (Dube Committee) and Task Force (Vidyarthi Committee) respectively, to formulate 'basic policy papers' for Tribal Development. In continuation to each of such documents, there have been a wide range of exercises to define specifics with each facet of the exercise of programme planning and programme implementation.

The contents of such documents, in combination, outline the details of 'the technology of planning'. We may clarify this is not a one point exercise, either in the vertical hierarchical order, from the Centre to the Block, or at the horizontal, time intervals, from the First to the Seventh Plan period. The technology of planning for TD in India has evolved through a complex set of experiences, from the First to the Seventh Five-Year Plan.

To emphasize the importance of technology of planning in the nature of performance of TD, we may explain that the most advisable approach to formulate realistic and pragmatic understanding of 'Issues and themes' of TD is to make a critical analysis of 'the technology of planning' which has evolved with TD, from the First to the Seventh Plan. Later in this section, I will discuss at some length what implies 'critical analysis' of planning, technology with reference to TD.

In its operational planning, technology includes the following components :

(1) Statement of *Ideology.*

(2) Definition of broad *Objectives.*

(3) Translating the objectives into specific *Targets,* (goals) intended to be achieved within the time period.

(4) Statements on *Strategy,* in terms of

 (a) Statements on the *Organization,* and

 (b) Statements on *Priorities* between the listed targets.

(5) Statements on *Information,* comprising

 (a) Initially, data for formulating programmes, and

 (b) Later, feedback through *Evaluation.*

The ultimate responsibility of TD, in the national context, has been entrusted to the Centre. There is specific mention of this in the Constitution. In view of some special reasons, the Constitution makes specific mention of the responsibility entrusted to the States of Orissa, Bihar and Madhya Pradesh. In its full operation, with reference to planning as well as implementation, TD is organized through an elaborate arrangement linking the efforts of the Centre with those of the States. This adds monitoring as one more important component in technology of planning.

In its full form, TD in India represents the combination of distinct, elaborate exercise in two directions, (a) the vertical coordination of the Centre to the ITDP and beyond, and at each of these levels, (b) full set of exercise involving every component of the planning, implementation, evaluation and monitoring.

Tribal Policy In India
(Paradigm III)

	Planning	*Implemen-tion*	*Evaluation*	*Monitor-ing*
Centre				
State				
ITDP				
Block				

(c) *Action Group*—A wide range of functionaries are involved with TD. They may be referred to as the functionaries involved with three broad categories of the action-component—planning, implementaion, evaluation, monitoring. In the action-frame (to borrow from Parsons), the responsibility and roles of the functionaries in each of the four categories (planning, implementation, evaluation, monitoring) operate through a complex, elaborate arrangement of organizations, at the Centre, the States, and the levels subsequent to it. At each of these three levels horizontally, there are elaborate, and again complex arrangements involving a wide array of Sectoral departments.

Tribal Policy In India
(Paradigm IV)

	Plann-ing	*Implemen-tation*	*Evalua-tion*	*Monitor-ing*
Centre (i) Planning Commission (ii) Ministry in the charge of TD (iii) Sectoral Ministry having component of TD				
State (i) Planning Board (ii) Sectoral Departments				

(d) *The Client Group*—This refers to the tribal communities in the country. These have been classified on the basis of (a) territorial location, and (b) socio-economic considerations.

On the basis of territorial location, the tribal population has been divided into three categories—(a) territories having a majority of scheduled tribe population, (b) territories having substantial tribal population, but as a majority group in only some particular administrative unit of the territory, and (c) territories having dispersed tribal population. Such classification have been made with reference to each State/Union Territory.

Again, in terms of their socio-economic levels, they have been classified as primitive tribes, displaced tribes, shifting cultivators, forest dwellers, etc.

Along with such classification it will be advisable to intersperse classification in terms of the following considerations : (a) the level of 'exposure' (as indicator to measure the nature of the proverbial solution, mobility, which will include territorial mobility as well as occupational mobility), (b) social demography and command over resources, and (c) mode of subsistence and level of technology.

Tribal Policy In India
(Paradigm V)

Socio-Economic Condition Location	*Exposure/ Mobility*	*Social Demo-graphyst Command over Resources*	*Mode of Subsistence Level of Technology*
Full concentration			
Pockets of concentration			
Dispersed			

Paradigms I to V, in combination, provide perspective of a comprehensive frame work for critical appraisal of TD, the formalized efforts organized by the Centre and the State/UT government. Such a critical appraisal of TD yields substantive set of issues for discussion.

In the discussion on 'Perspectives', this far an attempt has been made to disaggregate the relevant operational components involved with TD Programme. These components are relevant in making a critical appraisal of TD. The discussion on 'Perspectives' will remain incomplete if reference is not made to issues involved with 'achievements'.

The issues in mind emerge from a simple, obvious, hypothesis. In real life situation, however, the issues are involved with a complex array of situations.

Achievement of the objectives is one of the vital dimensions of any action-programme. There are two ways to perceive 'achievements', one, to perceive it in terms of the *effective implementation* of the itemized programme constituting the action-programme, and two, to perceive the 'achievements' in terms of the *impact* of the programmes and assess thereby the nature and extent to which the objectives have been achieved.

Evaluation is vital for any action programme. The feedback information from evaluation is useful at two levels. In the more immediate level, information from evaluation is utilized to improve on the implementation of programmes. In the broader context, information from evaluation is helpful to re-examine the orientation with which the objectives have to be defined.

"To promote economic interests, and to protect social injustice and exploitation", are the directive principles contained in the Constitution. The structure, the contents and dynamics of the Indian Society in 1950, has fast transformed. Between 1950 and 1990, the tribal communities find themselves in a phenomenally transformed societal situation. The efforts from TD have made their impact in attending to their economic interests and protecting them from social injustice and exploitation, but alongside this the situation has become compounded with the changes in the wider national context, with industrialization, urbanization, and the many other changes which have come along with these. Hence, evaluation of achievements should not remain confined only to the evaluation of the programmes itemized in each plan, under different Sectors. We will try to return to some more discussion on this, later in the paper.

In 1985, when formulating tribal development for the Seventh Plan, the objectives for the Sixth Plan were recalled, and with reference to this the achievements made during the Sixth Plan were revised. The broad approach of the TSP (for all practical purposes taken synonymous with tribal development) strategy was greater emphasised on four specific *objectives* : (a) raising of productivity levels in fields of agriculture and other land and forest based activities, village and small industry, with a view to enable a targeted number of families to move above the poverty line;

(b) development of the *human resources* and upgradation of education;

(c) elimination of exploitation in the fields of alienation of land, money-lending, debt-bondage, trade, forest, excise; and

(d) development of adequate *infrastructure*.

When opening for the Seventh Plan Strategy, it was felt that during the Sixth Plan period rich dividends had been reaped in the shape of a more integrated approach to *planning and implementation*, larger financial allocation both by the Centre and the States and considerably large physical achievements in amelioration of poverty targetted groups as also in the general and social service sectors. Among the important *contributions* of the TSP strategy over a period of years has been the gradual *evolution of the content* of family oriented programmes for *eradication of poverty*. The emphasis on family-oriented and beneficiary-oriented schemes during the Sixth Plan has had perceptible impact in substantially boosting up the number of tribal families economically assisted.

It was explained, the 'rich dividends' came through the adoption of the TSP approach and all that came along with it. It was, however, felt that there were not *a few lapses and shortcomings*, which in other words reveal the *weakness in the policies* and their implementation in the earlier plan periods.

With the TSP now as the mainstay of TD, and with the elaborate details which have been codified in regard to the operation of the TSP approach, if the achievements are much short of what we expect to achieve, most of the attention will remain involved with the operational details of TSP, and it is within this that we will try to locate 'what is eluding us'.

The short-falls in tribal development, or all that eludes us, has come to tribal development through the following three broad reasons :

(1) Disorientation in the Interpretation of the Objective.

(2) Inadequate Institutionalization of the Programme.

(3) Inefficiency in Technology of Planning.

Disorientation in Interpretation of Objectives : The genesis and the etiology of tribal development in India is from the Constitution. It spells out two distinct objectives, (a) protection from exploitation and (b) economic development. As students of social phenomena, it should not be difficult to appreciate that these two objectives imply a series of competing, and, at times, contradicting objectives.

(i) Where is the 'disorientation', what is its nature and what brings it, and

(ii) What are the implications of such 'disorientation' on Tribal Development ?

Let us examine the answers to these two questions. We may begin with straight answers to each of the two questions, and then examine each of them with some elaboration.

(a) The 'orientation' is with the political leadership, with the development planners, and with the academics, with the academics, with each of them individually, and more seriously, in all that flows through their inter-influence.

(b) According to dictionary definition, 'disorientation' refers to situation of 'incomplete context', 'disorganized sense of direction'. It is a situation of this nature which has come to get involved with (a) how each of the three—the political leadership, the development planner, and the academics perceive the central objectives of tribal development—elimination of exploitation and raising the level of economic development, and (b) the indicators in terms of which they describe the needed action and evaluate the achievements.

By now, the political leadership, the development planners, and the academics, each of them have arrived at a stage of perceiving the two objectives in misplaced contexts, and consequently, defining each of them in terms of fragmented indicators. In sum, it reveals a situation of *incomplete knowledge*.

(c) The reasons for such incomplete knowledge is more social and contextual rather than intellectual. Each of the three have their respective reasons.

(a) The political leadership, (specially those who are in power and these are the one that shape tribal development) have to oscillate between two sets of considerations. When on the platform of the political party, for obvious reasons, 'elimination of exploitation' receives prominence, and along with this, the urgency to reach the client-group (the tribals) as the beneficiary through family-oriented, poverty eradication programmes. On different occasions, when the political leadership finds themselves in office of power and decision making, the set of considerations have to be much beyond the population they emphasize rapid economic development. This brings the disorientation among the political leaderships. We will come to some details on this later in this paper.

The development planner, for all practical purposes, is the kingpin of tribal development. In the first instance, 'development planner' represents a wide array of functionaries, from the Planning Commission to the offices of the different Central Ministries, and within this, most importantly, the Ministry of Home Affairs/ Welfare, which during each Five-Year Plan Period, is entrusted with the responsibility to give shape to the national policy on Tribal Development, and from these to guide all those at the level of the State who are entrusted with the responsibility of TSP. The disorientation with the development planners is in the form of the mechanical approach they adopt in plan-formulation and programme-implementation. One of the traditions with development planning in India, and something which is getting deeply established, is the sectoral planning approach. In India we realize that while on the one hand there is the strong intention to attempt integrated development planning, but on the other hand we find that the development planner gets increasingly drawn to sectoral planning. As result, with the strong intention to approach planning from below, they are not able to work out from the shadow of the plan-definition as given by the Centre at the beginning of each Five-Year Plan.

There is another tradition with the development planners, which is getting established equally deep with them. Progress reporting is considered as an important responsibility of development planning. There has to be no debate on this, as such. In actual practice, for a variety of reasons, the quantification in progress-reporting exerts an overbearing influence on his definition of Tribal Development.

We may note, between the list of the four objectives, the achievements in respect of two of the objectives (raising level of productivity and development of infrastructure) can be evaluated in quantitative terms, while the mention of two other objectives (the development of human resources and elimination of poverty) which are complex in nature. In the first instance, achievements in respect to either of the two objectives, compared to the other two objectives, cannot be achieved through technological devices. Moreover, the stability as well as the level of relevance in the achievements in respect to these two objectives (elimination of poverty and development of human resources) depend on a set of complex across-the-system variables. It has been rightly realized by the planners that the development of 'inner-strength' has to be one of the clearly designated objective of Tribal Development.

With this before us, when we take a look at the indicators in terms of which the achievements of the Sixth Plan have been evaluated, we will note that out of the nine indicators listed, eight of them relate to achievements/weaknesses in the technology of planning, namely (i) the TSP is merely an agglomeration of State plans, (ii) very little consultation of tribal beneficiaries, (iii) arithmetical considerations in family oriented programmes, (iv) integration in administration of ITDP with other same level development programmes, (v) effective implementation of protective measures mainly those relating to exploitation, (vi) territorial and population coverage of the programme, (vii) enhanced input of appropriate technology, and (viii) improved monitoring and evaluation. As compared to this, we may note that only one objective 'improve the general awareness of the tribals/transcends beyond arithmatical achievement.

Inadequate Institutionalization of the Programme:

When any action programme becomes a well definable '*subject*', the success of such action programmes depends to a very large extent on the 'experts' and the 'professional institutions' for the subject. The institutionalization of a subject refers to combination of three components : (i) 'specialized knowledge' on the subject, (ii) the 'experts' with such specialized knowledge, and (iii) professional institutions which generate, exchange and communicate such specialized knowledge. It is the combination of these three components which bring precision and visibility to the definition of the subject, and more importantly, contribute to its success. As we have examined earlier, tribal development has the involvement of 'experts' from three distinct categories—the political leadership, the development planners, and the academics. Between these three, the role of the experts among the development planners and the academicians, and the contribution from these two in form of 'expert knowledge' and transactions of professional institutions is of crucial importance to the success of tribal development. It appears, tribal development in India had to suffer on account of visible deficiency in respect of each of these.

Civil servants form an important component of any development programme in India, and so also for Tribal Development. One of the characteristic features of the system of state civil servants in India is periodical transfers, with the understanding that they are 'generalists', and hence can be entrusted with the responsibility of any 'subject'. On account of this, the cadre of civil servants in India could not provide any 'experts' on tribal development. The 'generalists' could develop only fragmented expertise for obvious reasons. At times they were having responsibilities other than that of Tribal Development.

The contributions of such institutions as the Reserve Bank of India (through the Rural Credit Survey), the series of Agriculture Colleges in the country, the ICAR, the Ford Foundation, the FAO, in refining attentions towards rural development (RD) and in bringing out clear points for 'expert' knowledge, have gone a long way on stabilizing RD. As compared to this, the contributions from institutions like the Tribal Research Institutes (more than a dozen by now), the Anthropological Survey of India, towards generating 'expert' information on Tribal Development has been very dismal.

As regards the contribution from academic institutions, RD in India has received much from the Agriculture Colleges and Universities. In comparison to this, the University departments which have tribal development as a well defined subject in the syllabii, have not made much visible or meaningful contribution towards tribal development. The universities too have not been able to provide 'experts' on Tribal Development.

The Inefficiency in Technology of Planning:

As we have noted earlier in this paper, (i) planning from below, (ii) an integrated approach to planning, as away from the sectoral approach, and (iii) the vital significance of 'data' for realistic and effective planning, have been recognized as the key components of the planning-process. If we review how the planning exercise has been operating in India, it will not take much effort to find that development planning in India has very little to do with any three of these. A number of issues are involved with such three of these. A number of issues are involved with such realization, (i) issues relating to genesis and etiology and (ii) issues relating to the nature of deficiency with each of the three components listed above.

While planning from below is the approach we intend to follow in India, the overbearing influence of the Five-Year Plan as formulated by the Centre is something which vitiates the intentions.

In this connection, what needs to be understood is the sequence of conditions (or, more correctly, the compliment of situations), which contribute towards deeper, sustained establishment of the sectoral approach of planning discounting any visible effective effort towards integrated planning, from below. The role of the academics, and that of the professional institutions in initiating a shift from sectoral planning to integrated planning is of vital importance. The academics and the professional institutions (like the ASI, the TRI's, and the series of 'Development Study Institutes' in a number of States started under the agencies of the ICSSR) can build an intellectual atmosphere which will help to break the inertia in planning, so long deeply steeped in sectoral planning. The 'intellectual atmosphere' can come through various forms of wirtings readily intelligible and specific for the development planners. Such products from the academic and the professional institutions bring influence on the planning process and initiate some realistic efforts towards integrated planning. The beginning of such influences from the academic and the professional institutions will have to be 'from below', rather than attempting to influence (impress upon) the development planners at the centre (recall the Dube Committee or the Vidyarthi Committees referred earlier). Batch of these two committees have been able to achieve any thing other than integrated planning. The effective essence of the suggestions made by them have been 'reappropriation' in financial planning procedures. If the academics and the professional institutions associate themselves with local level planning processes through sustained, uninterrupted interest, a beginning towards integrated development planning can be made. What I have in mind is the 'adopted village' and the 'demonstration effect' approaches.

One of the most important, vital component for

effective and realistic planning has been 'data'. Unfortunately, this has been one of the weakest area in tribal development planning.

In relation to the nature any action-programme, the nature of the achievements from the programme depend to a large extent on (a) the organization of the programme, and (b) the 'expert knowledge' which evolves on the action-programme. Organization here refers to the structured hierarchical arrangement which is entrusted with the responsibility of conducting the action-programme. The 'expert knowledge' comes from two sources, the specialists/experts on the subject and from the professional institutions on the subject. In relation to TD, we may examine the experiences in regard to these.

The Organization of TD: Linked with every action programme is the structured arrangement which is expected to provide the action component of the programme. The constitution through Article 46 issues the 'directive principle' that TD has the responsibility of the 'state'. Through a set of Articles and Schedules the Constitution spells out the distribution of responsibility between the Centre and the State Governments. Articles 275, 340 and 164 spell out the distribution of responsibilities relating to general supervision, financial support, and designated responsibilities between the Centre and the States.

TD is as much a subject for the Centre as it is for the States. In fact, the on the ground appearance of the programme is a subject for the State government. In principle, there is a sharing of responsibility between the Centre and the States. Plan formulation is a responsibility for both the levels. The Centre is expected to provide the broad guidelines and spell out the perspectives, the States are expected to prepare a 'realistic' plan with reference to 'local conditions'. The planning exercise, in its full form has to be a judicious blend between 'planning from below' (all this may mean) and 'guidance from above'.

We may have a look at (a) the structured system that has taken shape at the Centre and at the level of the States, (b) how these function each individually, at the two levels, and (c) how they function in coordination.

At the Centre, the responsibility of TD has been held by one of the divisions of a Ministry. In any of these Ministries, the TD Division has been of rather minor significance in the charge of a civil servant of a middle rank. For a fairly long time the TD division was with the Ministry of Home Affairs, then shifted to the Ministry of Social Welfare, going back to the Ministry of Home Affairs and then returned back to the Ministry of Welfare. TD can be anyone's baby. This experience brings to sharp focus two points, (a) In view of the Statutory responsibilities through the Constitution, in the early phases, the responsibility may have been with the Ministry of Home Affairs, but later when it was realized that Welfare forms a major component of TD, the subject was assigned to the Ministry of the same name. By the Sixth Plan it had been made obsolutely clear that there will be a need for a shift in the orientation towards TD, the shift will have to be by approaching as a programme for economic development, rather than as a welfare-oriented programme. We may note that though there has been a shift in defining the orientation of the programme at the Centre, the responsibility of TD continues still with the Ministry of Welfare.

The other point we need to note relates to Centre-State relations in regard to development Planning. At the level of the State, the responsibility of TD is to entrust to a Ministry of the subject. In fact the Constitution makes this obligatory for the three States of Orissa, M.P. and Bihar. In sharp contrast to this, the Centre at no time had a Ministry on this subject.

With the States, the picture is sharply different, in quite some respects. Each State which has a sizeable tribal population does have a Ministry for TD. The three States of Orissa, M.P. and Bihar have such Ministry as part of the directives of the Constitution. The four North-Eastern States of Meghalaya, Mizoram, Nagaland, and Arunachal Pradesh do not have any such Ministry as each of these States are tribal majority, and hence every development programme in these States will have full bearing on tribal development. The States, like Gujarat, Maharashtra, West Bengal, Tamil Nadu, Karnataka, Rajasthan, Tripura, Manipur, Assam, Himachal Pradesh, Kerala, too have a Ministry for TD, (there may be local variations in the name of the Ministry). This stands in sharp distinction of what we have at the Centre.

The Centre has a guardian responsibility of giving a planned direction and thrust to TD. This has come to the Centre from the First Five-Year Plan onwards, for obvious reasons. By the Fifth Plan, with the introduction of the TSP approach, and all that the Centre had to contribute in bringing this, the compulsive of planning from above started getting deeply established. In this connection it needs to be noted that while on the one hand the formulation of plan by the Centre was the main guide for the States to formulate their plans, on the other hand, such exercises with the Centre were more in the nature of periodic formalities rather than an outflow from sustained, critical analysis. We may note how the 'informal' expert group and the task groups were formed on the eve of the Fifth Plan, and again, how the working Groups were formed on the eve of the Sixth and the Seventh Plan periods. On each of these occasions it was a sort of on-the-spot contributed official assembly of experts and functionaries whose names can be associated with Tribal Development. The exercise of plan formulation at the State is the influence, to a very large extent, by what comes from the Centre. Within this there is, however, a qualification. In its appearance, the plans formulated by the States may look like carbon copy of the plan as formulated by the Centre. The experience in this regard has led to the suggestion that 'The State tribal sub-plans should not be only be a compendium of tribal area project plans and tribal component of the programme of individual development departments but should also include programmes and outlays under important non-plan sectors having a developmental thrust....There is the feeling that the tribal sub-plan is merely an agglomeration of the State plan schemes taken up in the tribal areas. Central Ministries Plan schemes hardly feature in these documents'. In Tribal Development, there is always the suggestion for 'planning from below', in practice plan-coordination between middle and above even is non-existent. In planning the 'dissonance' between the Centre and the State lead to a complex set of situations bringing negative results.

On the ground, for many practical reasons, tribal development cannot be seen away from the programmes for rural development, such as IRDP, and the many other special purpose programmes. The multiplicity of development programmes beamed on the ground to a common area and its inhabitants distract the focus of tribal development, in many ways. Such situation confuses the planners, those involved with implementation on the ground, and in no less way, the recipient.

Today when much concern is shown on Centre-State relationship, shaping this as a subject of sharp debates and contests, the Centre-State relationship on development planning is one area which has received hardly any attention. So far no institutionalized system has been developed to give meaningful effect to this.

Expert Knowledge: As any action programme begins to get established through structured systems and well definable objectives (and relevance), over period of time three components evolve as indispensable requisites for the programme. The three components are (a) data, (b) experts and (c) professional institutions.

The introduction of the TSP approach led to the preparation of a visible data base for planning. Each of the State with TSP component was induced to conduct bench-mark surveys for the tribal areas and the tribal populations. By now all such data has become outdated, it needs to be updated, and additionally, put to serious analysis. 'Data' as base for planning refers to wide array of 'information', of different orders. The information has to be quantitative as well as qualitative. It has to have situation profiles, impact analysis, programe evaluation. The preparation of such information sets will involve deep attention to a series of conceptual and methodological exercise. It is any body's knowledge that feedback data on tribal development is near to non-existing. It may be a fact hard to agree more as when we are presented with list of an impressive corpus of literature on 'tribal development studies'.

For any action programme like tribal development, 'experts' come from two sources, from the governmental agencies and from the academic institutions.

One of the reliable methods to locate 'experts' is (a) to read the names of members nominated to official committees, (b) identify those associated with the preparation of official documents, (c) held official responsibilities, (d) authored 'learned writings containing substantial references to the subject, and (e) programmes involved with organising syllabi on the subject for academic. The contributions from 'experts' have been more ceremonial and discrete than substantive and sustained.

The bearing of professional institutions on the shaping the thrust and contents of rural development in India, from the CD approach to the IRDP approach, is a living example of the vital responsibilities which such professional organizations can assume. We have the chain of TRI's located in many of the States, and we have the Anthropological Survey of India. It is rather not very encouraging to note that any of these institutions have made hardly any appreciable contribution towards facilitating development planning.

As mentioned earlier, the TSP approach is referred to as the watershed in tribal development. This started with the Fifth Five-Year Plan, 1974 onwards. The period 1968 to 1972 may be taken as the preparatory period for formulating the TSP approach. The experiences from tribal development from the First to the Fourth Plan had started giving clear indications that a fresh look will need to be taken to the approach to tribal development, the strategy and the organization. It is interesting to note that this was the period when the anthropologists in India were also realizing that there is a need to take a fresh look towards their academic discipline, anthropology, and the classic subject of their discipline, tribal studies.

Much of the disorientation in the subject and its dismal performance came to anthropology in India through the over bearing influence of rapid commercialization of social research in India. Between the different social science disciplines, anthropolgy distinguishes itself from others through four distinctive characteristics of subject (i) the study of the tribes, (ii) integrated bio-cultural approach to the study of man, (iii) micro-study, and (iv) intensive field work approach. After Independence the rapid commercialization of social research in India came through the introduction of the Community Development Programme and the efforts of the PEO of the Planning Commission and the Ford Foundation to obtain ethnographic and evaluation information. A number of anthropologists were commissioned for such studies. And this initiated the process of disorientations. The intensive field work approach got compounded with survey method, tribal studies started getting compounded with (non-tribal) village studies, and the integrated bio-cultural approach started getting discounted in face of attractions for 'comparative sociological approach'. Through the sequence of events, as result, anthropology in India started getting farther away from meaningful, realistic tribal studies, and more so, tribal development.

Anthropology in India can contribute well and purposively towards tribal development if it attends to, to begin with, three broad directions (i) exercises to generate and develop relevant information, (ii) exercises to generate alternate perspectives of development, and (iii) provide 'experts' on tribal development. As an action programme, Tribal Development has to depend on two sets of data, (a) base line data, and (b) impact and evaluation data. The preparation of such data will expect a serious reorientation in the approach to research methodology. Anthropologists can assume the responsibility to prepare data profiles, situation analysis reports, operationalize 'development' in terms of social indicators and scales. The preparation of alternate models of development will expect a complex set of conceptual and methodological exercises. Some of the classical orientations which the subject will need are designing. The classical notion of 'development' which remains confined to the sub-culture of the discipline will need to mature out in terms of inter-disciplinary approaches. To be realistic as well as pragmatic in the conceptual outputs, anthropologists may have to examine with increasing rigour the conflict model of society.

In this paper I have tried to bring out some of the issues and themes involved with 'tribal policy'. We will need to postpone for another occasion a fuller discussion on 'tribal development and anthropology-issues and themes'.

3

Colonial Hangovers and Democratic Imperatives—A Study of Tribal Policy in India

Sachchidananda

India has been the home of a large number of ethnic communities from times immemorial. The cultural diversities between the different communities were immense. The British stumbled across this reality in the early years of their empire building. Their first brush was with the Paharias who lived in Jungle-terry, an undulating upland in what is known now as the Santal Pargana Division in Bihar. Forced by unprecedented famine in the early seventies of the eighteenth century, they took to raids on the plains people until they were brought under control by Augustus Cleveland between 1778-84. In order to pacify the Paharias and establish peace in the region, Cleveland hit upon the principle of indirect rule. The Paharia *Sardars* were given a monthly subsidy and assigned the responsibility of maintaining peace. The region was withdrawn from the jurisdiction of ordinary courts. Serious cases were taken to a Hill Assembly (Council of Chiefs) which met twice a year for dealing with sessions cases. Rules were drawn up for the work of the assembly. From

1782-1827 this arrangement continued. Although in 1827 the special regulation was repealed on the recommendation of James Sutherland, the government made it quite clear that the Paharias were not to be disturbed in their possessions in the free enjoyment of hills. In 1832, the government set apart a total area of 1366 square miles in the Santal Parganas for the settlement of the Paharias. This area was known Damin-i-Koh (skirt of the hills). However, by the middle of the 19th century, the area became the main concentration of the Santals.

Another experiment in indirect rule was made in the Kolhan government estate after the first Kol insurrection. In this area a set of rules known as Wilkinson rules was framed by virtue of which the HO village headman and divisional headman were given powers not only for the collection of revenue but also police powers for apprehension and arrest of offenders. This region was outside the purview of police and regular courts.

After the second Kol insurrection the entire Chotanagpur area was placed under an officer called Agent to the Governor-General. In 1854 it was to be administered as a non-regultion area. Dalton the first Commissioner of Chotanagpur, was of the opinion that the complicated machinery and civilised laws was unsuited to the backward tribals. After the Santal insurrection of 1855, the Santal Parganas including Damin-i-Koh was constituted into a separate district.

Such administrative arrangements were a precursor of the Scheduled District Act which was passed in 1874 whereby the local government was empowered to declare in respect of the tracts specified in the Act what enactments were to be and were not to be enforced and to notify the application, with modification or restrictions if necessary, of any inactments in force at the time in any part of British India. These tracts were known as Scheduled tracts and included areas in Assam, Rajasthan, Andaman islands, Bengal, Santal Parganas, Chotanagpur, some pockets in Maharashtra, Central Provinces, Madras and some areas in Punjab and United Provinces. The policy to be followed in the scheduled areas was to protect the interests of the tribal people. In Santal Parganas the government forbade sale and transfer of land either privately or by orders of court. In some areas hereditary serfdom was abolished. The village community system was fostered and efforts were made to prevent the rights of the tribes passing on to the non-tribals. Similar protective measures were taken to protect the tribals from exploitation, particularly in respect of land and forest.

The British government was inclined to leave the tribes alone. Attention was only given to them when on account of various grievances they rose in revolt and created a law and order problem. The first reaction was to crush the rebellion and to establish peace and then to look into the grievances of the tribals and remedy them to the extent possible. The policy of leaving them alone could also be attributed to the fact that the task of administration in the hills and forests in which the tribals lived was difficult and unrewarding. From the end of the 19th century onwards, throughout the country, the struggle for Independence was building up and it was necessary to keep the tribals away from it. Besides these reasons, a number of administrative officers sincerely held the view that the tribal people did not need any intervention and were better off and happier as they were. Such an attitude was not specifically basic and was not shared by all the colonial administrators. This view was probably inspired by Rousseau's image of the noble savage. There was a feeling that contact with civilisation has, the world over, impaired the fine qualities of the tribals.

Such a view may be characterised as the paternalistic view in which the ruler considers himself as the parent or the guardian of the community. The community itself is regarded as so undeveloped that it does not know its own ailments and maladies. It is left to the parent or guardian to take adequate care about the health and well-being of the ward. Such an attitude is not new since it finds a mention in the Dhauli Rock edict of Emperor Ashok. It goes without saying that chastisement or punishment of the community is very well within the perview of the ruler as it is in the overall interest of the people. Since the tribal communities were less developed than other communities, the administrative system of the latter would not suit the interests of the former. It is for this reason that tribal areas were converted into non-regulated areas where they were either left alone with their traditional rulers or village headmen under indirect rule or put in charge of rulers with extensive powers so as to enable them to look after tribal interests in a better way.

The policy of isolation was, however, never followed uniformly. The tribals were exploited by landlords and money-lenders and cheated by merchants. There was no check on these elements entering the tribal areas. Social workers were forbidden to work among them, while foreign missionaries were given all facilities and even encouraged in their efforts. The belief in the happy care free, noble savage was a myth. In many parts of tribal India, people did not have enough food. They suffered from serious diseases and mortality was high and their life was distracted by internecine fueds, conflicts, slavery etc. Serfdom was common and punishments were cruel. Thus life was not happy or idyllic in all tribal areas.

With the growth of humanitarian ideals of a welfare state, it is no longer possible to segregate a large section of the population. No government can afford to neglect them. After Independence political necessities and the democratic processes set into motion by the constitution, made the development of the tribals a concern of the nation. Thus after Independence the so called policy of isolation was neither possible nor desirable.

When the Montague Chelmsford reforms were on the anvil, it was realised that there were certain backward areas in the provinces where the people were primitive and there was no material on which political institutions could be founded. These were the areas specified under the Scheduled District Act of 1974 possibly[1] with certain additions. The government of India Act 1919 empowered the Governor-General-in-Council to declare any territory to be a backward tract and with the sanction of the Secretary of State to direct that the Government of India Act shall apply to the territory with such exceptions and modifications as may be prescribed in his notification. He may direct whether any Act of the Indian legislature shall not apply to the territory or shall do so with some modifications. Finally 19 areas were declared backward tracks. These backward tracks were divided into two groups with respect to the legislative authority of the provincial and central legislature. In respect of one category, the legislatures could not enact any law applying to them. The Governor-General-in-Council or the Governor-in-Council could apply any of the general enactments to them with necessary modifications. For the second category, the legislatures might pass laws but they could come into operation on such date and with such modifications as the Governor-General-in-Council or the Governor-in-council might direct. This dual classification was accepted by the Indian Statutory Commission. The first category was known as the wholly excluded area and the second category was known as areas with modified exclusion.

The question of excluded areas wholly or partially evoked a long and interesting debate in British Parliament. When the Government of India Bill 1935 was being discussed, Major Attlee, who was a member of the Simon Commission remarked. "We ought to err on the side of inclusion (in the schedule) and not on the side of exclusion". This was necessary to save the concerned population from the exploitation. Lord Eustace Percy[2] called the backward excluded areas a 'neglected garden'. He remarked that it was very difficult to keep back in cold storage the aboriginal population and wondered how far it could be led on towards absorption in the wider community round it. Mr. Butler[3], the then Under-Secretary of State of India warned against indiscriminate exclusion as it might go against the interests of the people. Earl Winterton[4] believed more in assimilation than in isolation and warned against creating chronological zoos. Ultimately, the two categories of excluded and partially excluded areas stayed on in the Government of India Act of 1935. The list in which both categories were embodied was the Government of India Order 1936. The main difference between the two categories was that the governor is required to exercise his function in regard to an excluded area in his own discretion. In regard to a partially excluded area, it is not so required and he may seek the advice of the ministers in this respect. The position of ministers in this regard is similar to that in the case of the normal portion of a province. The expenditure in an excluded area is non-votable but in case of the partially excluded areas it is votable. The partially excluded area and its administration is the special responsibility of the Governor. In respect to this area the advice of the ministers is not binding on the Governor. There was only a slight difference in theory between the political status of an excluded area and a partially excluded area. The difference could be great if the relations between the Governor and the ministers are such that he relies on them and does not invoke his special responsibility to act in his own discretion. Secondly, the demands in case of a partially excluded area must by submitted to a vote of the legislature, though the vote may not ultimately affect the demands. Thirdly, discussions could take place in the legislature in respect to partially excluded area without the Governor's previous assent.

This policy of protecting the tribals through the constitutional expedient of an excluded area or a partially excluded area evoked a protest from the politically conscious Indians and was strongly resented by them. It was indicative of the distrust of the Indian leadership on whom power was to devolve through the Government of India Act 1935. It was also interpreted as a desire to drive a wedge between tribals and non-tribals.

The Indian National Congress[5] at the Faizpur session (1936) expressed its views as follows:-

"This Congress is of the opinion that the separation of these excluded and partially excluded areas is intended to leave out of popular control, the disposition and exploitation of the mineral and forest wealth in these areas and to keep the inhabitants of these areas apart from India for their easier exploitation and suppression. This Congress holds that the same level of democratic and self governing institutions should be applicable to all parts of India without any distinction".

In the mid-forties when the negotiations for the transfer of power were in progress, the administrations became active to ensure the protection of tribal interests. Sir John Hubback[6], who had long experience of working in tribal areas in Bihar and Orissa, prepared a note on backward tribes at the instance of the Viceroy in 1944. He was of the opinion that the British government had a moral responsibility for the protection of the tribals even after the transfer of power. He recommended that the Indian government should allow the employment of officers for the uplift of backward tribals who would work under a British High Commissioner. Hubbock also suggested the formation of a three-member committee consisting of an administrator, an anthropologist and a missionary to oversee the administration of tribal areas. The Secretary of State for India was critical of the recommendations of Elwin that the tribals should be kept in reservations. He was doubtful about the political morality of maintaining the tribals as museum pieces.

T.S. Rutherford[8] who was governor of Bihar in mid-forties was against any form of intervention in tribal affairs by the government of India. He indicted the policy towards tribals in the following words:-

"We have not done much for them beyond a certain amount of protective legislation which functions effectively when the officers responsible are really sympathetic."

Ultimately, the proposal regarding the removal of the tribes from the jurisdiction of the provincial governments and their transfer to the control of an outside authoity fell down as it was impracticable. It was conceded that if India was fit to govern itself, she must also be able to look after her aboriginals. It may be mentioned that in all the discussions about the management of tribal affairs, the tribals were no where in the picture. The Adibasi Mahasabha hardly attracted any notice. Its leader Jaipal Singh did not plead the case for political autonomy for the tribals.

During the debates in Constituent Assembly Indian nationalist opinion was mainly shaped by Mahatma Gandhi and Pandit Nehru. Mahatma Gandhi's interest in the tribal problem was largely influenced by Thakkar Bapa. Tribal welfare was one of the items included in Gandhiji's fourteen-point reconstruction programme which was drawn up in January 1942. He believed that the Adivasis could not be neglected. He had intensely disliked the policy of isolation and status quo and the concept of the Excluded areas. In 1946 he said that he regarded as a "matter of shame that the Adivasis should be isolated from the rest of the nation of which they were an inalienable part. If a social worker was prevented from social service to the Adivasis, he should be prepared to go to prison. Under Gandhiji's inspiration a number of voluntary agencies were formed for social service in Gujarat, Bihar, Assam and other states. To some extent these activities brought some tribals into the mainstream of the national movement. These organisations became the channels for the spread of the ideas of nationalism and freedom. In course of time, a nationalist perspective on tribal problems emerged in contrast to the isolationist approach of missionaries and administrators.

Nehru's[10] perception of tribes was shaped by their early participation in different Congress sessions. In December 1937, Nehru met for the first time a mixed group of tribals from the North-East. He did not like the idea of segregating the tribal people from the rest of the country. He emphasised the unity of India and considered the concept of excluded areas as undesirable in course of a talk with the representatives of Chittagong Hill tracks in July 1945 at Simla. However, Nehru's enthusiasm about unity of the country in relation to the tribals began to wane during his visit to Assam in December 1945. He came to realise that the tribals needed a great deal of assistance from the government to shed their backwardness. They have also to be given protection to save them from exploitation. He began to feel that such groups needed autonomy and freedom to shape their lives as they liked. Thus Nehru's tribal philosophy moved from uniformity to protection and then to autonomy.[11]

Before Independence, Nehru was incensed at the British policy of segregating the tribal people through the concept of the Inner line. No person from outside could enter the Inner line without the permission of the district authorities. Acquisition of lands by outsiders was strictly prohibited. After Independence he saw the dangers of the open door policy as he observed 'it is between these two extreme positions that we have to function'[12]. This led to a middle of the road position for Nehru on tribal affairs. In the historic Objectives Resolution in the Constituent Assembly he made a strong plea for adequate safeguards for minorities, backward and tribal areas. During the subsequent debates he took the position that the tribal people should be protected in every possible way and that they should be governed by their customary laws. Despite stringent criticism in the Constituent Assembly, Nehru did not yield on the question of Inner line which continues to be in operation in Arunachal Pradesh, Mizoram and Nagaland.

Earlier Nehru was not in favour of giving reservations to the tribal people. It was Dharni Dhar Basumatri who impressed both upon Gandhi and Nehru the need for such a privilege. Gandhiji immediately agreed and wrote on a piece of paper "If reservation for these communities is not given, I have to undertake another fast." This made Nehru to give in and other members of the Constituent Assembly had to reluctantly agree to give tribal people this privilege. Nehru was against imposition of some other way of life on the tribals. He wanted them to develop on the lines of their own genius. He did not regard them as backward from the cultural point of view and wanted all Indians to view cultural diversity with respect.

The quintessence of Nehru's policy for tribals, popularly known as the *Tribal Panchsheel,* is expressed in the foreword he wrote for the second edition of Verrier Elwin's book 'Philosophy of NEFA (1960)'. It is a pity that in his own time and more so after him, administrators did not follow these principles as a matter of faith, although planners and policy makers paid lip sympathy to these sentiments. Administrators in different parts of the country did not take the trouble of discovering the genius of each tribal community and the differential patterns of its growth. They did not avoid imposing the same kind of scheme on the tribals as in non-tribal areas. The full play of market economy led to a decline in their traditional arts and crafts and to the imporvishment of the people. The pattern of education spread in the tribal areas alienated them from their own culture and made them second rate poor copies of people belonging to the advanced community of the same region. Tribal interests in land and forest were not effectively protected. For the more primitive tribals it affected the life support system through a shrinkage of resources for survival.

It would be useful to analyse the continuities as well as the departures in the tribal policy. During the colonial period and after Independence the continuities are all too apparent. This was largely due to the impact of Thakkar Bapa and Jaipal Singh. The interaction with all these leaders totally altered the perspective of the makers of the constitution. They were induced to provide for excluded and partially excluded areas, special protections for the tribals as well as reservations for them. The debates in the Constituent Assembly do not reveal any reappraisal of the previous stand taken by nationalist leaders in the matters of tribal welfare and protection. As many as twenty articles and two special schedules take care of the tribals. Article 46, in particular, provides for the promotion of educational and economic interests of the scheduled tribes and others and also their protection from social injustice and all forms of exploitation. Article 275 provides for grant from the Union to certain states for tribal development.

During the colonial period the administrators felt a sense of moral responsibility for the protection of the tribals to the point of their exclusion from fast moving political processes. They had no perception of the larger issues of social change and economic development and some of them even thought that status quo was good for the natives. While there was some point in stressing protection and the principle of full or partial exclusion was embodied in the constitution, the guarantees for protection had to be combined with programmes for rapid development which did not figure in the colonial regime. During the earlier regime the stress was on cleavages in Indian society such as between the tribes and castes. In free India the emphasis was on bringing the tribals into the mainstream. With the grant of universal suffrage, the tribals were given an opportunity for shaping their own destiny through the political process. The transformation in tribal areas was to be organised not through schemes of tribal welfare but through a process of participatory development in which the tribal leaders had a definite say. Thus the continuities and discontinuities in the tribal policies of the colonial government and in free India are clearly marked.

In the new Constitution, the Fifth and the Sixth Schedule were put in for the administration of the tribal areas. The Fifth Schedule applies to the tribal majority areas in eight states in middle India and the Sixth Schedule relates to the tribal areas of the North-Eastern region. The distinguishing feature of the scheduled areas is that the executive powers of the state extended to them under the Constitution is not absolute. The executive power is subject to the provisions of the Fifth Schedule. The executive of the union has the powers of giving directions necessary for the administration of the scheduled area and provides for drawing up and execution of schemes essential for the welfare of scheduled tribes in the state under Article 339. In the context of special responsibility of the Union Government, the governor has been assigned a special role and has been suitably empowered in relation to the administration of scheduled areas and the development of tribal people. He is required to draw up an annual report on the administration of scheduled areas and submit it to the president. The Governor may by public notification, direct that any act of parliament or legislature of the state may not apply to the scheduled areas or part thereof, or shall apply subject to such modification as specified in the notification. These provisions are so strong and comprehensive that the Fifth Schedule has been regarded by some legal authorities as a constitution within a constitution. The governor has also been given the power of making the provisions retrospective in effect. There are no qualifying clauses whatsover to circumscribe these provisions.

The executive powers of the Union under the constitution must be read with its special responsibility for providing necessary financial assistance to the states for raising the level of administration of the scheduled areas and the execution of such schemes as may be necessary for the development of tribal people.

These comprehensive provisions, however, have not been operationalised. No attempt has been made to elaborate as to what will constitute good government for these areas. The report of the governor is usually a compilation of sectional developmental activities. The report does not throw any light on the administration of scheduled areas. Such routine reports have not evoked any interest in the Union Government nor have they formed any basis of remedial administrative action. No attempt has been made to identify the deficiencies in the administration although it is well known that they do exist.

It was decided to use the Fifth Schedule for providing necessary administrative frame work for supporting the economic thrust and ensuring peace and good administration in the Scheduled areas. In pursuance of this decision the Constitution was amended in 1975 and the jurisdiction of the Fifth schedule was made co-extensive with the tribal majority areas covered in the tribal sub-plans. But the primary purpose of this amendment has suffered for want of any action to evolve a suitable frame for peace and good government in tribal areas and the issue of any guidelines from the central and the state governments in this regard. The special role of the governor which has developed in the states about the functioning of the governor in relation to his responsibilities for the administration of scheduled areas has been missed. The Governor acts on the advice of state cabinet and thus the Central govenment does not have the benefit of independent judgement about the situation. It is, thus natural that the report of the Governor, the only link between the tribal areas and the government, reflects only the perspectives of the state government. This report is neither prepared nor subjected to critical examination with the view to identify the problems and to take corrective measures.

Planned development of the tribals commence with the launching of the Five-year plans and the setting up of Community Development project. In course of time, community development was extended to cover the far flung tribal areas. During the First plan the main emphasis was to induce processes of change in all aspects of tribal life through community development. Attempts were made to secure people's participation and to create motivation for the acceptance of planned change. A large number of innovations were introduced in tribal areas to achieve a better standard of living while preserving their own cultural forms. During this period the emphasis was on providing immediate relief to the general mass of the population who were denied amenities of life during the colonial rule. At the same time, effort was also made to build up the productive infrastructure for future growth.

During the Second plan, 43 Special Multipurpose Tribal blocks were created in areas of tribal concentration. In each of these blocks, besides Rs. 12 lakhs which was provided for a C.D. block, an additional amount of 15 lakhs was provided by the Home Ministry as an additive. Thus, resources were poured in so that maximum development could take place. Top priority was given to the promotion of education followed by communication, agriculture, animal husbandry and health care. Additional outlays were provided so that the pace of development could be accelerated and the gap between the tribal and other area could be narrowed.

On the recommendation of the Elwin Committee for the evaluation of the SMPT blocks these were converted into Tribal Development blocks during the Third plan. By the end of the Fourth plan, 500 T.D. blocks covered all the tribal areas with two-third concentration of tribal population. During this plan financial assistance from the Central and the state sectors came more freely. More emphasis was given to food production and individual farm product plan was taken up. Economic upliftment was given top priority followed by education, health, housing and communication. During the Fourth plan more emphasis was given to the regional approach. Six pilot projects covering 40 thousand tribal families were created. These projects were agriculture oriented with stress on providing agricultural inputs like implements, fertilisers, seeds, irrigation facilities, etc., besides developing veterinary services, fisheries, etc.

The Fifth plan adopted the integrated area development approach. It was during this plan that the tribal sub-plan approach was introduced. This approach had three components:-

(a) Integrated tribal development projects for tribal areas with fifty per cent or more S.T. population.

(b) Modified area development approach for pockets having a total population of 10 thousand and an S.T. component of 50% or more.

(c) Projects for development of primitive tribal groups.

The tribal sub-plan is implemented with resources from :-

(a) State plans

(b) Special central assistance

(c) Flow from the central sector/centrally sponsored scheme.

(d) Institutional finance.

The purpose of special central assistance was to act as an additive and catalyst for spurring financial investments by the state government and financial institutions. This is allocated to the states on the basis of total S.T. population in the state and proportion of the area occupied by S.T. population and inversely proportional to the net domestic product of the state.

During the Sixth plan the percentage of planned funds of central ministries earmarked for tribal development out of the total plan allocation ranged between 4.8% and 12%. Institutional finance is an important ingredient of beneficiary oriented scheme programmes. The subsidy amount is available from Central or State funds. However, institutional finance has not emerged as a significant support to tribal development.

In the Seventh plan promises were held out for stringent anti-exploitative measures along with pushing up socio-economic development. The care of small primitive tribes was high on the agenda. Remedial measures were proposed for the alienation of tribal land on account of putting up of irrigation dams, factories, mines, etc. Suitable rehabilitation measures have to be taken for the displaced tribals. Planning has to be judicious mix of beneficiary oriented programmes, women, resource development and infrastructural growth. Three million tribal families were to be assisted for building up a sound economic base. It was realised that the protective legislation for the tribals was to be more rigorously pursued. Tribal families living in the forest villages have to be given full rights. Special care has to be provided for tribal women. Importance is to be given to the ethos, needs and aspirations of specific tribal groups while keeping the state and national priorities in view. More attention has to be paid to planning from below. The co-ordination between government and voluntary agencies has to be improved. It is to be seen that the dependency of the tribals on the government is reduced as far as possible and the beneficiaries are duly involved at the planning and implementation stage.

It was expected that the tribal population would benefit by the general development programmes in the normal course. Special Central assistance was to supplement these efforts so that the pace of development could be speeded up. But the hopes in this regard were not fulfilled. As the benefits of the general programme did not percolate to the tribals and the supplemental programmes, in fact supplanted them. The sub-plan strategy was intended to usher in integrated development cutting through sectoral hurdles. A number of poverty alleviation programmes were taken up through the ITDP projects. As a result of these steps the proportion of the tribal people below the poverty line has gone down. 3.46 million scheduled tribe families were covered during the Sixth plan period. However, the process of deprivation has pushed back a large number of people to the unorganised sector towards the margin. Unequal access to development opportunities have engendered a feeling of relative deprivation which is acute and pervasive.

A review of the working of the tribal sub-plan approach has revealed that it has been seen as an area development plan rather than as a strategy for the development of tribals. Between 1985-89, 37% of the total outlay under the TSP from the state plan was utilised for infrastructure development. In Bihar, M.P. and Orissa this expenditure was above 50%. There is more stress on quantitative investments rather than on qualitative achievements. Beneficiary oriented programmes have received a much lesser share. It is no where above 20%. The sectoral allocation of the T.S.P. does not reflect the felt need of the people and as such, has not created the desired impact.

There has been multiplication of administrative agencies for the implementation of the TSP both at the state and the project levels. The Project Officer in the ITDP has been reduced to a role of co-ordinator. In the absence of financial and administrative powers he finds it difficult to perform even his limited functions. The ITDP has not been accepted as a unit for planning. The schemes are implemented without being adapted to the needs of the tribals. The relationship between the ITDP and the District Rural Development Agency, both working in the same areas, is not clear. This creates a confusion in the public mind.

In some tribal areas there has been a revolution of rising expectations. Even though some tribals have made rapid progress, they are actively aware of their relative deprivation. The interests of the weaker and less articulate section of the tribal population has generally suffered. No effort has been made to bring the tribals close to the administration so that the latter is more responsive to its needs and aspirations. The voluntary agencies working in tribal areas who have much experience and enjoy the confidence of the local people could be actively involved in the entire process.

The complex problems facing the scheduled tribes can be tackled smoothly if we empathised with them and take a holistic view of life. It is not always possible to put a dividing line between developmental and non-developmental facets of administration. If one does so, they may lose their true import and become even dysfunctional. Experience has shown that the development plan for particular tribal areas has to be drawn with the social and economic parameters. There are wide differences between resource rich and resource depleted areas. The cultural differences between communities have also to be kept in mind. There may be a broad framework for tribal development at the national and the state level but to operationalise them uniformly at the ground level is frustrating and even dysfunctional.

In spite of legislative and administrative measures, it has not been possible to do away with all forms of exploitation. Professor N.K. Bose, the then Commissioner for Scheduled Castes and Tribes, in his report specifically mentioned this. He attributed the failure in this regard to the mode of production in our society.

The TSP strategy should be restructured and refined to ensure adequate quantification for TSP, adaptation of schemes to suit the needs of tribal people, adequate assistance to each family and participation of tribal beneficiaries. The programme should be efficiently monitored and evaluation of outcomes should be conducted. The participation of the people in programme planning, implementation and evaluation is a must.

Development is a dynamic process, The advancement of a community is not to be assessed with reference to some indicators but also in terms of its relative position in the national economy. Hence, the growth of the economy and the share of the community in question should be kept in view. New opportunities in the organised sector have gone to people with better education, skills and command over economic resources who are close to the corridors of power. Except the gains made by the tribals through reservations, their position in the national economy has gone down.

In a recent move the government has abolished the post of the Commissioner of Scheduled Castes and Tribes who was appointed under Article 338 of the Constitution to oversee the implementation of the tribal policy. Its functions have been taken over by the Commission for Scheduled Tribes and Castes which has been given statutory powers. However, the annual reports of the Commissioner or the Commission which are laid on the tables of parliament have not evoked any lively debates among the members. This indifference to the cause of these weaker sections of population is unfortunate.

This brief review of the quest for the tribal policy for India clearly demonstrates the need for fresh thinking in this regard. We have moved from the paternalistic approach to the welfare approach and from them on to the development approach which is characterised by participation of the tribals in the decision making process. This is essential to bring the tribal people in the mainstream of national polity and to effect social economic and emotional integration with them.

REFERENCES

1. Parliamentary Debates. Fifth Series, Volume 301.
2. Ibid.
3. Ibid.
4. Ibid.
5. Quoted in K.S. Singh 'Tribal Society in India' Manohar, New Delhi, 1985, p. 112.
6. Ibid, p. 114.
7. Ibid, p. 115.
8. Ibid, p. 116.
9. Ibid, p. 178.

10. Sachchidananda: 'The Legacy of Nehru and Tribal Policy in India' in "The Legacy of Nehru", G.B. Pant Institute, Allahabad (forthcoming).
11. Ibid, p. 3.
12. Elwin Vevviev: Forthote 16 Forward: A Philosophy for NEFA, Shillong, 1964.
13. Barthakor P.B.: Dharnidhar Basumatari, Veteran paliamentarian 'The Sunday Sentinal', Guwahati, June 18, 1989.

4

Tribal Policy and Issues

Bhupinder Singh

It is said that India does not have a tribal policy. It is not clear what "policy" is supposed to stand for when this question is asked. Evidently, a policy must have certain objects in view with reference to which it is framed. For instance, there is a national forest policy, a national industrial policy and so on. Currently, there is talk of a national agriculture policy; if and when it comes about, it will help the perspectives of agriculture experts, the implementing machinery, the farmers, etc., that is, all those who are intimately connected with agriculture. But it is difficult to conceive of a policy for Maharashtrians, Bengalis, Tamils and so on. Nevertheless, there is a point when the question of tribals is raised. The scheduled tribes form, by and large, the weakest link in the chain of the diverse ethnic and linguistic groups constituting the Indian society. As a consequence, their treatment by the state and society has to be given careful thought and consideration, leading to a package which could, perhaps, be denoted by "policy".

Irrespective of the fact whether there is an established tribal policy or not in the form of a neatly-tied desiderata package, elements of it are strewn here and there. First and foremost, the basic charter is contained in the Constitution. There are several provisions. Article 46 of the chapter on Directive Principles of State Policy is the lode-star. It calls for protection of scheduled tribes from social injustice and exploitation as well as promotion of their educational and economic interests. Even the Fundamental Rights like prohibition of discrimination on grounds of religion, race, caste, sex or place of birth in Article 15 and equality of opportunity in matters of public employment in Article 16 have been watered down to accommodate the needs of scheduled tribes. Article 275 relating to grants from the Union to certain states is open-ended in so far as devolution of financial resources for development schemes for scheduled tribes and raising the level of administration of Scheduled Areas are concerned; constitutionally, no constraint on resource availability for development purposes and administrative machinery for such measures is conceived. Then there is the over-arching Fifth Schedule relating to the administration and control of Scheduled Areas and Scheduled Tribes. But, apart from the administrative aspect that it deals with, its importance lies in the legislative measures that it enables to promulgate; the Governor's powers in this regard are sweeping. The paternalistic approach embodied in the Fifth Schedule is capped by empowerment of the Central Govt. to give directions to states (a) as to the administration of Scheduled Areas in para 3 there of and (b) formulation and implementation of welfare schemes for STs in Article 339(2). The ingredients of tribal policy are, therefore, unmistakable, though tucked away in different parts of the Constitution. They need to be pieced together to infuse coherence. It is noteworthy that they touch vital socio-political and socio-economic aspects.

It is sometimes argued that a tribal policy should be a cultural construct. Not unnaturally, cultural anthropologists set great deal of store by cultural elements in a tribal policy; maybe some feel that a tribal policy should basically concern itself with cultural ethos only of the tribal population. There is lot to be said in favour of such a view, as the nexus between culture on the one hand and political, economic and social state of tribal societies on the other, is close and inextricable. This view finds considerable sustenance in the present-day global emphasis on preservation of culture and life-style of tribal communities along with their modernisation. Whether this is, *ipso facto,* feasible or not is a moot point. The time and attention devoted to it in the earlier times is evidence of the importance in which it was held at one time. Nevertheless, that this aspect of the tribal horizon has not slipped from the view is evident from the first of the five principles of *Panchsheel,* whose validity is not doubted even today, according to which development should be along the lines of genius of the tribal community and nothing should be imposed on them. The preservation of culture and assertion of tribal identity have become the *liet-motif* of the charter of demands of tribal communities progressively during the post-independence era. If a conscious policy has to be devised, it should, in consequence, have cultural component as one of its important dimensions.

In the context of revivalist currents lashing the tribal societies today, to what extent is it possible for these societies to assure themselves preservation of their identity and culture ? The question had evoked lively interest among the social scientists, but since a majority tended to look at the evolving societies as outsiders from a distance, it was of academic value to them. It was not often that a social scientist involved himself so much in a study-society that he felt more than a theoretical interest. In India today, some of the ethnic societies have become conscious of the juncture in history they are placed in. It will not be surprising to learn from a probe that the question has started vexing them. Their response to the ongoing metamorphosis induced by modernistic forces will be highly instructive and should be studied carefully.

Integration and Identity

The question of doctrine of integration versus assimilation has been discussed times out of number. There have been comments on what "mainstream" can possibly mean in the context of the idea of integration of the tribal societies into mainstrean. It is not profitable to continue to dwell on the controversy. But there are one or two points which need consideration. Firstly, it cannot be forgotten that the progenitors of both "assimilation" and "integration" belong to the non-tribal sections. The tribals whose destiny is sought to be tied up with such dogmas, have had no share in shaping them. A unilateral frame is not only inequitous but also liable to carry bad faith. It can and, in the present circumstances, does arouse indignation. The second point to be considered is that a tribal policy should take full cognizance of the differential attributes of different scheduled tribe communities: not only is each scheduled tribe community grounded in different historical, environmental, linguistic and cultural milieu, but it has also evolved into different stages of socio-economic development. In a sense, each community has a unique personality and identity. No doubt, a policy takes note of the diversity of conditions and attempts to make a pronouncement comprehending an entire specturm. Nevertheless, the tribal scenario is so vastly differentiated that the pitfalls in policy-making are needed to be kept in view.

The factor of great diversity of tribal situation has

special relevance for the planner and the administrator. Apart from the fact of different tribal communities arrived in disparate stages of socio-economic development being rooted in a variety of cultural moorings, the quantum and quality of resources of their physical environment have to be reckoned with. Some tribal communities are encysted in comparatively affluent resource environment, while some inhabit impoverished affluent resource environment, while some inhabit impoverished resource regions. The planning and development policy can ignore these differences at the peril of relevance and utility.

The policy can state the objectives. For the achievement of the objectives, the means and instruments have to be spelt out, as also the change agent. Further, the milieu in which the dynamics of change are embedded has to be clearly understood. Certain parameters of the milieu may promote and hasten change, while some others may impede and stall it. The most important parameter in the milieu is the attitude of the people towards development and development agents. How do the tribals react to development measures in vogue ?

Planned Development

The history of post-independence planned development is embossed with a paternalistic stamp. The community development movement started, no doubt, with the idea of "involvement" of people in different programmes; the Tribal sub-Plan concept commencing in the Fifth Five-Year Plan period called for tribal "participation". In actual fact, both "involvement" and "participation" have been not more than mirages. The ruling classes have, more often than not, proceeded on the assumption that they were acting in the best interests of the people and tribals. But the results of the efforts of the past four decades have been lack-lustre. This is not to decry the achievements in certain fields.

For instance, the quantum-jump in the level of food-grains production is credit-worthy, though in the lack of affordability on the part of a certain percentage of the population of two square meals a day, self-sufficiency seems more illusory. The point is that these decades we have experimented with the idea of planned development being an official programme with the people in tow. The results are clear. One would like to ask now whether it is possible to make it more a people's programme. Fears are expressed that such an experiment could be beset with enormous pit-falls, an important one being that it could lead to concentration of power and wealth without accountability in a minority, leading further to wastage of public resources. Such criticism overlooks the fact that the present system is benighted on that very score. A change may not be worse. Optimists feel that empowerment of the people could, on the one hand, impart the right direction to the development processes and, on the other, evoke a much higher degree of people's response. In any event, having given enough latitude to the ongoing experiment, it might be worthwhile turning to another. The imperatives of democracy also demand that power should reposit in the people.

For quite some time, the air has been thick with the talk of decentralisation of powers. In a small number of states, statutes have been framed to make decentralisation a reality. But other states have yet to translate the word into deed. Further, it is necessary to be wary of the contents. Decentralisation should not lead to concentration of power from one higher tier to another intermediate tier. If it is to be meaningful, the devolution should permeate all rungs, from the highest through the middle tier to the grass-roots, linked organically. In other words, one tier should not feel the loss or gain at the cost of another. Power should not get concentrated in one tier. The step-down and step-up series should have rational relationship, mutually supportive and reinforcing.

It bears reiteration that in a bottom-up development process interacting with top-down national vision and goals, the contents of plans and programmes become realistic, responding to people's needs as well as to national priorities. At the grass root level, the prospective tribal beneficaries should be able to project their needs and get them incorporated in the block plan and ITDP project report. In implemention, they should have even a more direct role. Cultivation, and more specifically shifting cultivation, could, in such circumstances, be backed up by upgrade technology; they could participate in school building construction, social forestry, well construction, road construction, etc. Should beneficiary-participation of this nature occur on a big scale, the entire process would receive an elan.

The Fifth and Sixth Schedules

The Constitution offers two paradigms of politico-administrative framework for tribal areas and tribal people. In fact, the principles behind the two paradigms can be treated as arch-stones of a tribal policy. They are contained in the Fifth Schedule of the Constitution which embodies a paternalistic interface between the state and the tribal, and the Sixth Schedule whose provisions epitomize devolution of authority in certain spheres for autonomy and self-governance. Considering the lowly position in society occupied by the tribal population, a sincere paternalistic attitude after independence could not normally have been misconstrued, though it contains within it seeds of patronising arrogance. Clearly, its need should keep on waning in proportion to the advancement of the scheduled tribe people. The self-governing devolution in the Sixth Schedule is supposed to allow free play to the genius of the tribal communities, which developed, largely in isolation over aeons, their own concept of autonomy. In today's tribal scenario, both are valuable assets, particularly useful for the Central Indian mass of tribal people who need both paternalistic care and endogenous growth. Both these concepts can be regarded as mutually-consistent critical ingredients of a tribal policy.

But paternalistic care and endogenous growth are approaches only, though important without doubt. The direction in which the state should move vis-a-vis tribals is prescribed in Article 46 of the Constitution. In it the state has been enjoined to protect the tribals from exploitation and injustice on the one hand and to promote with special care their educational and economic interests, on the other. In delineating the two areas, the constitution-framers placed their fingers on the central nerve. The populist compulsions of the present day politics have spawned a stream of rhetoric on the two clauses of the Directive Principle, but matching action in the field is scarce. The lackadaisical executive performance in the field, could in a sense, be interpreted as erosion of the sanctity of a directive principle of the Constitution. If a directive principle has not attracted sincerity of purpose, one is liable to ask the question whether a policy would. Nevertheless, this is no alibi for non-evolution of a policy, if otherwise justified. But the policy should comprehend and may concordantly transcend the two dicta of the directive principle.

Working of Sixth Schedule

As mentioned earlier, the Sixth Schedule confers a degree of autonomy on the District Councils constituted in certain states of the north-east. They have powers, inter alia, to legislate on certain subjects, administer justice to a certain extent through village councils or courts, collect and impose taxes as specified. While the general design of autonomy does enable the people of the concerned districts to make laws, administer justice and perform other sundry acts through their own institutions "in accordance with their own genius", two points need consideration. The first relates to financial arrangement. According to Clause 13 of the Sixth Schedule, "the estimated receipts and expenditure pertaining to an autonomous district which are to be credited to, or are to be made from, the Consolidated Fund of the State shall be first placed before the District Council for discussion and then, after such discussion, be shown separately in the annual financial statement of the state to be laid before the Legislature of the State". It appears that these provisions have not been followed in entirety in the State of Assam. The Autonomous District Councils have voiced the grievance that, as a rule, no opportunity for discussions of financial position is afforded them nor adequate weightage given to their views by the state government. On the contrary, they are presented with a financial *fait accompli.* Secondly, the provision in clause 16 of the Sixth Schedule conferring power on the state government to dissolve a District Council has been resented, as it is liable to be misused. It seems that the two devices need to be implemented in a spirit of mutual understanding, respecting the autonomy implicit in the Schedule. However, in actual working, friction seems to have developed between the autonomous District Councils and the State of Assam. This matter needs examination.

Plains Tribes of Assam

According to Article 244 of the Constitution, the provisions of Fifth Schedule apply to the administration and control of the scheduled areas and scheduled tribes in any state other than the States of Assam and Meghalaya. Thus, the Fifth Schedule does not cover ST people of Assam, in plains or in hills. Further, the protion of the tribal areas in the States of Assam, Meghalaya, Tripura and Mizoram. The Sixth Schedule covers only two hill districts of Assam, i.e. the North Cachar Hills district and the Karbi Anglong district. The plains tribes in the State of Assam have been left out from the Sixth Schedule. Thus, the provisions of both the Fifth and Sixth Schedules are denied to the plains tribes of Assam.

Dealing with the question of plains tribals, the North-East Frontier (Assam) Tribal and Excluded Areas Sub-Committee remarked in their report (1947) submitted to the Advisory Committee on Fundamental Rights, Minorities, Tribal Areas, etc. of the Constituent Assembly, that "the population of the plains tribals which is being gradually assimilated with the population of the plains, should for all practical purposes be treated as a minority". They recommended that measures of protection for their land and reservation of seats in provincial legislatures should be undertaken. They hoped that the question of their representation and protection would be considered by the Minorities Sub-Committee. They made these observations notwithstanding the fact that the question of plains tribals did not concern the Sub-Committee directly.

More than four decades have elapsed since the Bordoloi Committee envisaged assimilation of plains tribes and their treatment as minority. In the first instance, the two propositions do not appear to be consistent. In any event, the important point is that, as of today, the several plains tribes of Assam have not lost each its distinct identity. As a matter of fact, the pride in self-identity and cultural traditions has been on the increase. This is true of almost all ethnic groups in India. But, presently, it has a special significance in the Assam and Central India context. In Assam, the demand for Bodoland and in Central India the demand for Jharkhand have been raised. Further, some other tribal groups are groping towards autonomy for self-management and self-expression. Ethnic states have been established earlier in the North-East like Nagaland, Mizoram, Meghalaya. From hindsight, it appears they have been the product of *ad hoc* decisions. A well-thought policy which encompasses all short-term and long-range repercussions and ramifications may have to be hammered out.

The Fall-out of Development

It is necessary to look back in retrospect at the tribal scenario which is the sum total of the development and other processes operating during the past four decades. In doing so, the fact that these processes have been polar has to be appreciated. The development impulses have been generated at the ruling end and transmitted to the "beneficiary" which in reality is the ruled end. The object of planned development in tribal areas, as indeed elsewhere, is to promote socio-economic growth and to improve the quality of life. The results are remarkably visible in those tribal areas where "development" has been at the highest pitch, with the largest investment. This is clearly demonstrable in the central belt having a concentration of water, forest and mineral resources, which coincidently is also the zone of concentration of tribal population viz. Bihar, Orissa, Madhya Pradesh, Maharashtra and Gujarat. In these central highlands, major, medium and minor projects in hydel, mining, industrial, etc., fields have been located in tribal lands and, as a consequence, tribal families have been displaced from their agricultural and habitational lands. Large tracts of forests have been felled to make room for these projects and townships. Large sections of migrant population have been imported for running them. A hoary agro-forest culture has been relentlessly destroyed and replaced by a crassly modernistic industrial culture. The victims are the autochthons who have been robbed of the basic means of livelihood, i.e. land, water and forest. Cut off from their traditional moorings and alien to the new totally materialistic culture, they have been adrift for generations. Hopefully, they will adapt themselves more and more in future.

The question is pertinent: what has development in such tribal regions meant to (a) the general national economy and (b) to the tribals living therein ? The general economy has perhaps gained with the establishment of hydel (like Damodar, Subarnarekha, Hirakud) projects, mines (all over Chottanagpur, Orissa, M.P.), steel plants (like at Bokaro, Rourkela, Bhilai, Viskhapatnam) and other industrial complexes. Indeed, some of the mega-projects of the central zone Ruhr of India contribute in employment. But, *pari passu*, tribal life and culture have received serious shock and damage. Once the lords of land and forest, the tribal folks of the region have been deprived of both these resources. Further, unlettered and unskilled, they have been unable to participate in the modern economy. In the result, what has promoted national economy has spelt their disaster. A policy should attempt reconciliation.

Incidentally, one might consider here the second principle of the *Panchsheel*. It calls for respect to be shown to tribal rights on land and forests. It seems that this principle was inscribed with a degree of prescience. No doubt, the question of the basic resources of tribals, land and forests, would have been important in Nehru's days; nevertheless, it cannot be gainsaid that its relevance has grown enormously with the passage of years and today it is critical. There has been so much erosion of these two resources on account of both private land-grab and state acquisition, that it has driven the economy of many tribal socieities to desperate straits. Whereas this *Panchsheel* should have been complied with as an article of faith in a tribal policy, it has been observed more in breach.

One has to be clear about the directions and implications of the on going planning process in tribal areas. It may have been possible so far to overlook and brush aside the effects on the local population, particularly a vulnerable section like the tribals. But is it feasible much longer to ignore the grave fall-out of economic policies on the local population ? To understand the situation in its fullness, it is necessary to cast a glance at the way the processes have worked in different tribal areas in the world. Accounts suggest that in pursuit of mineral, water and timber interests, national majorities in different countries of the globe have been pushing the tribal minorities, very often miniscule, to the brink of economic penury and starvation, at a short length from ultimate extinction. The struggle has been unequal. The tribal minorities have not had the capacity to withstand the onslaughts. In our own country, the marginalisation of tribal communities all over is discernible. It comes out in bold relief in certain parts where industrialisation has been advancing mindlessly, as in Central India. The stage of extinction would, perhaps, never be reached here, because of in-built constitutional and political checks. That itself could be a negative point, since it creates a situation similar to that of a patient in a prolonged coma. In the contemporaneous tribal situation, particularly in Central India, there are some hopeful signs. The angry and frustrated tribal communities of Jharkhand area have risen in reaction. They like to see the end of neo-colonial exploitation of the region's resources. But they have had to travel a long arduous way since the era of destitution to the present day.

In the welter of the tension and strife in the society, the mass of scheduled tribes are getting marginalised. But there are some vulnerable groups among them who are being pushed out of the nation's consciousness altogether. It may be a fact of contemporary history that some volatile and aggressive tribal communities have been able to press for and succeed in acquiring ethnic territorial units and some tribal communities of Central India have continued to agitate for politico-administrative rights. But, it is a mis-apprehension to infer that all tribal groups are cast in aggressive mould. Distinct from the few groups thus visible on the horizon, is the comparatively inert mass of tribal people across the length and breadth of the country. Most of the groups composing the mass are hardly articulate. There are some among them whose members live out their lives without ever having come to the notice of the non-tribal sections of the society and even neighbouring tribal societies. Some of them have been labelled infelicitously as "primitive tribal groups". They could be called "primary groups". Each of them is numerically rather small, some consisting of a few hundreds only. Many of them are afflicted with rather painful problems of health and nutrition. The Birhor and Pahariyas of Bihar, the Juang and Hill Kharia of Orissa exemplify. They call for urgent attention. Health and education are the entry points for their ministration. Several plans have been afoot, but none has really been imbued with adequate understanding and empathy. It is a vital area of human concern.

Scheduling and Descheduling

As per clause (1) of Article 342, a Presidential notification was issued in 1950 containing the names of tribal groups and communities deemed to be "Scheduled Tribes" in relation to a particular state or union territory. Subsequent amendements to the list of scheduled tribes have been carried out by Parliament in accordance with clause (2) of the Article. It is remarkable that there has not been a single case of exclusion from the list (descheduling) while additions (scheduling) have been made over the years. It speaks of the manner in which political processes have operated. Soft electoral politics rule out possibilities of exclusion, while pressures for scheduling mount beyond resistance. Merit of a proposal is thus pushed into background.

There is another facet. By the very nature of the case, it is difficult to evolve any objective and foolproof set of criteria which would enable slot a group or a community as a "tribe" beyond doubt. Instrinsic ambiguity and vagueness characterise the task of categorisation, enhancing proneness to popular pressures. In such an event, greater reliance on experts views becomes imperative. In fact, if we have to avoid *ad infinitum* expansion of the scheduled list, extending into greyer areas, the findings of the expert bodies should be made mandatory.

Policy and Basic Law

Ultimately, a tribal policy will perhaps mean different things to different people. It can not be circumscribed to one aspect. It should have a pan-ethnic character. Issuing from government and as an embodiment of the will of the society, it should touch on all vital aspects: political, social, economic, environmental, educational, cultural, etc.

The eighties have been a period of unprecedented turmoil for the Indian Republic. Passions have run high over many issues, many "isms". The poisonous roots of cleavage and potential conflicts buried under nationalism during pre-independence times and put safely behind in the early post-independence era, have been spreading. The forces of communalism, linguism, regionalism, casetism, etc. have been receiving such support that they do not hesitate to bare their fangs. Many issues have erupted into violence and bloodshed and the experience has been traumatising. A number of questions have come to the fore. Are the provisions in questions have come to the fore. Are the provisions in the Constitution adequate to meet the emerging situations ? Or, notwithstanding their adequacy, the failure lies in their being ignored ? Does the Constitution possess adequate political ambience to provide for interplay of diverse forces, still uniting them under the shield of one multi-religious, multi-regional, multi-linguistic, multi-caste, multi-ethnic, etc. society ? If, on examination, it is found that the constitutional spaces do not accommodate multiplicity of political entities and movements, there should be no bar to a fresh look at the Constitution. Notwithstanding acceptance of the Constitution as a repository of perennial philosophy and goals, it should not remain impervious to contemporaneity. Should the need arise, it has to be adapted to changing times, while remaining anchored to the verities.

5

Approaches Of Gandhi And Nehru To The Tribal Problem Of North-East India During The Colonial Period.*

B. Pakem

* This paper is based on the present author's papers on "Gandhi and the Tribals", in *Tribe,* (Tribal Research Institute, Udaipur), Vol. VI,, No. 4, 1970, pp. 12-20; and on "Jawaharlal Nehru's Tribal Panchshila and the Hill People of North-East India : The Policy of Segregation-A Critique", a Seminar Paper on *Jawaharlal Nehru and the Disadvantaged, Shillong,* September 25-26, 1989.

5

Approaches Of Gandhi And Nehru To The Tribal Problem Of North-East India During The Colonial Period*

[illegible]

---

* This paper is based on the present author's papers on "Gandhi and the Tribals" in Tribe (Tribal Research Institute, Udaipur), Vol. VI, No. 1, 1979, pp. 11-26 and on "Jawaharlal Nehru's Tribal Panchsheel and the Hill People of North-East India: The Policy of Integration" [illegible] Jawaharlal Nehru and His Contemporary [illegible], September 22-25, 1989.

The two great national leaders of colonial India, Gandhi and Nehru, while dealing with the bigger issues of dependent India, did not fail to appreciate the smaller issues like the problem of the tribal people of the country. Both of them could not visit the tribal areas of North-East India due to the British policy of isolating the tribal people with their inner line regulation and other restrictions imposed by the administration. But both of them could meet the tribal people because the latter on their own, desired either to have consultation with or just to catch a glimpse of them. The role of these two leaders as Indian freedom fighters reached the ears of the tribal folk and quite a number of them went to meet them whenever they happened to visit Assam.

The first indirect contact of Gandhi with the tribal people of North-East India was in 1926 during the Pandu Session of the Indian National Congress. On returning to Calcutta, an arrangement was made for him to halt for sometime in all the major intermediate railway stations. It was at the Bongaigoan railway station that Gandhi met a group of forty Bodo-Kachari boys under the leadership of Shri Dharinidhar Basumatari. Gandhi could spare his valuable time in having an exchange of pleasantries with those tribal boys. During such an exchange it transpired that Gandhi had an intimate knowledge of the tribal people of North-East India, particularly on the Bodo-Kachari.(1) Ten years later, that is in December 1937, Nehru also, for the first time, met an assortment of the tribal people of North-East India like the Garo, Lalung, Kachari, Khasi, Mikir (Karbi), Miri, Naga and Rava, and was immediately attracted by them.(2) In spite of the short duration of their visits to Assam, their attitudes towards the tribal people indicated their great concern for even any small tribal community of the country.

Regarding the approaches of the two leaders to the tribal problem of North-East India we cannot but try to understand the same in the context of their approaches to the other tribal sections of the country as well. The main problem was whether the tribal people were to be left to themselves or should be integrated with the majority of the country. While both Gandhi and Nehru agreed to provide protection and safeguards to the tribal people, their respective approaches appeared to be quite different from each other. In between the two extreme poles of seggregation and integration, Gandhi pursued a "missionary" approach and Nehru adopted a "middle course" approach. The goal may be the same but there is a difference between the two approaches.

First, let us take up Gandhi's approach to the tribal problem. The missionary approach of Gandhi was essentially an avoidance of imposition of any kind of integrative processes on the tribal people. The tribal people should only be gently guided towards the national goal so that with their own will, would ultimately be integrated with the other people of the country.

It was in 1938 that Gandhi, perhaps for the first time, encountered the problem of the tribal people, or rather the problems of Indians because of the tribal people. In that year, Gandhi visited Bannu in the North-West Frontier province on October 25. On that occasion he was told that the tribal people used to raid and plunder the Indian merchants and other businessmen who went for trade to the neighbouring tribal areas. When these merchants and businessmen sought Gandhi's advice, he preached them the sermon of "non-violence" as the "surest, infallible method of self-defence".(3) At the same time, Gandhi realized that mere non-violence as a weapon of self-defence would not serve the purpose as the tribal people would then have taken advantage of the passive attitude of such Indians towards them. He, therefore, suggested a more positive attitude towards the tribal people by saying that; "If I had my way, I would go and mix with tribes, and argue it out with them, and I am sure they won't be impervious to the argument of love and reason".(4)

The sermon of non-violence, love and reason to the tribal people was further emphasised by Gandhi in his speech in the *sanctum sanotorum* of the *dargah* at Mehrauli on January 27, 1948. Gandhi expressed his shock at the attack on the Parachinar Refugee Camp by the trans-border tribesmen. But at the same time Gandhi cautioned the people against being carried off their feet by the news of the attack. He said that they must regard it as a test of their faith and added: "They must never allow even such incidents to rekindle in their hearts the sentiments of retaliation or revenge. They should instead proclaim to themselves and all concerned that they were out not to demand blood for blood—that was the way to suicide—but to confront with love even the murderer".[5]

At this point, one would argue that excluded tribal areas are very much in existence today as it was during Gandhi's time. So, how is it possible to speak the language of love and reason to the tribal people ? It is true that we still have certain tribal pockets where non-tribal people have no free access. But what Gandhi meant was not really a question of free access to the tribal areas, but the manner of dealing with the tribal people while coming into contact with them. Trade and commerce is one of the means of communications between the tribal and the non-tribal people even in the absence of any free access to the tribal areas. But in the context of North-East India, the question is whether the merchants and businessmen from the plains have really spoken the language of love and reason in their commercial intercourse with the hill people.

At this stage, one would perhaps argue that Gandhi wanted, therefore, to confine such contacts between the tribal and non-tribal people only at the level of trade and commerce in the border *hats* at the foothills. But, Gandhi went further and expressed the necessity of going into the excluded tribal areas in order to serve them. While addressing a crowd of workers in the Midnapore district of Bengal on January 2, 1946, Gandhi said: "If the Government prevented him (a worker) from going among them (the tribal people) he would simply disobey the order. The Government might put him into prison; he would welcome it. It would be a most auspicious beginning for his work. The very fact that he had gone to prison, in order to serve the *adivasis* would enshrine him in their hearts".[6]

The central point in this statement was, however, not so much for a free access as to the spirit of service to the tribal people. Even by landing oneself in jail and not in the tribal areas, according to Gandhi, the spirit of service to the tribal people would enshrine him in their hearts. In such a process, though there was no physical contact between the tribal and the non-tribal people, nonetheless the meeting of minds and hearts between them could take place. This had been one of the approaches of the missionaries to the tribal people which Gandhi did not lose sight of.

Earlier, in the same meeting, Gandhi had sorrowfully remarked about the attitude of the Government of India to the tribal people. He was strongly against the Government of India Act, 1935 which had separated the tribal people from the rest of the Indian population by providing Excluded and Partially Excluded Areas under the direct administration of the government and not through the system of provincial autonomy. He did not hesitate to condemn such attitude in strong terms by saying that: "It was a shame that they allowed them to be treated like that. It was up to them to make the Adivasis feel one with them".(7) Gandhi's teaching of making the tribal people "feel" one with the rest of the country is quite pertinent in as much as the emphasis is on the feeling and not on the joining of the tribal areas with the non-tribal territory. So, without this objective of the tribal feeling, the opening up of the tribal areas to the non-tribal people would be as undesirable as the exclusive right of the politicians, the administrators and the academicians to speak, and sometimes feel, on behalf of the tribal people.

Gandhi continued the same theme about the tribal people during his visit to Assam in the early part of 1946. At a prayer meeting on Janauary 10, 1946 he incidentally referred to the hill people of Assam and said: "Today the Adivasis had been put into watertight compartments by the Government and they were classified as tribal people. It was their shame that they should be isolated from the rest of the nation of which they were an inalienable part. Here in Assam was a vast field for the constructive programme. If one was prevented from rendering silent service to the Adivasis, he should prefer to go to prison as prison-going would even in itself advance their cause."(8) This clearly revealed the deep concern of Gandhi for the welfare of the hill people of North-East India. Gandhi's "silent service" of the missionary, was more important in breaking the "watertight compartments" rather than by forced political and administrative integration by the politicians and the bureaucrats.

Gandhi had so much faith in the loyalty of the hill people of North-East India to India. This simple faith or belief of Gandhi in the integrity of the hill people was clearly evident from his statement in an interview with the two Congressmen from Assam who went to meet him on behalf of Shri Gopinath Bordoloi, the then Prime Minister of Assam, on the issue of the grouping Plan. We all know about the attitude of Gandhi on the problem of Assam regarding the plan and how he inspired and encouraged the people of Assam to reject it. On that occasion which took place on December 12, 1946, Gandhi remarked that: "The hill people are with you if you act on the square".(9) In other words, the tribal people should always feel that they could expect fair dealings from the non-tribal people. This statement of Gandhi had produced such an effect on the leaders of Assam, particularly on Shri Bordoloi, that the hill people in general were satisfied with their fair dealings regarding the provisions for constitutional safeguards in the post-independence period. Gandhi had very rightly observed that: "The tribesman cannot be the bogeyman that he is represented to be. He is human just like you and me and capable of responding to the human touch, which has hitherto been conspicous by its absence in dealing with him. I did not find that their nature was essentially different from human nature elsewhere. Give to the tribesmen all the love that you are capable of, and you will have theirs in return".(10)

Gandhi was quite aware of the difficulties that the tribal people would have confronted with the non-tribal people in the Indian society after independence. The tribal people would be one section of the minorities, who may be ostracised by, in Gandhi's word, "a hopeless minority"—the caste Hindus. As a friend of Harijans, the scheduled castes, and the scheduled tribes, his vision of a new India was to see that all the facilities should be provided to all classes fo the society including the lowest section. In a speech on June 12, 1947 at a prayer congregation, on how free India should act, Gandhi posed a challenge to the caste Hindus by saying that: "Will they recognise and do their obvious duty and give place to the least in the Union by affording them all the facilities to rise to the highest status ?"(11)

The phrase "the least in the Union" indicated the influence of Ruskin's ideal in his "Unto this Last" on Gandhi's thought and feeling on the disadvantaged section of the society.(12) He could not simply accept without proper evidence the charges against the scheduled castes and scheduled tribes as being communal. On the contrary, he was convinced that apart from other factors it was the communalism of the "hopeless minority" which was more intense than the communalism of others. It was this sort of communalism which was responsible for disintegration in an otherwise integrated India. Gandhi had earnestly hoped for an integrated India in which all, including the "hopeless minority", the Harijans, the scheduled castes, the scheduled tribes, and the other religions, cultural and linguistic groups, should be equal partners. In the case of the tribal people, the question of integration arose only because they were then looked upon by the majority more as aliens than Indians.

Gandhi, however, had never treated the tribal people as aliens. But if the tribal people felt themselves to be aliens, then Gandhi would not stand in the way of such a feeling. This was very clear from his meeting with the Naga delegation which visited him at the Bhangi Colony in New Delhi immediately before independence, when the Nagas proposed to declare their independence one day earlier than that of India's. On that occasion, Gandhi said: "Nagas have every right to be independent. We did not want to live under the domination of the British and they are not leaving us. I feel that the Naga Hills are mine just as much as they are yours. But, if you say that they are not mine, the matter must stop there. I believe in the brotherhood of men, but I do not believe in force or forced unions. If you do not wish to join the Union of India, nobody will force you to do that".(13) But when the Naga delegates pointed out that Sir Akbar Hydari, the then Governor of Assam, was threatening to do exactly that, Gandhi exlaimed: "Sir Akbar is wrong ! He cannot do that...I will come to Naga Hills; I will ask them to shoot me first before one Naga is shot".(14) Unfortunately, Gandhi was assassinated before he could send his mission to Nagaland.

Immediately after independence, Gandhi further nicely dealt with the problems of minorities. When at a prayer meeting on August 29, 1947, he was asked whether the minorities, say a Bengali in Bihar, would have recognition, apart from religion, Gandhi replied that, "an Indian was a citizen of India enjoying equal rights in every part of India...But...a Bengali must merge in the Bihari...He must never be guilty of exploiting Biharis, or feeling a stranger, or behaving as a stranger in Bihar".(15)

Now, if Gandhi were asked whether a majority, say an Assamese, a Bengali or a Marwari, etc. in a tribal area of North-East India would have recognition as a minority, I am afraid it would not be farfetched to conclude that the answer would have been the same.

He would have said something like the one above, that is, a majority, say an Assamese, a Bengali or a Marwari, etc. must merge in the tribesmen. He must never be guilty of exploiting the tribesmen, or feeling a stranger, or behaving as a stranger in the tribal areas. This would ensure a harmonious relationship between the tribal and the non-tribal people. Recognition of a minority by the majority, whether religious or otherwise, is one thing; and recognition of a minority (majority community) in the tribal areas by the tribal peole (minority community) is quite a different matter. And it is precisely because of this fact, that a confusion has gradually crept into the relationship between the tribal and the non-tribal people.

Till the end of his life, Gandhi had never lost his faith in the tribal people. Just four days before he was assassinated, in an interview with Kingsley Martin on the Kashmir problem, Gandhi made his last statement on the tribal situation in the country. He said: "I would accept a challenge of conquering the tribal areas, but as a non-violent man. I would not bribe them; I would serve them. Have not missionaries allowed themselves to be eaten by cannibals?"(16) Thus, throughout, Gandhi's attitude towards the tribal people was to approach them through the spirit of service, love and reason—the missionary approach.

Now, having discussed the missionary approach of Gandhi at some length, let us turn to the "middle course" approach of Jawaharlal Nehru to the tribal people. We shall limit the treatment of this subject to the colonial period only. True, the term "middle course" was used by Nehru after independence,(17) yet his ideas on the matter could be traced to the colonial period when he was confronted with the trivial question of whether to leave the tribal people to themselves or to integrate them with the rest of the country. As the following events would indicate, in fact, Nehru in dealing with tribal affairs during the colonial period was vascillating between the two extreme poles of isolation and integration. That was during the colonial period, Nehru appeared to have spoken on the need of segregating and integrating the tribal people in the same breath.

The first contact of Nehru with the tribal people of North-East India was during December 1937. Though he could not visit Shillong and other tribal areas, yet he met many tribal people like Garos, Lalungs, Kacharis, Khasis, Mikirs (Karbis), Miris, Nagas and Ravas. Concerning these people he said: "They deserve every help and sympathy".(18) Nehru had thus outlined his strategy in dealing with the tribal people of North-East India right from the day of his first contact with them. In the same account on these people he hoped that, "our provincial assemblies will do everything in their power to remove their disabilities and to encourage education and industry among them".(19) From strategic planning Nehru had quickly moved to tactical operation in that he not only expressed sympathy over the backward conditions of the tribal people of North-East India but also sought agencies for the removal of such undesirable conditions.

Nehru did not, therefore, like the idea of segregating the tribal people of North-East India from the rest of the country. His mind was already set on the theme of complete unity of India even much earlier. During August 1937, he wrote: "The unity of India must be maintained in the Constitution. The unity, both geographical and cultural, is a potent fact of Indian history, and political and economic unity has also become essential for us...Under the Government of India Act 1935...there is no uniformity".(20) Thus, Nehru talked of "geographical and cultural unity", "political and economic unity", and of "uniformity" in the country. He again emphasised this point in relation to the undesirability of "excluded areas" in a talk with the representative of the Chittagong Hill Tracts on July 15, 1945, at Simla, by saying that: "We are in complete agreement with you. We do not want any excluded area in our country".(21)

But all Nehru's talks about "unity" and "uniformity" began to change with his second visit to Assam during December 1945. In his speech at Shillong on December 17, 1945 he said: "There are tribal areas in Assam and in other parts of India which are backward and which need a great deal of assistance from the Government. The Khasis are quite capable of looking after themselves culturally, but not in the economic sphere. Their community is too small. Naturally, they will have to be given the largest protection so that other people may not come from outside and exploit them".(22) Now from "unity" and "uniformity" of earlier year, Nehru turned his attention to the need of giving "the largest protection" to the tribal people of North-East India. A dent has thus been made in his ideal independent India where "uniformity" or integration and "protection" or segregation would have to co-exist.

Hence, with the dawn of independence Nehru had become mellowed while dealing with the delicate matter of tribal affairs. In fact, it was during his second visit to Assam that he had authored the concept of tribal autonomy if "uniformity" and "protection" were to co-exist. In the same speech in Shillong he said: "It is also expected that within the provincial units, autonomous units, composed of people of distinctive groups will be set up. These smaller units will be given autonomy to shape their lives as they like. The whole point is that we want to give the fullest measure of freedom to the individuals and to every distinctive group of people within the large framework of the nation".(23) This is indeed the highest point of development in Nehru's tribal philosophy—a development from the concept of "uniformity" to "protection" and then to "autonomy" as "the fullest measure of freedom" to the tribal people of North-East India.

Nehru had not only authored the concept of tribal autonomy which was the foundation stone of the autonomous district councils but also envisaged the need for having a separate tribal areas department under the government of Assam for linking the autonomous units with the larger framework of the nation. Continuing his speech in Shillong with particular reference to the Khasi community, he said: "I would like to emphasise again that it may not be possible for them (the Khasis) to have the same type of growth which may be possible in India as a whole because they are too small in number. This is the reason why the Government should make special efforts to raise the standard of life of these tribal people. I would however, add this that I would not like to impose upon them the same type of growth which may perhaps be adopted by the rest of India. My point is that the Government should and must have a special department to deal with the tribal people to protect them and help them to grow".(24)

The above account on Nehru's approach to the tribal problem in North-East India is only to show that immediately before India's independence, Nehru was quite allergic to the British policy of segregating the tribal people. A policy of segregation was adopted by the British in relation to the hill people of North-East India through the concept of an Inner line. Beyond an Inner line no person from outside the area could move without permission by the district authorities. Possession of land by outsiders and non-residents was strictly prohibited. Further, there was minimal administration in the area and the Christian missionaries were not only allowed but also encouraged in their religious propagation and philanthrophic works. The policy of segregation was so much rigidly enforced that even the leaders of the Indian national movement could not penetrate the area. Quite naturally, therefore, Nehru viewed that kind of policy with deep resentment. At the same time he also saw the dangers of assimilation. That's why, later on, he observed: "It is between these two extreme positions that we have to function".(25) This amounts to a middle-of-the-road position in tribal affairs on the part of Nehru.

This middle-of-the-road position taken by Nehru was to be found in his same speech in Shillong when he said that, "the ultimate protection is to leave them to protect themselves. I am quite sure that the largest amount of autonomy will be given to every distinct group. It is difficult for me to say before hand what that quantum of autonomy will be. At the same time it should be understood that smaller communities cannot by themselves undertake larger economic development. They must be tagged on to larger groups in these matters. But there is no reason, whatsover, why they should not enjoy complete autonomy in the matter of cultural development".(26) This position was further reinforced by the historic Objectives Resolution moved by Nehru in the Constituent Assembly on the fifth day of its first session on December 13, 1946. In the Resolution we find among the objectives a provision which says: "wherein adequate safeguards shall be provided for minorities, backward and tribal areas and depressed and other backward classes".(27)

True, this provision remained only an objective which aimed at the policy of integration. But when we come to the debates on the other relevant provisions in the draft Constitution, Nehru made it clear that the existing laws relating to the protection of the tribal people should continue. While intervening in the debates on the Interim Report of the Committee on Fundamental Rights on April 30, 1947 he said: "I completely agree that the tribal areas and the tribal people should be protected in every possible way and the existing laws should continue and may be, should be, added to when the time comes".[28]

Now, one of the existing laws was, and which is still in operation, the Bengal Eastern Frontier Regulation, 1873 which stipulated an inner line beyond which there should be a segregation of certain hill areas in North-East India. Despite criticisms against the inner line from many quarters,[29] Nehru did not yield and the inner line policy was continued, and is still continuing in Arunachal Pradesh, Mizoram and Nagaland. Even in the other hill areas where the inner line Regulation was not in operation, the idea of Nehru, as per his Objective Resolution, was that "safeguards" should be provided. In other words, Nehru was not quite ready to immediately assimilate the hill people. He was far sighted enough in not provoking the hill people into believing that he was all out for imposing things on them. At most he would only like to tag them to larger political units for reasons of viable economic development.

Thus, a study of the approaches of Gandhi and Nehru to the tribal problem of North-East India during the colonial period indicated certain salient features. Both of them had never intended to leave the tribal people out of the Indian political system. Again, both the missionary approach of Gandhi and the middle course approach of Nehru to the tribal problem had converged at a point where sympathy, support and protection would be extended to the tribal people. The result was that in both the approaches, the idea of safeguards to the tribal people had been the main point of agreement. Of course, when we come to the question of reservation for the tribal people, it transpired that Nehru was greatly influenced by Gandhi's ideas. Still the two leaders could jointly agree on this point. It was reported that there was a time when all the Congress members of the Constituent Assembly were opposed to the idea of reservation for the tribal people and when Nehru had not yet made up his mind on such a vexed question. It was at that juncture that a tribal member from Assam, Shri Dharinidhar Basumatari, met both Gandhi and Nehru and impressed upon them the need of having a special privilege of such a reservation. Gandhi from his Bhangi Colony in New Delhi then wrote on a piece of paper, "If reservation for these communities is not given, I will have to undertake another fast".(30) On receipt of Gandhi's note, Nehru read it at the Congress Parliamentary meeting and all the members had to give in. That perhaps clinched the issue for Nehru personally to "reluctantly agree" to the provision for reservation for the tribal people.(31)

This kind of reluctance on the part of Nehru clearly revealed that he was not completely in tune with Gandhi's approach to the tribal problem. Even the concept of Gandhi's trusteeship(32) in relation to the tribal people was accepted belatedly by Nehru in 1956.(33) That is why his middle course approach is slightly different from the missionary approach of Gandhi. While Nehru's middle course approach had never, even for a moment, conceded the right of the tribal people to leave the Indian Union, Gandhi's missionary approach, on the other hand, would confer on the tribal people even the right to keep their independent status.(34) But in all fairness to Gandhi, we have also to point out that what he had actually emphasised was that while granting this right, India should try the missionary approach in bringing all the tribal people within the Indian Union by avoiding "forced unions". In any case, both Gandhi and Nehru while agreeing either to bring or to keep all the tribal people within the Indian Union, a kind of tribal segregation would still be necessary so that the tribal people could develop themselves according to their own genius.

Gandhi with his intense love for the tribal people did not live long after India's Independence and Nehru, with his seventeen years of service to the nation after Independence, had struggled very hard in uplifting the living conditions of the tribal people by trying to combine both the above pre-independence approaches. Subsequent administrations after Nehru while eagerly speeding up the process of integration are yet to give up the approaches of Gandhi and Nehru. So far, both the approaches, with certain pitfalls, have been able to survive and constitutionally, territorially, politically, and administratively the tribal people of North-East India have been fully integrated. What remains now is only psycholgical integration which the present administration would do well in learning the utility of the approaches of Gandhi and Nehru to the tribal problems. It is true that the tribal situation in the country has changed considerably, but the indispensable elements remain the same. By looking to the tribal people no longer as a social category but as a stage in the social formation,(35) the present administration should be in a better position to complete the final phase in the process of integrating the tribal people of North-East India.

REFERENCES

1. Barthakur, P.B., "Dharinidhar Basumatari: Veteran Parliamentarian", *The Sunday Sentinel*, (Guwahati), June 18, 1989, p.2.
2. Gopal, S., (ed), *Selected Works of Jawaharlal Nehru*, (Orient Longman, New Delhi), 1981, Vol. 8, p. 492.
3. Tendulkar, D.G., *Mahatma*, (Bombay, 1954), Vol. IV, pp. 360-61.
4. *Ibid.*
5. *Ibid*, Vol. VIII, p. 340.
6. *Ibid*, Vol. VII, pp. 36-37.
7. *Ibid.*, p. 34.
8. *Ibid.*, pp. 45-46.

9. *Ibid*, p. 337.
10. *Ibid.*, Vol. IV, pp.360-61.
11. *Ibid*, Vol. VIII, p.14.
12. Gandhi had paraphrased Ruskin's title to "Even Unto These Last". See *Harijan*, Vol. I, No. 6, March 18, 1933, p.4.
13. Phizo, A.Z., *The Fate of the Naga People : An Appeal to the World*, (London, 1960), pp.2-3
14. *Ibid.*
15. Tendulkar, *op.cit.*, Vol.VIII, p.340.
16. *Ibid.*
17. Elwin, Verrier, *A Philosophy for NEFA*, (P.C. Dutta, Shillong), 1964, Second Edition, Reprint, p. 207.
18. Gopal, F.n.2.
19. *Ibid.*, p.498.
20. *Ibid.*, p.599.
21. *Ibid.*, Vol. 14, p. 48.
22. *Ibid.*, p.271.
23. *Ibid.*
24. *Ibid.*, p.272.
25. Elwin, F.n. 16, Foreward.
26. Gopal, F.n. 21.
27. *Constituent Assembly Debates*, Vol. 1, December 13, 1946, p. 59.
28. *Ibid.*, Vol. III, April 30, 1947, p. 454.
29. The inner line has been criticised as the "museum specimen approach". Apart from the members of the Constituent Assembly, journalists like Harish Chandra was very embittered about the line, and the Indian geo-politician K.M. Panikkar suggested the settlement of the Himalayan range. See Choube, S.K., *Hill Politics in North-East India.* (Orient Longman, Calcutta), 1973, pp.180-187.
30. Barthakur, F.n. 1.
31. *Constituent Assembly Debates*, Vol.VIII, May 26, 1949, pp. 329, 331.
32. This should not be confused with Gandhi's economic principle of trusteeship in *Harijan.* Vo;. V, No.2, February 20, 1937, p.2 and Vol. VII, No. 45, December 16, 1939 p.1, In fact, his first use of the term "trustees" was political in nature. On October 14, 1909 he wrote a letter from London to one Mr. H.S.L. Polak who was then in India: "Then the British rulers will be servants and not masters. They will be trustees and not tyrants, and they will live in perfect peace with the whole of the inhabitants of India". See *Collected Works of Mahatma Gandhi*, (navajivan Trust, Ahmedabad), 1963, Vol. IX, p.481.

33. *Lok Sabha Debates,* Vol. VI, Part II, July 30, 1956, Col. 1518.
34. See F.n. 12.
35. For a detailed discussion on the changing concepts of tribe, see Roy Burman, B.K., "Issues in Tribal Studies", *ICSSR Newsletter,* (Indian Council of Social Science Research), New Delhi, Vol. XIX(1), April-June, 1988, pp. 19-25.

6

Approaches to Tribal Development and Experience

C.B. Tripathi

The tribal communities in India present a broad spectrum of diversity. The number of the scheduled tribes is about 461. Amongst them we have the Negrito, the Proto-Australoid, the Mongoloid and the Mediterranean. The Scheduled Tribes speak about 105 languages and 225 subsidiary languages. Besides, the tribes speaking Dravidian and Aryan languages, we have a good number of tribes who belong to the Austro-Asiatic family of language the latter include Kol or Munda speeches like Santhali, Mundari, Ho, Korku, Savara, Gadaba, etc. of Central India, Khasi of Meghalaya and Nicobarese of the Nicobar Islands. From the point of view of economy, the tribal communities have amongst them primitive people engaged in hunting and food gathering, pastoral people and nomads, shifting cultivators, settled agriculturists, artisans, plantation, mining and industrial labour. In Koraput district we find the spectacle of co-existence of primitive groups like Bondas and Didayis as well as tribals belonging to different communities working in the HAL factory at Sunabeda manufacturing MIG engines. There is wide divergence in the economic and educational status of the tribes from region to region.

Various Approaches to Tribal Development

In such a situation the strategy for tribal development will differ from region to region and even from tribe to tribe. However, a moot question is as to what the objective of tribal development is. I will briefly discuss the approaches of the British colonial rule, the Gandhian workers, a section of anthropologists whom we might in the current parlance call fundamentalists and the school of thought broadly influenced by Nehru.

British Administration in Tribal Areas

The East India Company faced serious troubles as it decided to extend its control over tribal areas. Several administrative measures taken by it led to the destruction of the communal land tenure and impaired the social solidarity of the tribal village in Chhotanagpur. The tribal proprietors were reduced to the position of tenants-at-will and evils of landlordism and racketeering prevailed. The oppression of the tribals led to successive risings of the Mundas in 1789, 1807, 1812, 1819-20 and 1831-32. The Kol rebellions of 1817 and 1832 were caused by the oppression of the aboriginal and the illegal deprivation of their rights by Hindu and other outsiders introduced into the villages of the plateau under the aegis of the British rule, either as landlords or their agents or as tax collectors, excise men or the police. In Bengal too several rebellions took place like the Chuar rebellion among the Bhumij of Manbhum in 1795-1800, the Ganganarain revolt among the Bhumij in 1832-33 and the Santhal rebellions in 1835-36, 1854 and later. Subsequently, Siddu and Kanu became national heroes of the Santhals and Birsa Munda who led a religious movement and revolted against the British in 1895 was deified as Birsa Bhagwan. In Orissa the Kondhs had rebelled in 1846. In the 20th century the most famous movement was the Tana Bhagat movement among the Oraon in 1914. The Tana Bhagats took active part in the non-cooperation movement launched by Mahatma Gandhi. There were tribal revolts and uprisings in the other parts of the country as well.

Dr. J.H. Hutton, writing on the impact of the British administration in tribal areas observed:

> "Far from being of immediate benefit to the primitive tribes, the establishment of British rule in India did most of them much more harm than good. It may be said that the early days of British Administration did very great detriment to the economic position of tribes through ignorance and neglect of their rights and customs. Many changes have been caused incidentally by the penetration of the tribal country, the opening up of communications, the protection of forests and the establishment of schools, to say nothing of the openings given in this way to Christian Missions. Many of the results of these changes have caused acute discomfort to the tribes".

Commenting on this Prof. G.S. Ghurye observed that "the acuteness of discomfort was very often so great that it led to apathy, indifference, moral deterioration and even a decline in population".

The Scheduled Areas and Scheduled Tribes Commission appointed by the President under Article 339 of the Constitution and headed by Sri U.N. Dhebar (1960-61) summed up the impact of the British Government's policy on tribals in these words:

> "It resulted in reducing the tribals to a state of penury in most parts of India. They were at the lowest level of literacy except in certain parts. Their lands were heavily encumbered and a good portion had already passed into the hands of non-

> tribals. Their rights in forest were definitely encroached upon. Outside elements introduced for the purpose of Government and forest work continued to exploit them. On many an occasion reforms were ordered but all these proved futile".

The British Government finally decided on a policy of segregating the tribes into special areas where their lives and interests could be protected. With the passing of an Act in 1874, tribal areas were specified into 'Scheduled Districts' to segregate the tribals in order to protect them. These areas were reconstituted at the time of the Government of India act 1919 and finally in 1935 more stringent provisions for a special treatment of the tribal areas were incorporated by converting them into 'Excluded and Partially Excluded Areas'. Upto 1947 numerous Acts and regulations were promulgated and reforms introduced. This policy of segregation of the tribals is often referred to as 'National Park' policy. One wonders if one of the covert objectives behind this policy was to prevent the animistic tribals from becoming Hindus while encouraging Christian missionaries to work in these areas.

Gandhian Workers

Thakkar Bapa (Sri A.V. Thakkar) was moved by deep human concerns and prepared an outline for the welfare of the tribals. He created a band of dedicated and selfless workers whose activities were mainly confined to spreading of education and organising tribal cooperatives for their economic uplift. However, their impact on the basic issues of exploitation of the tribals was marginal. In the matter of education they started with lofty ideals of *Gurukula* sytem, basic education and moral environment. A spirit of sacrifice and self-reliance pervaded these institutions but in later years after Independence the Ashram Schools, increasingly dependent on Government grants-in-aid, hardly remained the ideal institutions they were supposed to be. There was not much to distinguish most of these institutions from normal schools except that these provided residential facility even at the primary stage. A particular set of norms and values was sought to be imposed upon the tribal children which were often not in consonance with the traditional life of the tribals. To quote an instance, almost all these institutions banned non-vegetarian food for the inmates.

Anthropologists

Anthropologists have been a much misunderstood tribe. In 1960 I worked in the office of the Dhebar Commission as a (Senior) Research Officer for a few months. In one of the meetings of the Commission the desirability of associating anthropologists with its work was being discussed. Sri Dayabhai Naik, a close disciple of Thakkar Bapa and a member of the Commission, observed that they did not need any people to measure the head and the nose of the tribals. So that was the perception of the role of anthropologists by a well known social worker as late as 1960 ! What more surprising was the fact that Dr. Verrier Elwin, who had written several popular monographs on the tribes and was recognised as a leading anthropologist in the official circles, lustily supported the view of Sri Dayabhai Naik. Perhaps he did not want another (Indian) anthropologist to be associated with the Commission.

Barring a few exceptions, the University community of anthropologists has not adequately interested itself in the life and problems of the tribals and its acquaintance with the same is academic and often outdated. In October 1963 I participated in the first special orientation course on tribal development at the National Institute of Community Development, Mussoorie (since shifted to Hyderabad and renamed as the National Institute of Rural Development). A number of distinguished professors addressed the participants. Three professors of Anthropology, on different dates, had only the text book story of the 'Golden Stool' from an African tribe to offer as an illustration of applied anthropology. The participants wondered whether anthropology had no practical utility in the Indian situation.

I suspect that some of the academic anthropologists still suffer from the old romantic perception of the tribal and his problems. They would like the tribals to be left alone irrespective of the level of their economic and cultural development. I shall narrate an experience. The Bondas of Koraput District have attracted a number of foreign and Indian scholars. Bonda women were traditionally required to keep their heads shaven permanently and were not permitted to wear any proper clothes. While their breasts were covered by scores of strings of beads, the lower part of the body was only partly covered by a small piece of cloth known as *ringa* and woven by Bonda women themselves. Use of a large size cloth was not permitted by tradition. Now during the last four years or so, a slow but revolutionary change is taking place in the Bonda society on account of the initiative taken by a Bonda woman, Lakshmi, who was unanimously elected Sarpanch, and who, after visiting Bhubaneswar during the Adivasi *Mela* on the eve of the Republic Day, decided to do away with these traditional taboos. Now quite a few Bonda women and girls have started wearing *sarees* and also growing hairs and the tribal society has not taken any action against this group of Bonda women. Sometime back. I mentioned about this change to an anthropologist who expressed surprise that being an anthropologist I appreciated the change. I told her that if a primitive tribal group accepted a change willingly or took initiative to bring about a change in its traditional practices, it was to be welcomed.

For anthropologists like the one with whom I had this encounter. I wish to coin the description 'fundamentalists'. Whether this section of anthropologists really want the tribals to be preserved as museum specimens or not, it is clear that it is not possible to do so. The transformation is taking place and its pace will only be quickened in future. It is the job of the anthropologist to suggest the direction and the pace of this transformation.

Nehru's Tribal 'Panchsheel'

The informed and correct approach towards tribal development was laid down by Pandit Jawaharlal Nehru, the first Prime Minister of independent India. In his foreword to the second edition of 'A Philosophy for NEFA' by Dr. Verrier Elwin, Panditji wrote on October 9, 1958:

> "We cannot allow matters to drift in the tribal areas or just not take interest in them. In the world of today that is not possible or desirable. At the same time we should avoid over-administering these areas and, in particular, sending too many outsiders into tribal territory. It is between these two extreme positions that we have to function. Development in various ways there has to be, such as communications, medical facilities, education and better agriculture."

Pandit Nehru added that these avenues of development should be pursued within the broad framework of the following five fundamental principles:

(1) People should develop along the lines of their own genius and we should avoid imposing anything on them. We should try to encourage in every way their own traditional arts and culture.

(2) Tribal rights in land and forests should be respected.

(3) We should try to train and build up a team of their own people to do the work of administration and development. Some technical personnel from outside will, no doubt, be needed, especially in the beginning. But we should avoid introducing too many outsiders into tribal territory.

(4) We should not over-administer these areas or overwhelm them with a multiplicity of schemes. We should rather work through, and not in rivalry to, their own social and cultural institutions.

(5) We should judge results, not by statistics or the amount of money spent, but by the quality of human character that is evolved.

These five principles have since come to be known as Tribal *Panchsheel.*

Constitutional Safeguards for the Scheduled Tribes

The Constitution contains a number of safeguards and provisions for the Scheduled Tribes. Here I wish to mention only a few of the important ones. Article 46 in the chapter on Directive Principles of State Policy states:

> "The State shall promote with special care the educational and economic interests of the weaker sections of the people, and, in particular, of the Scheduled Castes and the Scheduled Tribes, and shall protect them from social injustice and all forms of exploitation".

A separate chapter containing only one Article, i.e., Article 244, is devoted to the Scheduled and Tribal Areas. Pursuant to this Article the Fifth Schedule to the Constitution contains provisions regarding the administration and control of the Scheduled Areas. At present there are eight States having Scheduled Areas, viz., Andhra Pradesh, Bihar, Gujarat, Himachal Pradesh, Madhya Pradesh, Maharashtra, Orissa and Rajasthan. Similarly the Sixth Schedule contains detailed provisions regarding the administration of the tribal areas in the States of Assam, Meghalaya, Mizoram and Tripura. The District Councils and the Regional Councils set up under the Sixth Schedule are democratic, autonomous and powerful bodies.

A very important provision is contained in Article 275(1) which runs as follows:

> "...there shall be paid out of the Consolidated Fund of India as grants-in-aid of the revenues of a State such capital and recurring sums as may be necessary to enable that State to meet the costs of such schemes of development as may be undertaken by the State with the approval of the Government of India for the purpose of promoting the welfare of the Scheduled Tribes in that State or raising the level of administration of the Scheduled Areas therein to that of the administration of the rest of the areas of that State."

Two Constitutional provisions, *viz.,* Article 339 (2) and paragraph 5(1) of the Fifth Schedule, deserve special mention. According to Article 339(2) "the executive power of the Union shall extend to the giving of directions to a State as to the drawing up and execution of schemes specified in the direction to be essential for the welfare of the Scheduled Tribes in the State". I am not aware of any single directive having been issued by the Government of India to any State Government so far. Similarly paragraph 5(1) of the Fifth Schedule reads as follows:

> "Notwithstanding anything in this Constitution, the Governor may by public notification direct that any particular Act of Parliament or of the Legislature

of the State shall not apply to a Scheduled Area or any part thereof in the State subject to such exceptions and modifications as he may specify in the notification and any direction given so as to have retrospective effect."

Thus the Governors of the States having Scheduled Areas have been vested with extraordinary powers to act in the interests of the tribals. This provision has been utilised so far by only one State, Andhra Pradesh, and that too only as recently as 1986 when the State Government issued orders that henceforth all the vacancies for the posts of teachers, forest guards and Village Officers (same as Patwari, Lekhpal, Talati or Karnam in other States) in the Scheduled Areas will be filled up by appointing only local Scheduled Tribe persons.

Five Year Plans

Upto the end of the Fourth Five-Year Plan the welfare of the Scheduled Tribes was mainly taken care of under a tiny Plan Sector, *viz.,* Welfare of Backward Classes Sector. The percentage of investments in the tribal areas out of the total Plan expenditure during this period was as follows: First Plan 1%, Second Plan 0.9%, Third Plan 0.6%, three Annual Plans (1966-67 to 1968-69) 0.6% and Fourth Plan 0.5%. In 1954, 43 SMPT (Special Multi-purpose Tribal) Blocks were started supplement the community development programme in the tribal areas. The Ministry of Home Affairs appointed a Committee under the chairmanship of Dr. Verrier Elwin to review the working of the SMPT Blocks. In its report submitted in 1960, the Committee recommended that to take up and sustain intensive programmes in the tribal areas Tribal Development Blocks with a smaller area, (150 to 200 sq. miles) and smaller population (about 25,000) should be set up. By the end of the Third Plan there were about 500 T.D.

Blocks covering about 40% of the total tribal population.

In the Fourth Plan a series of programmes addressed to specific target groups like small farmers, agricultural labourers as also specific areas like drought prone regions were taken up to check the process of growing disparities between different sections of the community and also between different regions. A programme for tribal areas was also taken up on a pilot basis in areas of special agrarian unrest, with the establishment of 6 Tribal Development Agencies (TDAs) in Andhra Pradesh, Bihar, Madhya Pradesh and Orissa. Towards the end of the Fourth Plan two more TDAs were created in Orissa in areas not based on any agrarian unrest. This programme envisaged a comprehensive frame comprising protective measures, economic development and social services. In actual practice, however, these agencies confined themselves to agricultural development programmes with only additional investment on arterial roads.

A Study Team on Tribal Development Programmes under the chairmanship of Sri Shilu Ao appointed by the All India Committee on Plan Projects, Planning Commission, submitted its Report in 1969 and observed that the scheme of T.D. Blocks was inadequate for dealing with the complex problems of tribal development. These Blocks were too small to function as the basic unit for planning and implementation. The main problems of tribal communities according to them related to indebtedness, land alienation, educational backwardness and inadequacy of communication. They called for vigorous action to implement the recommendations of the Dhebar Commission and for preparing comprehensive tribal development programmes with larger resources commensurate with the size of the problem and overall national development effort (Sivaraman Committee Report, p. 14).

Tribal Sub-Plan Concept and Strategy

In the first four Five-Year Plans it was expected that benefits would accrue to the tribals in due proportion under various developmental programmes. In practice, however, the T.D. Block programme and schemes taken up under the Welfare of Backward Classes Sector which were expected to be supplementary in nature substituted the developmental efforts of the sectoral programmes. The review of the tribal situation on the eve of the Fifth Plan brought out that some tribal communities were far ahead of other groups, both educationally and economically. In a few tribal areas, industrial and mining complexes had been established which did help the people living in those areas getting some benefits but this was a mixed blessing. In other areas, while some communities still continue to be at the stage of hoe cultivation, quite a few of them have taken to settled agriculture and adopted the plough culture. The rich resources of some tribal regions were attracting substantial population from outside. The pressure of population in other regions was forcing some tribal communities to migrate seasonally or permanently. Thus, it became clear that no single solution could be expected to have universal applicability in all tribal areas. Each tribal area presented more or less unique situation in terms of resources, people, social constraints, infrastructural development, etc.

The approach and strategy for tribal development in areas of tribal concentration and that for dispersed tribal population had to the quite distinct. In the former case some elements of area development have to be incorporated in any plan even when it may be exclusively designed for people's development, particularly in the backward areas where infrastructure was not developed. However, development of the physical potential and infrastructure need not necessarily lead to the development of the tribal people and, on the contrary, they have often to face backlash of development. Therefore, infrastructural development has to be suitably adopted as a part of the bigger package of programmes. Thus, a concept of 'area development with focus on the development of tribal communities' was accepted for the tribal areas. Besides, the primitive tribal communities were treated as a separate group for whom a very flexible approach of development was to be evolved keeping in view the conditions of each primitive community. Intensive development of dispersed tribals was to be taken up in the second phase.

The important features of the new Tribal Sub-Plan approach were as follows:

(i) The development in the tribal areas has to be conceived in comprehensive terms. The resources for development should be pooled and the priority within these resources worked out with reference to the needs of these areas. Problem-solving approach with clear objectives should be adopted, making the system flexible so as not to compromise on basic objectives.

(ii) The development of the tribal areas has to be an integral part of the total development of the State and the nation. The major thrust of their development has to be provided by the various sectoral authorities themselves. The basic investment for development of tribal areas, therefore, should flow from the normal State Plan.

(iii) The special responsibility of the Union Government in terms of the Constitutional provision was also spelt out. Each central ministry is responsible for development of these areas in relation to its functional jurisdiction. They should review the tribal situation and provide necessary investments for their speedy development. However, all sectoral efforts in their totality may still not provide the full answer to their problems. It was agreed that the nodal and the residual responsibility would rest with the Ministry of Home Affairs at Union level under the Constitutional scheme. Thus, the roles of all partners in the development were defined and a mechanism for its translation in operational terms was also provided.

(iv) Another basic premise in tribal development is the recognition of the fact that the socio-economic situation may require a specific answer. The basic unit of planning and implementation, which should be homogenous and viable, was defined as an Integrated Tribal Development Project (ITDP). The Sub-Plan should be built from below and represent an organic build-up of project planning.

(v) The Primitive tribal communities should be identified and special programme with adequate flexibility built up for them.

(vi) The administrative system for tribal areas should be simple and over-specialisation discouraged so that the system was within the comprehension of the community which it was supposed to serve. Adequate administrative and financial powers should be delegated and responsibility at each level should be specific.

(Sivaraman Committee Report, pp.15-16)

For detailed information on the concept and strategy of Tribal Sub-Plan we may refer to two books by Dr. B.D. Sharma captioned 'Tribal Development: The Concept and the Frame' and 'Planning for Tribal Development'. An informative series of 'Occasional Papers' on the various aspects and policies of tribal development were also brought out by the Tribal Development Division of the Ministry of Home Affairs (now Ministry of Welfare).

The Government of India decided that the tribal majority States/Union Territories like Arunachal Pradesh, Meghalaya, Mizoram, Nagaland, Dadra and Nagar Haveli and Lakshadweep need not have a tribal Sub-Plan as the entire plan of these States/UTs was primarily meant for the tribal population constituting the majority. By the end of the Sixth Plan, 17 States and 2 Union Territories had adopted the TSP and 181 ITDPs, 245 MADA pockets (Modified Area Development Approach for pockets of tribal concentration outside the Sub-Plan area) and 72 special projects for PTGs (Primitive Tribal Groups) were in operation. The coverage of the Scheduled Tribe population during the Sixth Plan rose to about 75% of the total tribal population in the country from about 65% of such coverage during the Fifth Plan.

Review of the TSP

For the Sixth Plan the major objectives in the field of tribal development had been spelt out as follows in the Report of the Working Group on Tribal Development during Sixth Plan period:

(a) Raising the productivity levels in the field of agriculture, horticulture, animal husbandry, forestry, cottage, village and small industry, etc., so as to create an economic impact of an order which will enable a targeted number of families (say 50%) in the TSP area to cross the poverty line. With the household as the basic unit of planning in poverty reduction, the poorest and then the poor should be taken up on a progressive scale.

(b) Apart from the effort in the core economic sectors indicated in (a) above, education should become the key sector in the Sixth Plan period.

(c) The attainment of the objectives in (a) and (b) above would vitally depend on an adequate infrastructure for the creation of which there should be commensurate financial and physical effort.

(d) Concomitant with the aforesaid three-fold aims and, perhaps, the most important, assiduous exertions are necessary to eliminate exploitation of tribals in the fields of alienation of land, money-lending, debt bondage, trade, excise, forest, etc.

In the Report of the Working Group on Development of Scheduled Tribes during Seventh Five-Year Plan (December 1984) these objectives were elaborated and eleven important aspects emphasised in order to avoid the weaknesses in the policies and their implementation in the earlier Plan periods. Another good review of the new strategy of development may be found in the Report on Development of Tribal Areas (June 1981) by the National Committee on the Development of Backward Areas headed by Sri B. Sivaraman.

A number of sample evaluation studies undertaken by official agencies as well as independent research organisations have concluded that though the target for the Sixth Plan was to enable 50% of the tribal families below the poverty line to cross the poverty line, hardly 15% of the families assisted during the Plan period were able to cross the poverty line. In fact, no State is in a position to state categorically the number of families which have crossed the poverty line. The State Governments only indicate the total number of the families assisted and often there is double counting of the same families assisted under different programmes. The number of families assisted during the Plan period in many of the States exceeded the target but the net result in terms of improvement of economic condition had been rather disappointing. A large chunk of the beneficiaries were covered under the IRDP (Integrated Rural Development Programme) and other poverty alleviation programmes. The shortcomings noticed in the implementation of these programmes through various evaluation studies are too well known to be repeated here. Some corrective measures regarding selection of beneficiaries, quantum of assistance, etc., have been taken during the current Seventh Plan.

The two basic components of the TSP strategy, i.e., pooling of resources (funds) and single line administration in the ITDPs, have not yet been implemented by all the TSP States. The provision of a separate minor head in the budget of each developmental department does not ensure fulfilment of the objective. The position is better in the States like Andhra Pradesh, Gujarat, Himachal Pradesh, Madhya Pradesh and Maharashtra which have adopted a single demand number in the budget for the TSP. Similarly the single line administration has been introduced in right earnest only in Andhra Pradesh and that too since 1986-87.

Some States still do not do any realistic planning and resort to national quantification of funds in the different sectoral programmes. In one State a few years back a fiat was issued by the Chief Secretary that a cetain percentage of allocations might be shown as flow to the TSP and accordingly a uniform percentage was shown against almost all the schemes including a newly set up Sanskrit University. On the eve of the Conference of State Ministers on Tribal Development held on January 6, 1988, the Ministry of Welfare admitted that the ITDPs had not served the purpose of operational units partly because these had not been accepted as the basic unit of planning. The States should prepare and adopt ITDP-wise plans which may be amalgamated to constitute a State TSP. The benchmark socio-economic data relating to the tribal areas are also now available in most of the States in the Tribal Research

Institutes, some of which have computerised the data relating to households, villages, Blocks, ITDPs, etc. In the formulation of the ITDP plan the local tribal representatives including MPs and MLAs should be involved.

Administration of Tribal Areas

In almost all the States having tribal population there is a Secretary incharge of Tribal Development. In some States he is also the Commissioner of Tribal Development while in others there is a separate incumbent in the post of Commissioner. The Secretary/Commissioner is further assisted by the Director, Tribal Development or the Additional Commissioners. Madhya Pradesh has created Regional Tribal Development Agencies with a view to decentralising the functions and securing better coordination at the Project level. In Bihar a Regional Development Commissioner has been posted at Ranchi. He has full supervisory powers over all the sectors of development in Chhotanagpur area.

The role of the Project Officer of the ITDP has generally continued to be that of a coordinator. However, in reality they are finding it difficult to discharge even this function because of lack of adequate administrative powers. All officers at the Project/district level working in the ITDP should be placed under the direct charge of the Project Officer for all administrative and related purposes irrespective of the departments to which they belong. All of them should be considered as on deputation to the ITDP/ Tribal Development Department. The BDOs, being the officers directly responsible for the implementation of all development schemes in an ITDP, should also be placed under the direct control of the Project Officer. In Andhra Pradesh the Project Officer has been declared as an ADM and powers are being delegated to him in order to make the ITDP a single agency for developmental and regulatory activities.

Personnel Policy in Tribal Areas

The Maheshwar Prasad Group on Administrative Arrangements and Personnel Policies has in its report given a complete account of the weaknesses in the administrative structure in the tribal areas and has also listed out administrative and financial measures required for attracting the right quality of people to those areas. The States have, however, yet to formulate a comprehensive personnel policy for tribal areas taking into account the recommendations of the Maheshwar Prasad Group.

At present some of the personnel of the various departments posted in the tribal areas are not only indifferent but positively hostile towards the tribals. There are some bureaucrats who think that we are unnecessarily bothering about tribal development. Some at the lower levels state that the tribals are *jangali,* will never learn anything and the efforts of the Government to 'civilise' them are bound to prove infructuous. I wish to narrate two experiences. While I was working in the Culture Change Evaluation Project in Jaunsar-Bawar during 1955-56, I found that almost all the officials posted in that area had nothing but contempt and derision for the local people on account of their practice of polyandry. Similar is the attitude of many officials working among tribal communities having marriage customs and ritual practices entirely different from their own. Recently I had an opportunity of speaking to senior Indian Forest Service officers from different States at an orientation programme at the Administrative Training Institute, Nainital. That the forest and the tribal have a symbiotic relationship is by now a common cliche, yet the officers of the Forest Departments and the tribals are seldom amicable towards each other. However, I was not prepared for the shock when a Conservator of forests said quite passionately that it was high time for the Government and the community to decide whether they wanted the forest or the tribal to survive. According to him their co-existence was merely impossible. That gentleman forgot that the association of the Forest Department with the forest was only a little over hundred years old, during which period the net result had been only a tragic destruction of the forest wealth, while the association of the tribal with the forest had lasted for millenia with mutual benefit.

There is need for proper and intensive orientation of all the personnel at different levels posted or likely to be posted in the tribal areas so that they develop the right kind of attitude and spirit and also develop respect for the tribal culture.

The role of voluntary organisations in tribal development is indeed stressed in every official report or gathering. But hardly any effort is made to clearly specify the extent of that role or its details. Consequently, barring a few States like Gujarat and Maharashtra, the voluntary organisations in most of the States, which are dependent on Government grants-in-aid, are playing a marginal role. The role of the foreign funded organisations also needs a critical examination. Of late, a number of small groups of social activists have sprung up in the tribal areas where there is discontent amongst the tribals over one issue or the other. They usually enjoy the confidence of the tribals.

I am firmly of the view that there should be separate cadres/sub-cadres of officers for tribal development work in all the States having tribal population. Besides, there is need for raising corps of thousands of dedicated youth who might be given orientation about tribal life, culture and problems and imparted intensive training for tribal development work. It should be an autonomous organisation but vested with adequate powers to make a tangible impact within a given time frame. While their emoluments may not be identical with those of regular Government employees, their needs should be reasonably met. However, they must command the respect of the official agencies. Details of this proposed organisation for the tribal areas can be worked out and the programme taken up in a few States on a pilot basis.

Some Important Problems

Education

The rate of literacy among the Scheduled Tribes in 1981 was 16.35% as against 41.3% in the non-SC/ST population. The respective figures of female literacy were 8.04% and 29.43%. The gap in literacy rates between the Scheduled Tribes and the non-SC/ST population increased from 22.5% in 1971 to 24.95% in 1981. Similarly the gap in female literacy rates increased from 17.4% in 1971 to 21.39% in 1981.

Replying to a question in Rajya Sabha on August 5, 1987, the Minister of Education informed that in 1982-83 the drop-out rate of tribal students in classes I to VIII was above 80% in 14 States/UTs, *viz.*, Andhra Pradesh, Assam, Bihar, Madhya Pradesh, Maharashtra, Manipur, Meghalaya, Orissa, Rajasthan, Tripura, West Bengal, Goa, Daman & Diu and Dadra & Nagar Haveli.

Several expert bodies have made recommendations in respect of tribal education, the last comprehensive exercise having been done by the Sivaraman Committee which made 44 useful recommendations. Several of these have been gainfully put into operation by some States, e.g., Andhra Pradesh, which has issued orders that in the Scheduled Areas only local Scheduled Tribe persons will be appointed as teachers in primary schools and if qualified tribals are not available in adequate numbers, even those who had studied upto the matriculation but had not passed that examination may be appointed and later sent up for training. It is a common knowledge that in several interior tribal areas primary schools exist only on paper, though non-tribal teachers have been appointed for these schools. They usually offer the excuse that they do not understand the speech of the tribals and vice versa. That is why all the experts emphasise that at least in classes I and II the tribal children should have the facility of receiving instructions in their mother tongue. Some State Governments have prepared text books in major tribal languages in their States. It is important that even where the text books are in the regional language, the teacher at least in the first two classes should be able to communicate with the tribal children in the local tribal speech.

Land Alienation in Tribal Areas

Under the Fifth Schedule to the Constitution regulations to control alienation of tribal lands have been promulgated in Andhra Pradesh, Bihar and Orissa. Besides, there are laws in 22 States/UTs to control alienation of tribal lands. Yet the Commissioner for Scheduled Castes and Scheduled Tribes observed in his 27th Report (1979-81): "It is rather disquieting that in spite of the necessary legislative measures taken by various States, the alienation of tribal lands is still taking place". He listed eight methods used by non-tribals for circumventing the laws for this purpose. However, the magnitude of the problem of alienation of tribal lands is not known accurately in the absence of reliable and up-to-date information from the States. In the above mentioned report he was able to give only partial information in respect of nine States furnished on the basis of registered cases of land alienation. There may be a large number of cases which have not been identified. The State Governments were, therefore, requested to undertake comprehensive surveys in the tribal areas where this problem was known to be acute, in order to identify the cases of land alienation. In some tribal areas the land has not even been surveyed so far. In Duddhi area of Mirzapur district the survey work had been taken up on the orders of the Supreme Court but it was reported that vested interests like non-tribal money lenders, with the help of musclemen, were dislodging the tribals from their ancestral lands and attempting to get their names recorded as owners of those lands. Besides the above cited 27th Report of the Commissioner for SC&ST, important remedial measures have been suggested in the Second Report (1979-80) and the Fifth Report (1982-83) of the Commission for Scheduled Castes and Scheduled Tribes, the Sivaraman Committee (which made 53 useful recommendations), the Working Group on Development of Scheduled Tribes during Seventh Five-Year Plan and the Annual Report of the Union Department of Rural Development for 1986-87.

Excise Policy

One of the worst forms of exploitation in the tribal areas is that of the practice of liquor vending. The Ministry of Social Welfare issued certain guidelines in 1975 for excise policy in the tribal areas. The main guidelines were:

(a) Abolition of the contract system of vending of liquor in tribal areas, (b) sale of liquor through Government agencies where the non-tribal population was mixed with tribal population, and (c) permitting tribals to brew their traditional liquor. These guidelines have not been implemented in right earnest in all the concerned States. Besides commercial vending through authorised agencies, there is a lot of illicit distillation. Till December 1984, Madhya Pradesh was yet to close down nearly 200 shops in the tribal areas and outstill shops in four districts of Orissa were continuing in the tribal areas. In 1984 itself when the Commission for Scheduled Castes and Scheduled Tribes visited Koraput, a senior official of the district stated that one could not hope for any development of the tribals of that district until the liquor shops were firmly closed down. Addiction to liquor was the single biggest cause of their ruin and the most blatant source of their exploitation by the powerful vested interests controlling these shops with the blessings of influential political bosses and with the physical support of gangs of musclemen brought from an adjoining State.

Rehabilitation of Tribals Displaced by Major Projects

So far there is no national policy on rehabilitation of tribals displaced by major projects like irrigation or hydro-electric projects, mining and industrial projects as well as national parks and games sanctuaries. According to information collected by the Commission for SC&ST in 1986 in respect of 119 projects only, the number of tribals displaced by these was nearly 8.14 lakh persons out of a total of nearly 16.94 lakh persons. The rehabilitation of these displaced persons has been quite inadequate due to various reasons. The emphasis placed on cash compensation as a major component of rehabilitation policy has proved to be wrong and against the interests of the tribals. The State Governments try to relocate oustees as individual households rather than as members of a community having social solidarity for ages. The problem is further accentuated as even the cash compensation is limited only to the people with proven legal ownership rights over the land and homestead.

The outdated Land Acquisition Act of 1894 does not take note of the tribals possessing land but without a legal title or of the landless tribals. It also does not take into account the loss of income from minor forest produce, fishing and hunting, etc., and the mental and emotional trauma on being uprooted from the abode of their ancestors and deities.

The guidelines issued by the Central Ministries and some Central Undertakings for resettlement and rehabilitation of oustees have remained expressions of intentions and objectives and have not been implemented seriously. Except for the States of Madhya Pradesh and Maharashtra which have enacted separate acts for rehabilitation of displaced persons, other States have continued rehabilitation of displaced persons including tribals in a perfunctory manner. The latest guidelines issued by the Bureau of Public Enterprises broadly touch upon the issues of land acquisition, compensation and rehabilitation. These guidelines have taken away the offer of employment given in the earlier guidelines of various Ministries to one member of every dispossessed family in the project.

Inadequate rehabilitation has been resulting in an acute deprivation and a sense of alienation amongst the tribals. The displaced tribals should not only be assisted to regain at least a standard of living enjoyed by them prior to displacement but it should be ensured that as far as possible their community life is not disturbed.

The most crucial current issue is that of the rehabilitation of the large number of people, mostly tribals, displaced or being displaced by the numerous projects on the Narmada. The Sardar Sarovar project alone is likely to displace about two lakh people. The Narmada Control Authority set up by the Centre is seriously looking into the issues involved but all the States concerned do not yet appear to be ready with comprehensive plans of rehabilitation.

Some Basic Issues

There appears to be lack of clarity about the ultimate objective of tribal development. It is often stated that the objective is to enable the tribals to join the mainstream of national life. What this mainstream is anybody's guess. To a Naga perhaps it is a dirty word. He is apt to tell people from outside Nagaland: "Ours is the mainstream. You are welcome to join it." The other expression commonly used in this context is integration. It again is open to different interpretations. What is perhaps desirable on the part of non-tribals is not to make any conscious or deliberate efforts to assimilate or even actuate the tribals. Let the non-tribals acquire some of the good and healthy traits of the tribal cultures as they expect the latter to acquire their own. This mutuality of healthy relations is not possible in a system based on exploitation. The processes of socio-economic transformation have got to be duly regulated.

The tribal society has largely been egalitarian and democratic. The tribal elite today have the only model of larger national life comprising socially and economically structured society where there are the poor and the rich. In the tribal areas we still have an opportunity of strengthening an egalitarian society. Development in the tribal areas should be so guided that deprivation processes do not set in. Dr. B.D. Sharma has observed that the entire question of tribal development boils down to two basic issues: (i) whether the traditional command of the community over resources can be preserved, and (ii) whether the egalitarian structure of the tribal communities can be retained and their social milieu can be taken advantage of to initiate a process so that socio-economic transformation can be negotiated without deprivation. This process cannot be superimposed but has to be stimulated by the tribal community itself which has a tradition of self-governance.

7

Nehru and Tribal Development in India

Buddhadeb Chaudhuri

The different tribal communities are found in most of the States of India. According to the 1981 census, the tribal population of India comprising 427 communities was 51,628,638 constituting 7.76 per cent of India's total population. However, ethnographic data on a number of tribal communities are lacking. Some of the large tribal communities are distributed in a wide region and often profess varied occupations. Again, a few tribal groups are divided into a number of subgroups which are practically distinct tribal groups. In many cases, some distinct tribal groups have identical names. Besides these, the scheduling of tribes has also created a problem as in many cases, a tribe may be scheduled in one State and not so in another State. For all these reasons, any classification needs careful endeavour. Still it can be said that these tribal communities belong to different racial stocks, speak languages of different families and show considerable variation in their basic economy.

Approach to Tribals

During the pre-Independence period, the British rulers mostly followed the policy of segregation and tried to keep the tribals isolated from the rest of the population. This isolation not only led to exploitation of the tribal population by the selected non-tribals like the money-lenders and contractors, but also helped the British rulers to exploit and enjoy the natural resources of such areas as the rest of population were not aware or concerned with the developments of these areas. A number of Acts were passed to keep some areas isolated or segregated like the Scheduled Tracts (1870), Scheduled District Acts (1876), Backward Tracts (1919), Excluded Areas and Partially Excluded Areas of 1936; Elwin also suggested the "establishment of a sort of National Park" (1939; 511-519) and minimum contact between the tribals and non-tribals. In 1941, he also suggested the idea of isolationism.

This policy of segregation not only promoted exploitation and served colonial interest, but also created a sense of separatism among the tribal groups with the rest of India.

This policy, however, was criticised by the nationalist leaders and social workers like A.V. Thakkar, and others who did not want the tribals to be confined in isolated and inaccessible hills and jungles.

Immediately after Independence, the same policy of isolation with certain modifications was followed. Gradually it was changed. The declaration of "a few particular areas of tribal concentration as Scheduled Areas and Tribal Areas" does not always indicate the isolation policy as the observation of Shri A.V. Thakkar as Chairman of the sub-committee, constituted by the Constituent Assembly in this regard shows that some form of isolation was suggested to check exploitation and not to keep the tribals isolated. It recommended "considering the past experiences and the strong temptation take advantage of the tribal simplicity and weakness, it is essential to provide statutory safeguards for the protection of the land," (Elwin 1963; 15-16). Gradually the approach and policy of assimilation, as a result of contact of the tribals with the non-tribals, and the integration of the tribals in the regional and national spheres were followed and no doubt, the policy and approach towards the tribals after Independence was influenced by Pandit Nehru to a great extent.

Nehru and the Indian Tribes

Nehru keenly appreciated Tribal culture. He was greatly impressed by its democratic ethos and sense of discipline. He observed, "They are an extemely disciplined people, often much more democratic than most others in India. Without a Constitution, they function democratically and carry out the decisions made by their elders or their own representatives almost without exceptions." He advised to approach, "this simple folk in a spirit of comradeship and not like some one aloof who had come to look at them, examine them, or make them conform to another way of life". He also strongly felt it a wrong approach, "to call some people primitive and to think of ourselves as highly civilised". Nehru was very much concerned with the tribal policy and tribal development, but consistently opposed any type of imposition or interference with their way of life. He felt that "if you approach the tribal people with affection, go to them as a liberating force and as a friend so that they may feel you have come not to take away something from them but to give them something... But, if they feel you have come to try to change their methods of living, then it is all completely wrong." He strongly felt that the main problem is not to provide facilities to the tribals, but to "understand these people, make them understand us and create a bond of affection and understanding between us". In order to preserve their traditional way of life and culture, he considered the language as an important factor and made it "perfectly and absolutely clear that Government would encourage the tribal languages to encourage and help them to flourish". Though Nehru was anxious for educational and economic development of the tribals, he strongly expressed the desire that "there would be no attempt to impose other's ways of life on them in a hurry". "Let the change come gradually and be worked out by the tribals themselves" (1957). Pandit Nehru strongly believed in the co-existence of numerous diverse cultures and thus felt that the tribal groups can become a part of integrated Indian nation. Integration of tribals and non-tribals is very crucial and for this the non-tribals need education as much as the tribals. The approaches to the tribal problems and development, as concieved by Nehru, are clearly stated in his Foreword to the Elwin's book, 'Philosophy of NEFA' (2nd Ed.), which really formed the basis of the national policy towards tribal development (1959).

In the name of development Nehru was against the imposition of anything on the tribals. Programme should be initiated considering the felt needs of the tribals where they should have the final say lastly, the customary rights of the tribals on land and forest, which they have enjoyed so long would be honoured.

Tribal Development : Meaning and Scope

Before discussing and reviewing the tribal development approach of the government, it is pertinent to know how the anthropologists view development and particularly their understanding of tribal development.

The term development is often used in the sense of growth indicating a quantitative increase or progress in production, income, consumption of food, etc. and thus giving emphasis on quantitative aspect ignoring the qualitative part of man. Belshaw, however, gave equal emphasis on social, cultural, economic and other aspects of life. He observed, "sociologically speaking, development should be looked upon as an organised activity with the aim of satisfying certain basic needs and to psychologically orient the tribals to adopt new skills, attitudes and life styles, so that they built up the inner strength, and appropriate social and cultural infrastructure to stand the pressure of the new situation and accrue benefits from the new programmes and maintain higher levels (1972). In a later article, he has considered the development as a positive change and observed, "development presents an increase in the capacities of a society to organise for its own objectives and to carry out its programmes more efficiently" (1977; 31).

Development, as has been observed by Beals and Hoijer, may be considered as those changes which are required but have minimum disruptive effects on the concerned population.

Vidyarthi (1981) observed that development means growth and change which includes both the material and human—the socio-cultural factors which are an integral part of the dynamics of growth. He felt, "while striving for the development of a group or an area, due emphasis has to be given to their traditional values and historical experiences." In fact, economist like Schumacher has also observed, "development does not start with goods; it starts with people and their education, organisation and discipline" (1977 : 157).

With reference to development, Mahapatra has also observed that real development should consider the needs, values and aspiration of the concerned population and local development are not likely to be in conflict with the national objectives, but at the same time, the local people's aspirations and potentialities should be honoured, respected and accommodated. He also felt that resistances to new programmes would be there if such programmes are not properly planned (1980). To Roy Burman, development activities particularly in the context of tribals should be concerned with,

(a) Satisfaction of minimum needs,
(b) Control and management of productive resources.
(e) Employment Optimisation.
(d) Broad based participation of the population in development process, and
(e) Socio-cultural and political aspect of national integration, (1986; 133).

Elsewhere he has suggested (1989) that anywhere development would lead to the reduction of regional disparity and help in the creation of self-reliant economy. Besides, it would lead to redistribution of income, equalisation of distribution of development benefits, reduction of social stratification and resource mobilisation without affecting quality of life and physical environment. Mahatma Gandhi also desired that the tribals should not live under anybody's patronage and should enjoy and equality of status and opportunity with others (Bose : 1968).

Thus a number of issues may be suggested particularly in the context of tribal development.

(1) Development includes both quantitative and qualitative change.
(2) Social and cultural aspects of the concerned population should be considered.
(3) Imposition of ideas and values, plans and programmes, and also priorities of work without considering the felt needs of the concerned population should not be made.
(4) Development should promote participation of the concerned population in the development process.

(5) Development should help in the elimination or at least reduction of various process of domination and cultural hegemony of ruling classes, equalisation of distribution of development benefits (growth with justice) and redistribution of income.

(6) Development should not only prevent alienation of the tribals over productive resources, it should also not affect the physical environment to any appreciable extent and the traditional customary rights of the tribals over productive resources.

(7) Development should not in any way affect the quality of life, but is expected to improve it.

Thus is we compare and examine the broad approach and type of tribal development visualized by Pandit Nehru and that suggested by the social scientists, particularly anthropologists and sociologists, it is interesting that the major issues are common. Thus, broad based participation of the concerned population in the development process and development on the lines of their own genius have been suggested and it has been recommended that nothing should be imposed upon them. Control and management of productive resources is another important issue and it has been advised that tribal rights over land and forest should be respected. Development is also expected to improve the quality of life.

Tribal Development

The different measures taken or programmes initiated in the context of the tribals may be broadly classified into three groups—(a) protective, which includes constitutional safeguards and also legislations restricting and regulating alienation of tribal over resources, particularly land, (b) mobilisation, which includes reservation in academic institutions, services and legislatives, and lastly (c) developmental, which includes a large number of programmes covering social services, health, education, economy, etc. (Roy Burman; 1989). Here, it may not be possible to examine and critically analyse all the programmes initiated or efforts made in the context of tribal development in different plan periods, but even if some areas are analysed this should no doubt reflect the general pattern and may indicate how far the broad approach and type of development visualized by Pandit Nehru, and also suggested by the social scientists have been fulfilled and translated into reality.

Tribal Development Programmes

After Independence, various efforts were made to improve the socio-economic conditions of the tribals and to sustain the constitutional safeguards given to them. A number of commissions, committees, working groups or study teams were formed from time to time to evaluate the condition of the Scheduled Castes and Scheduled Tribes. The annual reports of the Commissioner for Scheduled Castes and Scheduled Tribes from 1950 onwards, the report of the Backward Classes Commission and the various other reports including report published by the State Governments are available. The first study team was constituted as early as 1949. On the Criminal Tribes Act Enquiry Committee and a number of such study-teams or working groups reports are available including the very recent report of the Working Group on Development of Scheduled Tribes during Seventh Five-Year Plan, 1985-90. These study team reports, working group reports and similar other reports or discussions often guided and helped to reformulate the development strategy with reference to the tribals. The different programmes and schemes initiated by the Government during the different plan periods can be grouped broadly into six categories:

1. Economic, including agriculture, forestry, animal husbandry and small scale industry.
2. Educational.
3. Health, sanitation and family welfare.
4. Communication and housing.
5. Socio-cultural.
6. Political.

In the first plan, mostly as a part of Community Development Programme, various programmes were initiated with particular reference to health, communication and housing. In the Second Plan initiated in 1956, the establishment of 43 special Multipurpose Tribal Blocks in areas with tribal concentration for integrated tribal development was a significant step. Special emphasis was given to education in addition to health., agriculture, communication and housing programmes. In the Third Plan, these blocks were renamed as Tribal Development Blocks where major emphasis was given on economic development along with education, health, housing and communication. Allocation was also increased manifold and 489 Tribal Development Blocks were opened for integrated tribal development, each block covering about 25,000 population of which two-third belonged to the tribal areas. However, due to wider coverage, per capita expenditure went down. By the end of the Fourth Plan, 43 per cent of the tribal population were covered in 504 tribal development blocks. During this period, a number of special programmes were initiated for the poorer families or small-marginal farmers. Thus special attention was directed to the individual families during this period in addition to area-based programmes. However, the Task Force Report on Development of Tribal Areas has noted a proportionate decrease on expenditure on tribal programmes. Thus, in the First Plan, expenditure on tribal programmes was around 1 per cent which came down to 4 per cent in the Fourth Plan and 2 per cent in the Fifth Plan period.

The Fifth Five-Year plan was a landmark in the development planning for the tribal people because the concept of sub-plan for the tribal regions of a state within the overall frame of the state plan was initiated. The unit of planning was an Integrated Tribal Development Project (ITDP). In the Fifth Plan, 18 sub-plans were initiated covering 65% of the tribal population in India in 16 States and 2UTs. The preparation of annual sub-plan was a concurrent exercise with the State annual plans. The tribal sub-plan approach initiated in the Fifth Plan continued in the Sixth Plan basing on the geographical and demographic concentration of the tribals and also included Sikkim, besides the States and UTs already in the Fifth Plan. The main objectives were to narrow the gap between the level of development of tribal areas and others and to improve the quality of life of the tribal people; and to achieve these, economic programmes, protective measures, employment, education, health services, credit facilities were initiated and the importance of LAMPS was re-emphasized and strengthened. Attempts were made to cover the entire tribal population and tribals living outside the tribal concentrated areas were also included and in this Plan period about 75% of the tribals were covered where more investment was made and emphasis was given on amelioration of poverty, development of human resources, education, elimination of exploitation and development of adequate infrastructure.

Effects of Various Programmes

It is obvious that it would not be possible to critically analyse all the development efforts but, if a few of them are properly assessed and analysed, it would clearly indicate the trend.

Firstly, if the forest situation is examined, it is quite

evident that tribal customary laws regulating access to control and management of resources, particularly forest has been denied on the pretext of wider national interest and ecological consequences and commercial exploitation of forests has been promoted. In the recent past, forest has become an important source of earning revenue and increasing commercial exploitation of forest was needed. Besides timber, which serves the interest of the industry, to a vast majority of tribal population, forest is one of the main source of subsistence for them and it is mainly through the minor forest products. But in view of the various restrictions and regulations imposed from time to time their rights to collect fuel, fodder and minor forest products are very much restricted almost throughout India. It is well-known that there is considerable pressure from neo-colonial forces to mobilise the untapped resources and particularly in the context of forest, they are also interested besides timber in the minor forest products which are mostly enjoyed by the tribals to meet their various needs. The mobilisation of such untapped resources has resulted in the depletion of non-renewable resources adversely affecting not only the immediate interests of the tribals but also the long-range interest of the nation. Again, in the afforestation programmes, mostly those trees are planted which have commercial interest. These trees do not really help the tribals as they can neither generate employment opportunities locally nor help the local people to meet some of their daily demands. Again, such afforestation programme with mono-tree can also adversely affect the ecology which are often funded by international agencies like World Bank. The World Bank out of own interest may suggest that poor people cause deforestation and that for their own good, the forests must be removed from their control and made into commercially viable assets, but perhaps such a policy cannot be adopted by a welfare state. The commercial aspect should not be totally overlooked, but this should not be done at the cost of the tribals, the economy of whom largely depends on forests. A harmony is to be made between the two interests.

Again, some of the big dam projects and hydel projects are not only adversely affecting the forest ecology, the tribal population has not been the beneficiaries of such development programmes and the development programmes have adversely affected the environment where the tribals live. Singh has also noted that many of the development programmes have not benefitted tribal communities in the past, sometimes development had been at the cost of tribal interests (Bhupinder Singh; 1977 : 229-43).

The role of Bank, Cooperative Societies can also be mentioned here in this connection with reference to tribal development. Tribal economy is partly monetised but mostly non-monetised. It is to be examined whether the institutional finance is compatible or not with this economic environment. It has often been observed that due to various rules and regulations the tribals are not in a position to enjoy the benefits of such facilities.

The class formation among the tribal communities due to type of development strategy followed have been observed by many. No doubt a question may be asked, whether only community background should be considered or the community background along with economic condition should be the factors for consideration.

The failure of limitations of various tribal development programmes have been observed by many. In fact, even in the Government report, *Approach to Tribal Development in the Sixth Plan: A Preliminary Perspective*, it has been observed, "In the name of tribal developments we have spent a lot of money during the last several Plans, but when accounting was made at the end of the last period of the safeguards to the tribals in the Constitution, it was found that actual benefits trickling down to the tribals have not been consistent with the promise we have made...75% of the total benefits have not reached the tribals...we cannot have development at this rate." The Shilee Ao Team on tribal development programme have also expressed more or less the same view.

A few points may be said about tribal health. The so-called western medicine is promoted without critically examining its usefulness. The merits of the traditional tribal medicinal system is totally ignored. Insecticides and pesticides are encouraged even though the tribals have many useful plants to serve such needs and without their harmful effects.

It is not only in the context of forest that the traditional customary rights have been denied, it is also true in the context of land and unfortunately there were many instances where there was conversion from a local communal resource to a privately owned commercial resource.

If the tribal development strategy as visualised by Pandit Nehru and also the approach suggested by the social scientists are examined in the context of actual happening in tribal areas, a number of features would emerge which were neither suggested nor desired. It is obvious that the traditional tribal rights over land and forest are not always respected and they often cannot develop on the lines of their own skill and tradition. The involvement and participation of the tribals are rather limited and lastly, which is more significant, the type of development strategy is creating more dependence on welfare bureaucracy or welfare middlemen.

Unfortunately the progress or development of the tribals is not up to expectations for a number of reasons. As the programmes are plan-based and more emphasis is often given on the disbursement without considering the local felt needs, they often do not serve the real purpose. For making the development programmes really successful, one must be aware of cultural traditions, eco-system, economy, history and ethnic composition of the region. A number of studies have also indicated that the development has not taken place at a uniform pace. Thus some communities are more advanced than others or some families are enjoying most of the benefits meant for total community. The utilization and enjoyment is typically unequal at the communities as well as at the regional level. There is no doubt that this situation will lead to class formation among the tribals. In fact, it has already emerged. The economically well-to-do sections are also educationally more advanced and the emergence of a new elite section among the tribals who are otherwise known by the homogenous character, particularly in the context of various development programmes, is quite conspicious. In a number of situations, enjoying various benefits, some families of a few tribal communities have become economically well-to-do, purchasing land from other tribals at a much cheaper rate than the local market price. The lands owned by the tribals have also less market value because they cannot be sold to the non-tribals. Such well-off tribals often lend money to other less priviledged members of their tribes. The emergence of the tribal money-lender, except in North-East India, is a new feature and through it they greatly exploit the members of their own community. Though previously the tribals were equally exploited by the non-tribals, the unfortunate aspect is that the present type of exploitation has been possible partly due to the various development facilities extended to the tribals and their unequal utilization and enjoyment which has resulted in some sort of class formation in those communities which characteristically lacked any type of traditional hierarchy. Development does not necessarily mean only an increase in expenditure and generation of a situation which would increase exploitation. It demands some serious thinking and it is felt that while extending facilities in addition to area and community background, the class character should also be considered. Though the exploitation of the tribals and various governmental policies have often stimulated a number of tribal unrests, conflicts and tensions, there are reasons to believe that the developmental programmes are indirectly responsible for these movements as they are often initiated by the emerging tribal elities, who quite often try to organise the total tribal population in their own interest. It is to be seen that economic opportunities permeate a broad base of the population instead of being limited to an elite group.

REFERENCE

1. Belshaw Cyril S, 1972, Development: The Contribution of Anthropology, *International Social Science Journal*, Vol. 24.
2. Belshaw Cyril S, 1977, The Contribution of Anthropologists to Development, *Anthropology in Development Process*, Ed. H.M. Mathur, Vikas Publishing House, New Delhi.
3. Bose N.K. 1968, Precision in Applied Anthropology, in *Applied Anthropology in India*, Ed. L.P. Vidyarthi, Kitab Mahal, Allahabad.
4. Chaudhuri Buddhadeb (Ed.), 1982 *Tribal Development in India Problems and Prospects*, 1st Edn., Inter India Publications, New Delhi.
5. Dube, S.C, 1968 Approaches to Tribal Problems in India, in *Applied Anthropology in India*, Ed. L.P. Vidyarthi, Kitab Mahal, Allahabad.
6. Elwin Verrier, 1939 *The Baiga*, John Murray, London.
7. Elwin, Verrier, 1943 *The Aboriginals*, Oxford University Press, Bombay.
8. Elwin, Verrier, 1963 *A New Deal for Tribal India*, New Delhi (1st Ed. 1957).
9. Mahapatra L.K., 1980 Barriers to Development in Isolated Tribal Areas, *National Seminar on Tribal Development*. THRTI, Bhubaneswar.
10. Nehru Jawaharlal, 1952, Inaugural speech at the Conference of Tribes and Scheduled Areas held in New Delhi, 7th June, 1952, published in *Vanyajati* Vol. 22 No, 3 July, 1964.
11. Nehru Jawaharlal, 1954, Inaugural address, 3rd Tribal Welfare Conference, Jagdalpur, M.P. Published in the Report, Bhartiya Adimjati Sevak Sangha, Delhi.

12. Nehru Jawaharlal, 1959, Foreword to *Philosophy for NEFA*, (2nd Ed.) by V. Elwin, Govt. of Assam, Shillong.
13. Roy Burman B.K., 1989, Introduction in *Tribal Development in India*, Ed. Pati R.N. and B. Jena, Ashish Publishing House, New Delhi.
14. Roy Burman B.K., 1986, Strategy of Tribal Development, in *Tribal Development and its Administration*, Ed. L.P. Vidyarthi, Concept Pub.. N. Delhi.
15. Schumacher E.F., 1977, *Small is Beautiful*, Radhakrishna.
16. Vidyarthi L.P, (Ed.) 1968, *Applied Anthropology in India*, Kitab Mahal, Allahabad.
17. Vidyarthi L.P. and B.K. Rai 1977, *The Tribal Culture of India*, Concept Publishing Company, Delhi.
18. Vidyarthi L.P. and B.N. Sahay (Ed.) 1980, *Applied Anthropology and Development in India*, National, New Delhi.
19. Vidyarthi L.P. (Ed.), 1986, *Tribal Development and its Administration*, Concept Publishing Company, New Delhi (1st Ed. 1981).

8

Post-Independence Policies, Planned Development and Tribal Deprivation

Walter Fernandes

Development, particularly of the planned variety, is understood to mean progress towards a better quality of life than in the past. In the context of India, the first step is the abolition of poverty. This has been mentioned as the primary objective from the very first Five-Year Plan.

> The urge to economic and social change under present conditions comes from the fact of poverty and of inequalities in income, health and opportunity. The elimination of poverty cannot obviously be achieved merely by redistributing existing wealth. Nor can a programme aiming only at raising production remove existing inequalities. Only a simultaneous advance along both these lines can create conditions in which the community can put forth its best efforts for promoting development (Planning Commission 1951: 8).

Also the Second Plan insisted that its purpose was a movement towards equality (Planning Commission

1956: 236). The Third Plan was more explicit and stated that

> For India, the conquest of poverty has no short or easy answer. India does not have, as do some underdeveloped countries, oil or precious minerals or any single rich resource or export crop out of which it can largely pay for development. Nor does it have vast unexplored lands and untapped forests, such as have helped some countries in the past providing ready wealth and resources for their development...Further, India's is an old traditional society, rooted in thousands of years of history. Far-reaching changes in social customs and institutions are necessary–and have been started–to build up a technically advanced society which offers more equal opportunities for all (Planning Commission 1961: 7).

Similar statements have been made by all the Five-Year Plans. At the same time they have given two steps to achieve this. The first is raising the productivity in agriculture and industry. The second is attaining social equality through the combination of land reforms, *Panchayati Raj* and community development (Planning Commission 1956: 234-236).

However, most studies indicate that inequalities have increased rather than decreased during the decade of planned development. According to one study (Bandyopadhyay 1988: 77), the poverty ratio which was 56.8 in 1960-61 came as low as 45.2 in 1967-68 but was at 53.4 in 1979-80. The actual number of the poor went up from 202.21 to 272.00 millions in the two decades. These are official figures and other studies put them much higher. Montek Ahluwalia (1978: 17), for example, concludes that the rural poverty ratio in 14 major States remained more or less unchanged during 1957-58 to 1973-74.

Inequalities have increased both in the industrial

and the agricultural sector. The number of landless labourers as well as marginal and small farmers has increased and the top decile has monopolised more land in 1981 compared to 1951. What is equally important is that these inequalities have increased both in income distribution (Bardhan 1974: 125-127) and in the ownership of assets. For example, the Sixth Plan document estimated that the bottom 20 per cent owned less than 1 per cent of the total assets in 1980 while the top 10 per cent owned more than 50 per cent (Planning Commission 1980: 8-10).

The most important aspect of the growing inequalities is their cumulative character. Certain groups have accumulated in themselves all the advantages while others have been victims of all the disadvantages of development. That is where the discussion on planned development and policies becomes relevant to the tribes. They belong to the resource rich regions and these are also the ones with the highest poverty ratio. For example, the resource rich State of Bihar has the highest poverty ratio of 55 per cent (Krishna 1981: 4-6)

That is what the present paper is trying to analyse. There has been much concentration in planned development on the resource rich tribal areas. Special provision has been made to protect their land and other assets. Despite this, their situation has deteriorated during the four decades of planned development. How does one explain this contradiction ?

In order to understand this situation, the present paper will begin with an analysis of Nehru's and other immediate post-independence policies concerning the tribals. It will then situate the present state of the tribals in the context of their transition from the traditional to the modern economy. We shall make an attempt to understand it by analysing their situation from the point of view of land and agriculture, industry and forests. We shall end with an analytical conclusion.

The Policy Concerning the Tribals

Controversies are again and again revived concerning the approach to the tribals. It is stated by some that guided by the advice of Verrier Elwin, Nehru suggested that the tribals should remain in their idyllic past and should be left alone and that the dominant groups have no right, whatever, to impose their views and values on them. This is stated, oftener than not, by those who hold the other extreme, *viz.* that they should be integrated completely into the mainstream. The reality is considerably different. Nehru as well as G.B. Pant, the main architects of post-independence policies concerning the tribals, as well as their adviser Verrier Elwin held a middle view. All of them agreed that matters cannot be allowed to drift but that the tribals have a right to make progress exactly like the rest of the nation. They cannot be preserved as museum pieces. On the other hand they should not be overadministered. They and the other minorities should be allowed to develop in their own way (Sharma 1978: 7-9). Nehru was specific on what he thought. He enunciated his *Panchsheel* for tribal development in his foreword to the book of Verrier Elwin (1955).

An aspect that comes out clearly in these policies is respect for their culture as against ethnocentrism that seems to guide the dominant sections. The policy is based on the assumption that

> It is grossly presumptuous on our part to approach them with an air of superiority or to tell them what to do or not to do. There is no point in trying to make them a second rate copy of ourselves...and to impose on them a particular way of life. (Gopalan 1982: 242).

The Approach of The Five-Year Plans

It is in the context of these policies that one needs to ask with Haimendorf (1980: 1-2), why do

> populations who for millennia persisted in a state of almost complete self-sufficiency, having developed their own way of life and cultural individuality without any need for outside assistance, have now to be protected and aided by government. This question appears to be all the more pertinent as only one or two generations ago many tribal communities enjoyed the advantages of a well balanced ecology fully in tune with the natural resources of their environment and could boast an overall quality of life superior in many ways to that of large sections of the Indian rural population. Adequate food supplies, a non-exploitative social structure, freedom from indebtedness and other forms of dependence on non-tribal outsiders, equality of the sexes and a remarkable tolerance in all interpersonal relations were outstanding characteristics of such tribal societies.

This can probably be explained from what a former member of the Planning Commission is reported to have stated. Every plan has the poetic part of the "chapter on objectives, approach and policy, often from the guiding principles of our Constitution. Having once gotten over this poetic preamble, the operational part got down to the serious business of ensuring the subversion of every one of them" (Gadgil 1983: 111). The same fate seems to have befallen the policy concerning the tribals. First of all, the Five-Year Plans were based on the assumption of the growth factor and higher productivity being combined with equitable distribution. Industrialisation was to be a tool to abolish poverty. Thus, after stating that the abolition of poverty should be the objective and that the *Panchayati Raj* and the involvement of the community were the means to attain equlity, the Second Five-Year Plan went on to say:

> Industrialisation is a means, not an end. But considering the need for initiating the process of sus-

> tained and more rapid progress in subsequent plans, it becomes almost an objective in itself. From the long-term point of view it is necessary to make a rapid advance in these sectors where the potentialities for further growth and the indirect benefits to other sectors are the greatest. It was with this end in view that the First Plan laid great emphasis on the development of irrigation and power in the country. In the Second Plan, a high priority must be accorded to the development of basic industries such as those producing iron and steel, machinery, electrical equipment and heavy chemicals...It is only by developing basic industries that a secure foundation for capital formation can be laid and the country made more independent of imports of vitally needed plant and equipment (Planning Commission 1955: Para 16).

The Same approach was proposed also by the Third Five-Year Plan. Its approach paper said among others:

> India's other highly promising road out of poverty lies in sharply stepping up production from industries, large and small. Because of its natural resources, India has very important advantages and considerable potential for industrialisation. Its known reserves of iron, manganese, bauxite are extensive. There is considerable coal, mica and atomic material such as thorium ores. Surveys and explorations have already shown the possibility of oil reserves. India's famous rivers have a potential for hydro-electrical power, perhaps among the highest in the world (Planning Commission 1961: 10).

Thus one notices a certain conflict arising already in the Five-Year Plans between equality and growth of the weaker sections, tribals in particular on the one hand and industrialisation-cum-productivity on the other. The ideal set in the plan documents is one of balance between the two. The reality is considerably different since a choice seems to have been made between the two because of the power equation in the country. This should be seen especially in the context of the slow evolution of a policy concerning the tribals.

While all the approach papers to the Five-Year Plans were clear on industrialisation and productivity as tools for the abolition of poverty, a policy concerning the tribals evolved somewhat slowly. The approach papers to the first three Plans do not mention the tribals directly but only refer to the problem of poverty among the "weaker sections". The tribals were not specifically mentioned though alluded to. On the other hand, industrialisation and productivity involved much greater exploitation of the resources in which the tribal areas were rich. This referred particularly to the forests, minerals and water. The human element was definitely mentioned but in the context of using "human hands and brains" for increasing the productivity of these resources. The framework of the Second Five-Year Plan (Part II. No. 20), for example, stated:

> The development of heavy industries would require fuller exploitation of our mineral resources, extension of transport facilities and rapid expansion in the number of trained personnel in the country. Concrete schemes for scientific training, mineral development and transport must, therefore, be worked out in advance of the projects for heavy industries. In the ultimate analysis all wealth is forged by human hands...The need for extensive surveys to discover additional mineral resources in the country can, therefore, be hardly exaggerated.

Though the rural poor, weaker sections and equality were mentioned in the other plans, it became clear by 1969 that there was a danger of planned development resulting in monopolies and concentration of power in a few hands. The approach paper to the Plan began by saying that monopolies over and greater command of resources by a few persons should be avoided through legislation and the licensing policies. It also stated that income disparities have to be avoided through fiscal measures. However, it was clear that a poor country cannot, as in a rich country, transfer income from the rich to the poor because whatever is saved has to be invested (Planning Commission 1969: 14). Hence, it stated that

> We have to reach the social and economic objectives through more rapid growth of the economy, greater diffusion of enterprise and of the ownership of the means, means of production, increasing productivity of the weaker units and widening opportuities of productive work and employment to the common man, and particularly the less privileged sections the of society. These measures have to be brought out in a number of different contexts and coordinated into effective, integrated programmes (Ibid: 15).

The solution suggested for this was area development and local level planning beginning with the State, region and the district. It continued that the handicaps of each one should be studied in order to "start them on the path of development". Cooperatives, adjustments of procedures of financial institutions and rural industries would be some of the means suggested.

It is in this context that for the first time the Scheduled Tribes and Scheduled Castes are mentioned specifically in an approach paper of the Five-Year Plans.

> The problems of Scheduled Tribes and Scheduled Castes have in addition some special features. The problem of Scheduled Tribes living in compact areas is essentially that of economic development of their areas and of integrating their economy with that of the rest of the country. The individual welfare approach or that of a schematic block is inap-

propriate in this case. Development plans must be formulated to suit the specific potentialities and levels of development of separate regions or areas...In both (SC & ST) the cases the special programmes meant for them must operate as additional programmes so that tribal blocks obtain from the general Plan outlays funds required for the development of basic infrastructure and their other needs can use the supplementary resources for specific programmes of economic development (Ibid: 16).

During this plan, to be specific in 1971-72, tribal development agencies were thought of. They were based on the SFDA and the focus was on soil conservation, land development and control of shifting cultivation and a subsidy towards a risk fund of cooperative institutions. Particular stress was to be laid on restructuring the cooperative institutions and providing consumption credit and debt redemption. It also stated that land records have to be updated in order to protect the tribals (Planning Commission 1973: 2.90-2.93).

In the Sixth Plan, for the first time the target was set of raising 50 per cent each of the Scheduled Castes and Scheduled Tribes above the poverty line. The Seventh Plan aimed to continue this thrust of socioeconomic development through the tribal sub-plans and by turning the blocks with a tribal majority into the integrated tribal development projects. It suggested human resource as well as infrastructure development, strengthening protective measures and forming LAMPS and other cooperatives and integrating the existing IRDP, DPAP and other programmes into them (Planning Commission 1985: 15.11-13; 15.15; 15.25-33).

Formal Versus Informal Economy

One thus notices that though an attempt is made to put tribal development and equality together with productivity and industrialisation, there is an in built conflict and contradiction between the two. As a result, the thrust has been mainly towards productivity and industrialisation and much less in favour of the tribals. Most studies indicate that the situation of the tribals has deteriorated.

That in itself was inevitable because what one notices through planned development is a transition from the informal to the formal economy. They are two systems with different foundations. First of all, the informal system of economy and political organisation on which the tribals depend, is based on an oral tradition and word of honour, and keeps it, trusting the others to do the same. Truth in this system is unambiguous, not evidential and gets legitimacy through acceptance by the community. The formal system, on the contrary, is individual-based and property and other rights are recognised through a written document.

The difference can probably be best understood by looking at a social system like marriage or economic in-put or property rights. To begin with the former, among many tribes as soon as a boy and a girl exchange a promise, they are allowed to live together. Their coming together is recognised as marriage though the formal ceremony may come much later. What is required is recognition by the community.

The second is seen in the Hindu marriage where only the word of honour of the two persons is insufficient. A witness is required for the couple to live together legitimation. The third step in the formal system is taken by the civil marriage which has to have individual living witnesses as well as a written document. The witness and legitimation by the community are of no avail to it. Only individuals and written material are recognised (Sharma 1978: 13-14).

The difference can also be seen in the concept of

property rights. Here too, the crucial factor is acceptance by the community. Before going into the ownership pattern, it is important to stress that the concept of property as understood today was absent in the traditional tribal society. Land, for example, is today understood, primarily or even exclusively, as an object of agriculture and construction. This is a capitalist view of property owned by the individual who has an absolute right over it. To the tribal whose life was centered primarily around land and forests, it was not property in that sense but a community resource. The descendants of those who first cleared the forests and founded a village have some special rights known as *Khuntkatti* among the Hos and other words elsewhere, otherwise land and other resources were held by individuals only in the name of the community. Common lands, wastelands, forests, ponds, gardens, etc. were a common property resources. The individual had only usufructuary rights over them (Pathy 1988: 84-85).

The way in which individuals availed of this property differed from tribe to tribe. What was common to all was that the title did not become hereditary but only the use of a given type of property was allowed. Among the Khasi, Jaintia and Garo tribes of Meghalaya, for example, the right of inheritance was from mother to daughter. Among the Khasis and Jaintias, the youngest daughter inherits ancestral property and among the Garos parents select their privileged daughter. But the inheritance is of the right to select the plot meant for cultivating land which belongs to the community. Any member of the community may cultivate it without paying a tax while outsiders have to pay a tax. In most cases even land that was acquired by an individual family would be considered community property when it passes to the next generation (Nair 1987: 27-29).

Also in Tripura, traditionally each individual family could cultivte the land required for its use but could not own it. Even the 1986 land tenure census book brought out by the government of Tripura, does not include *jhum* land in individual or government land because the individual can only use it for *jhum* but does not have any right over it, not even over its timber. Traditionally, the king was not the *zamindar* of *jhum* land. Even when the king claimed right over the rest of the land, the *jhum* land was controlled by the village. The family was free to choose the plot it required from the area earmarked for shifting cultivation, cultivate it for a year and leave it fallow for five years to let bamboo grow (Mishra 1976: 70-71).

The *Khuntkatti* rights of the Munda and Ho tribals, and the community rights of the Khasis, Garos, Jaintias, Tripura, etc. are true also about the tribals elsewhere in India. Land and forests had a corporate character also among the Hill Khondas of Orissa, the Bhils of Udaipur in Rajasthan, the Cholanaickams of Malappuram, the Mullakurumbas of Wynad and the Kurichans of Kerala and others (Roy Burman 1987: 396).

Some Implications

Firstly, because the natural resources like forests, land and water were community-based and were treated like a resource that is meant to be used for a living and not destroyed as a raw material, their society was equitable. By saying this, one does not mean that there was total uniformity among them. There certainly were differences. There was a hierarchy with greater honour given to the chief and some clans but not stratification which involves inequality (Sharma 1978: 11-12).

The second implication of a community resource rather than individual property was that their culture was conservation-oriented. Given the extent of their dependence on forests, for example, they developed a culture around it, that ensured a balance between human needs and environmental imperatives. They ensured this balance through the preservation of eco-systems such as the *sarna,* special protection accorded to economically indispensable species, religious myths and traditions linking many important trees, animals and birds to the ancestors or the origin and continuity of the tribe through the totem, rituals and customs based on the wrath of God if the norms were violated and social control mechanisms ensuring equitable distribution of the resources (Fernandes, Menon and Viegas 1988: 159-170).

The third implication is the relatively high status of women among the tribals compared to those in the mainstream caste society. One does not state that there was total equality. Most tribal societies are partilineal, though many like the Jaintias, Khasis and Garos are matrilineal. But even in partilineal communities, women had a much bigger decision-making role in the family and to some extent in society than in caste societies. Their main form of agriculture, *viz.* shifting cultivation can easily be called "female farming". The village elders, all men, would decide on the area to be cultivated. But most decisions concerning cultivation were taken by women who also put in more work than men. However, unlike in settled agriculture where tedious and back breaking jobs are done by women and what is considered physically strenuous work is allotted to men, in shifting cultivation while men do what is considered strenuous work, they share the tedious jobs with women. Since shifting cultivation plots are allotted to the family and not to individuals, women become full sharers in the operations. In their family they have the final word on their children's choice of a marriage partner, though the final approval is accorded by the group of leaders, all of them men. Divorce and choice of a new partner as well as widow marriage are allowed (Fernandes and Menon 1987: 75-84). Other studies have indicated that tribal women are more aware of their ethnic identity than men. Saora women retain their father's family name after marriage and often have decision making power. Their economic contribution to the family too is greater than that of women in caste societies (Pathy 1988: 179-182). One should add, however, that the Oraons and some other tribal groups of Chotanagpur and even of Western India who are settled agriculturists and do not practise shifting cultivation do not have communal ownership and do not seem to be as egalitarian as many others (Bhagat 1983: 4-6). But women's status among them is higher than that of their counterparts in caste societies, though it is probably lower than which women involved in shifting cultivation experience.

Implications for Planned Development

The fact that the tribals belong to an informal economy also has implications for planned development. A link between the two system could have been provided by the objectives set by Nehru, Verrier Elwin and G.B. Pant; they have to contrasted with the approach of the Five-Year Plans that belong to different categories. Planned development is based on the formal economy which is today, particularly in its capitalist form as practised in India, individual-based. Unlike the community resource of the tribals, the formal economy is individual property-oriented. In other words, even the natural resources cease to be for the common good and are the property of their individual owners. Profit orientation and productivity of this resource is the main criterion in using property. A social, political and legal system that requires a written document is superimposed on an illiterate community with its tradition of oral communication and mutual trust. The natural resource becomes a permanent asset of an individual and not the life support system of the community with individuals having usufructuary rights alone.

The formal economy recognises only the individual right based on a written record. Only the articultate and the literate are able to take advantage of it. But the State supports the formal system which alone is recognised and puts its legal and administrative power behind it. As a result, the interaction between the formal and the informal economy becomes a conflict between power and powerlessness. The tribals who belong to the informal system have been rendered powerless and are at the mercy of the agents of the powerful formal system (Sharma 1978: 14-15). The result of this transition and conflict between power and powerlessness is the deterioration of the tribal communities. Women are the worst affected since the natural resource-based informal economy is essentially a female economy.

One can see then that economic development of the tribal areas involves interaction between and clash of two unequal groups. The powerless group cannot resist the powerful one. In this unequal struggle, one would have required special protection of the tribals. That is what Nehru suggested in theory. In reality, however, the policies followed during his life time and strengthened later were geared to productivity. Industrialisation involved building the infrastructure of heavy industry that would feed the consumer sector. This would have to depend on the natural resources in which the tribal areas abounded. Higher productivity in agriculture depended, among others, on irrigation for which major and medium dams were planned, most of them in the tribal areas. Forests were to be used as raw material for several industries and industrialisation itself was to be encouraged in what were called backward areas to which category most tribal regions belonged. We shall look at the impact of each of these inputs on the tribals.

Industrialisation

A few years after the Rourkela, Bokaro, Heavy Electrical Corporation, Ranchi and many other industrial plants were built in the tribal areas, one noticed a cultural revival among the Chotanagpur tribals. Bhupinder Singh (1983: 97-99) attributes this to the destablisation caused by the uprooting of thousands of families often without resettlement; land alienation and other ill effects. The reaction of the tribals to their destabilisation and the break up of the traditional ties with their community and environment was to resort to a cultural revival. As mentioned above, the relationship between the industry and the tribals is one of power and powerlessness. Overwhelmed by the powerful external factors, the tribals at first revolted against their exploitation and when this could not be done, closed themselves in through religious or cultural revival. This revival and reaction of the tribals is a consequence of the nature of industrialisation in a Third World country like India.

In contrast with urban concentrations in industrial countries such enclaves have only very tenuous links with their environment because the economic activity prevailing in them is derived from an exogenous impact. The coalfield is only one instance of these kinds there are many types of enclaved, e.g. a port serving as an entry point for international trade, a military base maintained by a foreign power etc. The relation of such an enclave with its hinterland will be determined only by the demand for local labour and food. In exceptional cases even this relation may not exist if recruited elsewhere and food is brought in from abroad. The disappearance of such an enclave would not make much of a difference to the economy or its hinerland. If the enclave does have an impact on its environment this may not necessarily be a positive one, leading only to a distortion of the economy of the hinterland without generating economic growth (Rothermund 1978: 1-2).

In other words, the area was materially developed but the beneficiaries were outsiders. For example, iron was in use in many of the coal bearing areas right from the ancient times, even at the time of Ashoka. But it was made with charcoal, as such soft and malleable. Harder iron would have been possible with the use of coal. But it would also have required change of technology. When in the colonial times coal began to be used, the changeover was based on the need of the steam engines and textile mills owned by the colonialists and not according to local requirements. Hence, the mines developed as an enclave that did not really result in any major change in the hinterland. As an example one may mention that though a great amount of electricity is produced by the thermal plants with the coal mines in the Dhanbad district of Bihar, in the district itself electricity stops a few metres after the coal fields end (Ibid: 1-3). The same trend has continued even after independence. For example, out of 498 coal mines existing in the country in 1983, as many as 463 (92.97 per cent) were in the five states of Andhra Pradesh, Orissa, Madhya Pradesh, Bihar and West Bengal, most of them in their tribal areas. Briefly, more than 80 per cent of the coal mines were in the tribal areas (Fernandes, Das and Rao 1989: 66-67).

However, though raw material is taken from the tribal areas, local inhabitants themselves get little or no benefit from it. Most well paid jobs in the industries require skills and literacy which the tribals do not possess. The areas were opened up suddenly for economic activity but education was slow in coming partly because of official neglect and partly because of lack of motivation among the tribals. In itself, education may help mobility. But given the neglect and the low standard in these areas, the children who go to school lose out in the competition for jobs. The few who manage to get jobs, find themselves in a new world with socio-psychological barriers which they cannot always cross. Hence, they are misfits both in their society and in their relationship with the outsiders. As a result, given the alienating nature of the present form of education and lack of opportunities even afterwards because of their powerlessness, very few tribals are motivated to send their children to school. Consequently, all the new economic opportunities in the region are absorbed by migrants who are in touch with the mainstream outside for whose benefit the area is exploited. Moreover, contractors, middlemen and moneylenders accompany the outsider. As a result, the tribal slowly loses his land and other resources to the individual and written document-based formal system which enters the area where classes have not been formed, land is cultivated by the family according to its needs and legal rights according to their present understanding have no meaning in a society based on trust and the word of mouth and legitimacy by the community (Sharma 1978: 27-30).

That if such a clash of interests is not allowed and the tribals are prepared in advance to meet the onslaught, there is a possibility of their getting some benefits, is seen from a comparison between the North-East and Middle India. There certainly is a great amount of exploitation in the North-East and one is not certain about the future. But many more protective measures have been taken in the North-East and it has remained insulated for a relatively long time. Besides, missionaries have introduced inputs such as education and health facilities that have put the tribals in a better position than those in Middle India. As a result, the tribals in Nagaland and elsewhere have been able to retain most of their land, and tribes like the Apa Tanis have been able to take over local trade, join civil and defence services, and use the protective measures in their own favour (Haimendorf 1980: 3-6).

Even unskilled labour is not necessarily recruited from among the local population, not even from among those displaced by the project or those whose land has been alienated. When local labour is recruited, it is because of the possibility of giving them low wages, and the local population, in their turn, is forced to accept these conditions because of lack of any alternative.

> Recruitment of the tribals as industrial workers is a necessity experienced by both the sides concerned–the employer-industrialist and the members of the tribal community. The industry requires such unskilled and semi-skilled workers who can work for low or minimum wages. The tribals, in many cases, are also ready to offer their labour at this rate of wages, because in rural area they cannot get even this much wages. The tribals, in many cases, are also ready to offer their labour at this rate of wages in spite of hard and longer duties to be performed in the firm (Kabra 1987: 34-35).

Development and Displacement

A consequence of having a large number of mines in the tribal areas is displacement. It is not merely mines that are located in these areas, but also other industries. Because of the closeness of the minerals, two out of four major steel mills opened after independence are located in the tribal area itself and the remaining two (Bhilai and Durgapur) not far from it. The same is the case also with the major dams. Apart from the development projects, the wildlife sanctuaries that are meant for environmental protection are mainly in the forests of the tribal areas.

A major result of the location of these development projects and infrastructure is displacement. Because they are based predominantly in the tribal areas, a very large number of those who are displaced are tribals. While they form about 7.5 per cent of the country's population, they are more than 50 per cent among those displaced by the major dams and mines and form a substantial number of those displaced by industries.

A few distinguishing features of involuntary displacement by development projects since independence can be given. The first is that despite the immensity of the problem, an adequate data base is lacking. Not even official figures are available concerning the extent of displacement. Only a few case studies can be found. By extrapolating these figures and making a very conservative estimate, we came to a low figure of 185 lakhs displaced by development projects during the last four decades. 21 lakhs among them have been displaced by coal and other mines, 140 lakhs by dams and canals, 10 lakhs by industries and 6 lakhs by sanctuaries and parks (Fernandes 1991: 250).

The second aspect is the predominance of the tribals, *dalits* and other landless categories among the displaced. While tribals form about 7.5 per cent of the country's population, because a very large number of the biggest displacing projects like mines and dams are in the tribal areas, the percentage of tribals among the displaced is very big. Estimates put their number at about 40 per cent among them and probably it is much more (Government of India 1985: 18-21). What is much more important is the fact that the trend is increasing. More and more wildlife sanctuaries are being planned in the tribal areas. While they may not physically displace a large number, many inhabitants of the area are what can be called Project Affected Persons (PAPs) since their life support system is taken over by the sanctuary. Of approximately 12 lakh persons to be displaced by 20 major dams that are being planned or under construction, data concerning the percentage of tribals are not available for three and one will not have any tribal. The remaining 16 dams will displace more than 6 lakh tribals. In other words, more than 50 per cent of those to be displaced are tribals (Fernandes, Das and Rao 1959: 84-85). This seems to be the trend of the future.

A very large number of the others to be displaced belong to the category of *dalits* and other landless persons. For example, of the 19, 271 families (106, 000 persons) displaced in Maharashtra between 1968-69 and 1970-71, as many as 5, 703 families (31,000 persons or 29.62 per cent) were *dalits* and 9, 264 families (51,100 persons or 48.21 per cent) were tribals (Singh 1989: 93).

What one notices in this process is the struggle for another natural resource, *viz.* land. Because the land in the tribal areas abound in water and minerals, more and more of it is being alienated to the classes that are getting all the benefits of development at the cost of being marginalised. What one notices here is

> A series of changes in the use of land which are exclusive, that is, it is put to such uses that access to it as a resource is denied to those who enjoyed it earlier, either customarily or through legal entitlements. These changes in land use are the result of economic or State development and their outcome is not to intensify the use of and access to it as a resource, but to reserve it for exclusive use so that access to it is curtailed (Mankodi 1989: 139).

The tribals also happen to be the forest dwellers, the only people who do not have property rights in India. "There are two types of citizens in India: those governed by tenancy laws and those governed by the forest laws" (Singh 1989: 92). The tribals belong to this category. While others who occupy revenue land eventually become tenants and owners, those living in the forest areas do not get any right even after several generations. They can be displaced for public purposes (whose meaning has not been defined till now) and can be uprooted without any compensation. The *dalits,* on the other hand, are by and large landless but depend on the village as a unit by rendering their service much more than the landowners do. In other words, in the agricultural economy, land

> is not only a site–it is the prime means of production. As such it supports the owner, his servants, the village artisans, the merchant who buys the produce and a host of others. When the cycle of agriculture is disturbed, all these activities are disrupted and the livelihood of all the landless endangered. The Land Acquisition Act does not provide for such people (NCHSE 1986: ii).

The third aspect that stands out is that fewer than 30 per cent of those displaced by development projects during the last four decades have been rehabilitated. Compensation, obviously, has been given only to those who owned land while most of the tribals and *dalits* at most had a homestead. Resettlement has, for all practical purposes, been non-existent (Hansda 1983: 22-23).

It is in this context that displacement has to be understood. Those who pay for what is called national development are the assetless rural poor, a very large number of them tribals and the rest *dalits.* The displacing agency is also the one put in charge of their rehabilitation. Pressure on them is to complete the project in as short a time and as low a cost as possible. They are judged according to the cost-benefit analysis of the completion of the project and not the extent of rehabilitation of the displaced persons. As a result, they have little or no motivation to rehabilitate the displaced persons. This seems to be one of the reasons why the cost-benefit analysis is biased and does not take the social costs into consideration as can be seen in the present Narmada controversy (Paranjpye 1989).

An obvious consequence of this situation is what

Areeparampil (1989: 19-26) calls the dispossession of the indigenous peoples. They are deprived of their land and their very identity in order to support the development of a small minority outside the area. They are dispossessed of their land, their culture and of their community. It is not merely the infrastructure or the dam that displaces them. Whatever industry or other development project that comes into the area, begins a much bigger process of dispossession which continues through many other modes.

Impoverishment and bondage are the obvious consequences. Such impoverishment begins the process of indebtedness, further land alienation and bondage. More exploitation follows. For example, a study of the 1.5 lakh workers on the Asian Games construction projects in 1982 revealed that 30,000 of them were bonded labourers, all of them tribals displaced by deforestation and development projects from their habitat in Orissa and Chattisgarh in Madhya Pradesh (Fernandes 1986: 269). It is estimated that more than half of the 5 million construction workers in the country are tribals, mostly bonded labourers, displaced by the same processes.

Those who do not become construction workers and are bonded, cope with their displacement without rehabilitation by further destroying their environment. In our sample of 272 families in 16 villages of 6 districts in Orissa, 77 lived by selling firewood in 1983. Thirty years earlier hardly ten of them were selling firewood and their number had gone upto 18 in the 1960s. What is more important is that about 80 per cent of those living on the sale of firewood were persons displaced by the Hirakud, Salandi and other irrigation projects and not rehabilitated (Fernandes, Menon and Viegas 1988: 95-96). In other words, as a result of displacement without rehabilitation, one notices a transition from constructive to destructive dependence on the forests. Deprived as they are of their livelihood, and since they lack any other economic or employment alternative in the area, they have no choice but to destroy forests for their survival. This process has been noticed also in other states like Maharashtra. The tribals have been alienated from the forests and they have made the transition to destructive dependence.

The situation of dispossession is in itself not surprising. The very fact that even after 40 years, the country lacks a data base on a crucial issue of this type this in itself is a sign of lack of concern of the decision-makers concerning the groups that pay the price for the development of the urban upper classes. That the situation itself has not changed becomes clear when one studies the condition of preparation for future displacement as well as past resettlement. Studies of the oustees of the Pong dam, the Tehri dam and others have indicated that till almost the moment of submergence, the persons to be displaced did not have any information concerning either the area to be submerged, the number to be displaced and the type of rehabilitation planned (Ganguly Thukral 1989: 41-42). That the situation is similar also in the projects that are being planned, including the massive Narmada Valley, is obvious from several studies. To begin with the number of persons to be displaced, according to official estimates, Sardar Sarovar which is one of the 30 major dams to be constructed, will displace 45,000 persons (Verma 1985: 38) while according to another study (NIUA d.6) it will affect 1,08,118 persons.

The same type of callousness is noticed also in multiple displacement. In some cases, the host population where they are resettled does not accept them and they have to return to their native place as it happened with the Pong dam outees. But in their own group saw them as rootless since they had lost all their assets and were not able to settle down somewhere else. Hence, they had to leave the place once again.

In many cases multiple displacement is caused by lack of official policies or proper planning. The same group is sometimes displaced by different projects. Such, for example is the case of the Rihand dam ousees. In the early 1960s, 30,000 of them were displaced by the construction of the dam. Coal was discovered in the 1960s in the Jayant area where they were resettled and they had to move out again. In the 1970s, the government decided to have thermal plants around the coal fields and they had to leave the resettlement area once again. More were displaced when other industrial units or roads came up. In other words, many of them were displaced three or even four times in a 20-25 years span (Ganguly Thukral 1989: 47-48).

The Forest Policy

Closely linked to the industrial orientation of the present pattern of development is the Forest Policy. It is one more case of the power equation that goes against the rural poor, particularly the tribals, and results in the transfer of another natural resource from the powerless to the powerful.

In order to understand this transfer of resources, one should remember that like land and water, the forests too form an integral part of the informal community and natural resource-based tribal economy. In many cases as much as 50 per cent of their food came from the forests either as a result of shifting cultivation or from what are today called Non-Wood Forest Produce (NWFP) such as fruits and flowers and in the lean season tubers and roots on which they survived.

One major source of their food is shifting cultivation practised by at least 109 tribes in 233 blocks of 62 districts spread over 16 States and affecting one million hectares. Tribals form nearly 90 per cent of its practitioners. 9.47 per cent are estimated to be from the Scheduled Castes and 2.87 are others (Govt. of India 1982: 48). It is a way of life for a large number of tribals spread all over the country from the Malayalars of Malabar in Kerala, to the Baigas of Madhya Pradesh, the Naga tribes, the Khasis and Garos of Meghalaya, the Mizos of Mizoram, the Khonds, Saoras, the Pauribhuiyan and others of Orissa, and others elsewhere (Pati, Patnaik and Mohapatra 1984: 384).

An important feature of this form of agriculture is that it was practised on the slopes. Studies have shown that as long as it kept an 18 to 20-year cycle, it was environmentally the safest method for these areas, better than terrace or other form of settled cultivation. In reality, till the early 1950s, this was the length of the *jhum* cycle (Gangwar and Ramakrishnan 1987: 346-347). Only when bamboo forests were cut as in Tripura, a Five or Six-year cycle was followed since it was cultivated for only one year and bamboo is ready for cutting in five years (Mishra 1976: 75).

As mentioned above, it was essentially a community resource that was shared by individual families according to their need. The way of selecting the plot differed from place to place. In some cases the family chose a plot from the area selected by the leaders and in others the village community allotted the plot to each family. But what is common to all is that after use it reverted to the community. Another aspect that is common to all the tribals is that they had rituals of reparation before cultivation began to ask the pardon of *Banadevata* for destroying forests for human use.

The third aspect of shifting cultivation was that much more than the rest of the forest economy, it was a female economy. Women had much greater control over shifting cultivation than they can ever hope to have in settled agriculture. While in the latter tedious jobs are given to women, in the former they are shared by men. Besides, women have much greater control over the decision-making process in these operations than in the latter. It is true that even in shifting cultivation priority is given to one or the other sex in a given type of work. But there is a much greater family approach than in the latter (Fernandes and Menon 1987: 77-84).

Another major source of their food is NWFP. Together with *jhum* it contributed more than 50 per cent and in many cases nearly 80 per cent of the food of the forest dwellers. Hoffmann (1950: 179-187) mentions as many as 148 types of trees, shrubs, leaves, wild plants and potherbs used by the Mundas for food and many more for medicine, fodder, etc. 54 different varieties of herbs, plants and trees were identified as used for food by the Ho tribals of Singhbhum of Chotanagpur (Deeney and Fernandes). In Orissa we identified 83 species in 8 blocks in which the study was conducted (Fernandes, Menon and Viegas 1988: 151-153).

What one notices here is the close link between the forests and the tribals. They depended on the forests for nearly 80 per cent of their food, most of their small timber needs and other requirements like fuel, fodder and medicinal herbs. Given the extent of their dependence, they had developed a whole culture geared to treating them as a renewable resource. Their techniques of cutting trees and bamboos were geared to coppicing. Their traditions and social control systems ensured that the resource was treated as renewable (Menon 1987: 376-377).

This symbiotic relationship between the forests and the tribals has all but disappeared today and tribals now have made the transition from constructive to destructive dependence on the forest. In other words, while in the past they treated the forest as a renewable resource in whose use they kept a balance between human and environmental needs, today they cut trees for sale as firewood and as wage earners under contractors. In other words, they survive on the forest not by preserving it for posterity but by destroying it. The forest policy geared to industry has to be considered responsible for this transition. It is a purely growth-oriented strategy that speaks only of production without equitable distribution and sustainability. This lop-sided strategy that focuses only on production and not on enhancing their flow to the entire population, ends up by organising the flow of resources from the periphery to the few islands of prosperity created by this model of development (Gadgil n.d.: 4-5).

This model of development has turned the number of industries into the main criterion of progress. Industrial production was expanded without counting the environmental and human costs. Extra efforts were made in States that were considered backward, particularly if they were mineral and forest rich. Such, for example, is the case of states like Bihar, Orissa and Madhya Pradesh where many forests and mineral-based industries came up. Chattisgarh in Madhya Pradesh, for example, only had a few saw mills and no other industry worth the name at independence. In 1980 it had 1,361 small and medium industries, 541 of them forest-based. This does not include major industries like Bhilai and big mines like Dalli-Rajhara. Besides, it has several major dams and 12 new major dams are being planned in the seven districts with a catchment area of 10,000 sq. kms. (Fernandes, Viegas, Menon and Chandy 1988: 147-151). All these enterprises cause deforestation. In fact, the destruction of the forests begins even before an enterprise goes into production, with the building of the infrastructure in the form of roads, irrigation and hydro-electrical dams, townships, railway lines, etc. It is continued once the industry begins production since many of them use bamboo, timber, etc. as raw material. What the important is that this material is highly subsidised.

The widely accepted notion that industry must be encouraged at all costs was translated in practice into prescription that industry must be subsidised in every possible fashion. But this subsidy performance has to be at somebody's cost (Gadgil 1989: 15).

An example of this subsidy would be bamboo. In Orissa, in 1983, industry paid around Rs. 400 per National Tonne (NT, i.e. 2,400 running metres of industrial bamboo) and in Chattisgarh around Rs. 430 (Fernandes, Viegas, Menon and Chandy 1985: 106). In Karnataka, in the early 1960s, the West Coast Paper Mills of Dandeli in Uttar Kannada district was awarded bamboo at Rs. 1.50 per tonne when the commercial price was around 1,500 (Gadgil 1989: 35). In 1983, the price of bamboo given to the people in Orissa was around Rs. 1,800 and in Madhya Pradesh around 1,500 per NT. Similar statements can be made also concerning subsidies given to timber and other raw material used by industry which ensured the destruction of forests. The first aspect of this profit orientation is what is called sequential exhaustion of resources. The industrialist begins by a spatial sequence of accessibility. He clearfells the forests that are the closest to the village since they are accessible at least by a bullock cart. Once they are exhausted, they go to reserve forests further away and finally to protected forests from which the people get the rest of their small needs like bamboos, fodder and medicinal herbs. Then comes the sequence of distance. Once the forests in a given area are exhausted, they go to the next district or even the next State and finally to far away areas. For example, the forest-based industries of West Bengal that have depleted the resources in their State now extract more and more of them from Bihar, Orissa and the North-East. The industries of Andhra Pradesh depend to a great extent on raw material from Orissa and the Bastar district of Madhya Pradesh (Fernandes, Menon and

Viegas 1988: 189-195). The two paper mills of Karnataka began by removing bamboo from the most accessible block, then built a road to the next block and continued the process. After thus exhausting all the resources in the State, the West Coast Paper Mill went to the neighbouring State like Andhra Pradesh and finally to the distant areas of Garwhals in Uttar Pradesh and to Assam, Nagaland and Arunachal Pradesh in the North-East (Gadgil 1989: 16-17).

Then comes the sequence of the type of material used. Once bamboo is exhausted, the paper mills acquired rights to other soft wood and later to hard wood. The plywood factories began by exhausting desirable species like mango and later the more accessible deciduous forests and some of the evergreen forests and finally they have gone on to exploit other species (Fernandes fund). The third aspect of profit orientation is the type of techniques used. Traditionally, the tribals and other forest dwellers used techniques geared to coppicing. For example, normally they cut a few bamboos from each clump, at a certain angle and a few centimetres above the ground to ensure that the thorny cover of short branches formed at the base of each clump was not disturbed and thus prevented grazing in order to ensure the regeneration of bamboos. Usually, they cut only one or two culms from each clump (Fernandes, Menon and Viegas 1988: 188-189). The paper mills, on the contrary, follow what are considered economically viable methods prescribed by "scientific forestry". They clearfell the area by removing a much larger number of culms from each clump and do not leave the thorny cover for protection since the techniques would be too expensive for them. The removal of the thorny cover from the base exposes the tender shoots to grazing by cattle, pigs, monkeys, etc. Regeneration is thus prevented and the overexploitation of existing resources and prevention of regeneration ensures the process of depletion. At the same time, given the subsidies, the industrialist lacks the motivation required for reforestation since it is more expensive than the material he gets. As a result, deforestation is ensured.

As far as the tribal is concerned, this begins another vicious circle in his community. The village is deprived of its food from the forest that was the closest and has been clearfelled by the industrialist. The impoverishment that results, pushes the people into the hands of the moneylender who accompanies the forest contractor and industrialist. Land alienation and often bondage are the consequences. Given their impoverishment and absence of any economic or employment alternatives in the region, the tribals who had till then preserved forests for posterity are forced to overexploit it. First of all, the shifting cultivation plot is overexploited and the 18-year fallow period cannot be observed since they have been deprived of their other MFP and cultivable land. In Orissa *jhum* has been reduced to a 6 year cycle and in the North-East to about 12-years and it seems to be as low as 3 years in Western India. Deforestation and soil erosion are the consequences. At the same time, the tribal is forced to cut trees as wage labourer under contractors or for sale as firewood. With the transfer of these resources to the corporate sector, begins competition within the tribal community for the few resources that are still available to them. Consequently, their community breaks up and individualism sets in. This further deprives them of the mutual support they enjoyed in moments of shortages and that helped them to survive in times of droughts, floods and famines. The tubers, roots and other "famine food" disappears with the forest and the community that sustained every family gets weakened. Thus, the tribals are deprived both of the material and the human base that supported them in the times of shortages. Hence, with every shortage and drought their situation deteriorates much more than that of the others (Fernandes 1987: 432-435).

Consequences on Women

While all the tribals suffer, women are the worst victims of deforestation and of displacement. To begin with food, it was traditionally obtained from shifting cultivation which was controlled primarily by them. In the traditional division of work, it is the woman's role to make provision for basic necessities like food, fuel and water. Among the tribals, food was obtained mainly from the forests which were close-by. Hence, the economic demands of shifting cultivation and collecting firewood did not clash with the other household duties of the woman. With deforestation the distance of forests from the village has increased. This has destabilised the close social and economic relationship between the tribal women and the forests. In Orissa, for example, the distance of the forest has increased from an average of 1.7 kms 40 years ago to 7 kms. today and in Chattisgarh from 1.6 kms. to 3.1 kms. Everyday the woman has to walk this additional distance to collect MFP. Because of this extra distance, her children as well as older women are not able to accompany her. Traditionally, all worked together to collect MFP like *Mahua* flowers and other fruits that were close to the village. Hence, the housewife has to walk the additional distance but has less help. As a result, she works more to collect less food. While the tribes like the Saoras of Orissa have a common plate from which every member eats together (as such, discrimination between boys and girls is missing), in many other cases the housewife distributes food to the family. Studies have indicated that when there is shortage of food, the housewife feeds first her husband then the boys. After that follow girl children and finally herself.

When there is shortage she may even starve herself (Menon 1987: 378-380).

Briefly, the nutritional status of all the tribals has deteriorated but that of their women more than that of their men. Together with that, deforestation has resulted in the disappearance of medicinal herbs on which they survived for centuries. Given the distance of the primary health centres and because of the fact that they are open only during the day when the women have to be working, they do not have access to allopathic medicine. Moreover, the non-availability of medicinal plants has forced most *bhagats* into sorcery. Their failure to heal has led to the ritualistic killing of women as *bhutali* (witches). The threat of being identified as a *bhutali* is the Damocles sword that hangs over the head of every woman. The *bhutali* is man's ultimate weapon in the repression of women.

Moreover, the intensity of droughts is much greater in the forest areas, more particularly the tribal areas than in the others. First of all, there are indications that there is a close link between deforestation and droughts as indicated by studies in the Andaman and Nicobar Islands, Dibrugarh in the North-East, Chattisgarh in Madhya Pradesh and in the Southern states of Karnataka, Kerala and Southern Tamil Nadu (Meher-Homji 1988: 117-124). All these affect women much more than men since they are the ones who have to ensure the regular supply of water, fodder and fuel and it is these items that disappear the fastest in a drought year. With the break up of the community, she has lost the support she received from others in moments of scarcity and suffers the most (Fernandes 1987: 424).

In the whole process one notices the definite transfer of the forest resources to the corporate sector and the consequent impoverishment and deterioration of the tribal communities.

> These (industrial) communities are entirely structured and have well defined functional specialisation. The forests in this system represent as specialised a sector as a big steel plant. Steel plant produces finished steel while forests produce certain raw material which are necessary for producing other finished goods for satisfying certain specialised needs. The forests are part of a long 'assembly-line'. It would be immaterial to the industrial man whether the finished goods he uses are based on forest produce or on some other substitute (Sharma 1973: 60-61).

Agriculture and Land Alienation

It is in the context of the impoverishment of the tribal community that one has to search for alternatives. And one realises that the tribal areas have been neglected as far as economic and employment alternatives are concerned. This is what forces them to depend on the forests in a destructive manner as against their traditional constructive dependence. As mentioned above, the tribal areas are used as sources of forest raw material and of water for the major dams. However, studies indicate that as far as agricultural development is concerned, they are among the neglected areas. For example, Chotanagpur where the tribals are different from those in the rest of India, i.e., are settled agriculturists and do not practise shifting cultivation. They own on an average five acres or more land. Except for the Ho tribals, they do not have communal ownership today. Studies have indicated that they are open to new agricultural practices.

However, in reality they do not have access to these inputs. For example, the Chotanagpur plateau which has many major dams, has only 9.2 per cent of its cultivated land irrigated as against 25.4 in North Bihar and 67.5 per cent in the South Bihar plains. Availability of agricultural credit is 23.4 per cent in Chotanagpur as against 35.2 and 65.8 respectively in North and South Bihar plains. Similarly, the composite demonstration plots are 11.46 per cent in Chotanagpur as against 19.4 and 18.55 per cent respectively in North and South Bihar plains (Bhagat 1983: 11).

Apart from lack of infrastructural facilities, the high cost of the new technology makes it inappropriate for the poor tribal farmer. Hence, many tribals dilute the inputs such as fertilisers since they cannot afford the full quantity suggested. The diluted amount cannot deliver the results.

Moreover, most lands in the tribal *talukas* of Gujarat, for example, belong to what are called D & E categories, i.e. infertile. Thus, the poor quality of land, lack of infrastructural facilities and increasing drought ensure that the tribal does not get enough to eat from his land (Iyengar 1983: 27-32.)

Moreover, it is normally assumed that commercial crops raise the standard of living of a farmer. But this does not necessarily happen in the case of small and marginal farmers to which category most tribals belong. One can see it from the tribals in the Adilabad district of Andhra Pradesh. Most Gond tribals in this district have taken to cotton cultivation and the area under cotton has increased from 5,702 acres in 1921 to 38,724 acres in 1971 and to 60,000 acres in 1981, while paddy is cultivated in around 11,000 acres of tribal land. Nearly half the tribal cultivated land comes under cotton. On the assumption that they will be able to make enough money by cultivating cotton, they do not produce enough cereals and pulses for their own consumption. This forces them to depend on the merchant for half of their food as well as to market their cotton. That is where exploitation begins. Most tribals take *jowar* on credit from the merchants at lean season prices and repay in peak season prices. Thus, the tribal who grows cotton on about 2 acres gets about Rs 1,800 for four quintals he grows there. But around Rs. 900 have to be repaid for *jowar.* As the need for cash increases, the tribal grows more cotton with the hope of getting more cash and the area under food crops comes down. Moreover, cotton requires external labour inputs while food crops can be grown by the family. Briefly, as in other cases, also in commercial crops, the tribal does not have access to the forward and backward linkages and has to depend on the same moneylender. Consequently, even what could have freed him from the moneylender becomes one more source of his impoverishment (Reddy 1987: 38-47).

One notices once again the consequence of the transition from the informal to the formal economy without adequate preparation. Also land alienation has to be situated in the same context. Apart from the fact that the private ownership of land which is usually in the hands of men has lowered the status of women, the transition from the informal to the formal economy has resulted in a great amount of land alienation. The first factor we have mentioned above is impoverishment, indebtedness, land alienation and bondage. Besides, the very fact that there is a transition from an oral promise-based ownership pattern with legitimation coming from the community to a written document system ensures that the illiterate tribal is deprived of land. The process began with the introduction of *muttahdars* or *jagirdars* and finally *zamindars.* The process is getting intensified today because of indebtedness as well as the close link between the administrator and the vested interests. For example, at the time of the land settlement in 1968-69 in Orissa, the tribals were unware of the manipulative tactics employed by the *sundis* (liquor merchants) to whom they were indebted. Large tracts of their land was transferred to the non-tribals while the tribals, the original owners and cultivators, were rendered landless because of the collusion between the moneylenders and the revenue officers (Viegas 1987: 338-339). Similar cases are found in all the tribal areas as many other studies have indicated.

Lack of Exposure to Modern Inputs

It is in this context that one has to study the lack of exposure of the tribals to the tools of modernisation such as education and health. They are exposed to the exploitative elements of the formal system without any preparation. As a result they end up only as suppliers of low priced raw materials and cheap manual labour to the benefit of another class that gets all the benefits. The few who have access to formal education do not get enough of its benefits. On the other hand , a comparison between the North-Eastern States and middle India shows that the former remained isolated for a relatively long time and at the same time they were provided opportunities of education and health services. As a result, many more tribals in the North-East have got the benefits of development than those in middle India (Pathy 1988: 175-177). Education, together with the new frame for personal and social behaviour, provided by the missionary as well as their relative isolation seem to have combined to help the tribals in the North-East to cope with the transition from the informal to the formal economy. In most other cases education which improves upper caste values on them, also creats a crisis in them.

> This bouncing back of the educated is sociologically a serious problem. As formal education fails to provide a new frame of references, he (the tribal) becomes aware of the low economic condition of his group, particularly the scanty clothing and different social mores. This creates a psychological schism and he is torn between the two worlds. If a

youthful group loses respect for its own elders and is shy of its own social extraction, it cannot play the role of a catalytic agent for the healthy socio-economic change of a community.

It may be useful to contrast this state of rootlessness and non-belonging with social change initiated as a result of educational effort by missionaries. They provide him with an alternative–a new frame for his personal and social behaviour; not only that, they also provide the young with a new ideal, *viz.*, recasting of his social group in the image of the new religious ethic. This perhaps creates greater schism between him and the original group but he gets the care and the warmth of a new group and an ideal to work for, if he so wishes (Sharma 1978: 30).

Studies have indicated that except for the North-East and some areas like Ranchi district in Chotanagpur, in the rest of India literacy among the tribals is very low. This has been indicated by studies in Karnataka (Ramkumar 1983: 183-193), Maharashtra and other States, and is worse when it concerns women, particularly in the rural areas. As against more than 80 per cent literacy among urban upper class males, only 8.04 per cent of the rural Scheduled Tribe women and 24.52 per cent men were literate in 1981 (Fernandes 1985: 19).

Briefly, what one notices is not merely impoverishment in the past but the certainty of further deterioration in the future because of the lack of exposure to the reproductive inputs like education of the formal system. The resources on which they depended, particularly forests and land, are being alienated from them. At the same time, their culture is being devalued and they are deprived of their self-respect. Most anthropological and nationalist literature looks at the culture of the minorities from the majority, *viz.* ethnocentric point of view. That every culture has its own autonomy is forgotten and as a result the tribals who belong to a subordinate culture are not allowed to grow autonomously. They are deprived of the resources they have, alienated from their culture and are asked to join the mainstream without providing them with the exposure required to join it as equals. Its result is that they join the mainstream as subordinate bonded and wage labourers.

It is not surprising then that most recent tribal movements have been around their culture and land and for forests. The *Jharkhand* movement, for example, stresses the ethnic identity of the tribals when the reactionary nationalist groups try to Hinduise them (Pathy 1988: 161-165).

> Given tribal alienation from land and forests and from their culture, it is not surprising that behind almost all the tribal agrarian armed struggles the causes are interference of the British in their traditional cultures, exploitation of the tribals by the non-tribal traders and moneylenders, creation of Forest Policy, imposing restrictions on the exploitation of forest resources and finally the loss of tribal agricultural land to the non-tribals, perhaps the most crucial factor which adversely affected the economic life of the tribal communities. Further, the creation of *Zamindari* and *Jagirdari* systems made the tribal land owners tenant cultivators. Alienation of the tribals from their basic productive resource, i.e. the agricultural land and the oppressing conditions created by the feudal system and its inhuman treatment of the tribals could not but lead to protests through armed struggles....The scene in every tribal area of the country during the British period was almost the same—interference with the internal and traditional affairs, oppression and inhuman treatment, alienation from their basic pro-

ductive resources like land and forest was the order of the day. In all the cases of tribal insurgency or armed struggles during the period, the tribals chose rebellion or revolt as a last resort having failed to attract attention of the authorities through repeated appeals and even representations (Reddy: 1987: 6-7).

Colonial Economy

We do not need to go into the solutions attempted by the government. They have taken forms such as the Integrated Tribal Development Programme which have not made much impact and have it times resulted in the further impoverishment of the tribals and Scheduled Castes (Pais and Singh 1987: 38-42). What is important to remember is that the economy in the tribal areas has a colonial character which is continued and intensified by the post-independence government. This intensification can be seen in the Forest Policy. In 1854 when the first document on the forests was drafted, the tribals were given some rights in their traditional forests. In 1894 the Forest Policy turned them into "rights and privileges". The post-independence government would have been expected to undo the harm and give more rights to the tribals. In reality, however, the policy promulgated on 12th May, 1952 changed this to "rights and concessions".

Already in 1961, the Commissioner for Scheduled Castes and Tribes complained in his report that more and more rights were being taken away and only concessions were thought of. Though this was not accepted by the government, the National Commission on Agriculture officially suggested in 1976 the taking away of all rights and retention of only a few concessions according to the will of the State.

What is important to note is not merely that words have changed but the reality of colonisation has been intensified. One would notice this if one were to compare the analysis of the official Indian delegation at the UNCTAD VII with the reality in the tribal areas. At the UNCTAD: VII Conference, the Indian delegation complained about :

a. the low price of raw materials on which the economy of most Third World countries depends, and the refusal of the rich countries to fix their floor price for them;
b. protectionism and the bias against any processed product coming from the Third World by taxing them and allowing in only raw material;
c. refusing to deal with any cartel such as OPEC and dividing the Third World countries against one another;
d. what is due to the Third World in the form of higher prices is given to them by the rich countries as foreign aid which is in fact a loan that enriches the donor country at the cost of the receiver. What the Third World needs is better trade conditions and not aid.

When one studies the situation in the tribal areas, one notices that it is identical to the relationship between the Third World and the rich countries. First of all, like rich countries, that do not give a good price for its raw material, the tribals to whom the forest is a source of survival, are deprived of the little income they could get by selling their produce at a decent price by the commercial-industrial interests that try to make as much profit out of the misery of these groups as possible. The Tribal Development Cooperative Corporations whose declared objective is to improve the status of the tribals by functioning as conduits for the commercialisation of their products like MFP, are in fact sources of exploitation of the tribals and of revenue to the State. They are dominated by the same middlemen and other commercial interests (Fernandes,

Menon and Viegas 1988; 139-142). Secondly, like the rich countries that use the Third World only as a supplier of the raw material without giving it the opportunity of processing the raw material, also the upper classes in India treat the tribal areas only as suppliers of raw material for the enrichment of other classes. For example, *tendu* leaf is sold to the *bidi* makers outside the area and the tribal is used only as a cheap wage labourer. The TDCC in 1983 bought *sal* seeds from the tribals at less than Rs. 100 per quintal, sold them to industry at around Rs. 1,500 per quintal. No processing was undertaken in the tribal areas themselves. The same can be said about bamboos, timber and other products.

Thirdly, India complained about the rich countries dividing the Third World by not accepting any cartel like OPEC. The same happens in the tribal areas. Bamboos, *mahua* and other MFP are controlled by the non-tribal middlemen when in fact the State should have encouraged tribal cooperatives. At present the tribals in the Gadchiroli district of Maharashtra are demanding that they be allowed on a cooperative basis to use their traditional techniques of cutting and growing bamboo and supply it to the paper mill that is coming up. But this is not accepted by the State since the middlemen and contractors are in control. The State deals only with individual tribals and not with their community, thus weakening them further.

Finally, India complains that the rich countries deprive the Third World of their resources by not giving them good trading terms and compensate for this injustice by giving aid. The same happens in the tribal areas. Nothing is done to improve the terms of trade in the commercialisation of MFP, in the wage labour and the whole economic system that renders them further powerless. Instead, after rendering the tribals powerless and impoverishing them, official poverty alleviation policies like ITDP and IRDP are introduced. Because of the tribals' lack of exposure, also the benefits of these schemes meant for them go to the outsiders.

Conclusion

It is at this level that the policies have to change to suit tribal needs.

> A world in which poverty and inequality are endemic will always be prone to ecological and other crises. Sustainable development requires meeting the basic needs of all and extending to all the opportunity to satisfy their aspirations for a better life.
>
> Living standards that go beyond the basic minimum are sustainable only if consumption standards everywhere have regard for long-term sustainability. Yet many of us live beyond the world's ecological means, for instance in our patterns of energy use (WCED 1987: 43-44).

One has to speak about the sustainability of the forests. Today their use is not within their sustainable limits, be it for grazing or for raw material (Gadgil 1983: 113-334). We have seen the same happening to shifting cultivation, firewood and the environment in general. This results in shortages and competition. In the context of these shortages begins the competition. for scarce resources between the powerful and powerless classes. Obviously, the powerful corporate sector wins against the powerless tribals.

This process has to be reversed. The tribal has to be trained to face the formal sector. At the same time, the formal economy has to be adapted to the needs of their community. At this stage space does not allow us to make all the suggestions in this direction. Suffice it to say, that the meeting point of the two economics has to be not the individual but the community of the tribals. Their cooperatives have to be encouraged and they have to be built not on the system of the formal economy but on the tribal community. Their techniques have to be studied and updated and education geared to meet their needs. It is only by beginning with what the tribal has and updating it that their community can be helped to resist the negative impact of modernisation. Ultimately, the present type of modernisation that further impoverishes the already weak has to be questioned.

REFERENCE

1. Ahluwalia, M.S. "Rural Poverty in India 1956-57 to 1973-74 in *India; Occassional Papers.* Washington: The World Bank, 1979.
2. Areeparempil, Mathew. "Industries, Mines and Dispossession of Indigenous Peoples: The Case of Chotanagpur," in Walter Fernandes and Enakshi Ganguly Thukral (eds.), *Development Displacement and Rehabilitation: Issues for A National Debate.* New Delhi: Indian Social Institute, 1989, pp. 19-26.
3. Bandyopadhyay, D. "Direct Intervention Programmes for Poverty Alleviation: An Appraisal," *Economic and Political Weekly* 23 n. 26, June 25, 1988, pp. A77-A88.
4. Bardhan, P.K. "The Pattern of Income Distribution in India: A Review," in T.N. Srinivasan and P.K. Bardhan (eds.). *Poverty and Income Distribution in India* Calcutta: Statistical Publishing Society, 1974, pp. 103-138.
5. Bhagat, L.N. "New Technology and Agricultural Development in Tribal Areas: A Study of the Chotanagpur Region," in S.N. Mishra and Bhupinder Singh (eds.). *Tribal Area Development* New Delhi: Society for the Study of Regional development, 1983, pp. 3-20.
6. Deeney, John and Walter Fernandes. "Tribes and Their Dependence on Forests," in Walter Fernandes (ed.) *National Development and Tribal Deprivation* New Delhi: Indian Social Institute, forthcoming.
7. Elwin, Verrier. *A Philosophy For NEFA* (London Oxford University Press, 1955.
8. Fernandes, Walter. "Development and People's Participation: An Introduction," in Walter Fernandes (ed.) *Development with People: Experiments With Participation And Non-Formal Education* New Delhi: Indian Social Institute, 1985, pp. 1-36.
9. ---------. "Construction Workers, Powerlessness And Bondage: The

Case of the Asian Games," *Social Action* 36 n. 3, July-September, 1986, pp. 264-291.

10. ----------. "Drought In India: Its Causes and Victims," *Social Action* 37 n. 4, Oct-December, 1987, pp. 421-443.

11. -----------. "Forest Policy: A Solution To Tribal Deprivation?" in Walter Fernandes (ed.) *National Development and Tribal Deprivation* New Delhi: Indian Social Institute, forthcoming.

12. Fernandes, Walter, Philip Viegas, Geeta Menon and K.T. Chandy. *Forests, Evnironment and Forest Dweller Economy in Chattisgarh* New Delhi: Indian Social Institute, 1985. mimeo.

13. Fernandes, Walter and Geeta Menon. *Tribal Women and Forest Economy: Deforestation, Exploitation and Status Change* New Delhi: Indian Social Institute, 1987.

14. Fernandes, Walter, Geeta Menon and Philip Viegas. *Forest, Environment And Tribal Economy: Deforestation, Impoverishment and Marginalisation in Orissa* New Delhi: Indian Social Institute, 1988.

15. Fernandes, Walter, J.C. Das and Sam Rao. "Displacement and Rehabilitation: An Estimate of Extent and Prospects," in Walter Fernandes and Enakshi Ganguly Thukral (eds.) *Development, Displacement and Rehabilitation: Issues From A National Debate* New Delhi: Indian Social Institute, 1989, pp. 62-90.

16. 1991 "Power and Powerlessness: Denlopment Projects and Displacement of Tribal". *Social Action* 41 no. 3. July-Sept pp. 243-270.

17. 1992 "Forest Policy: A Solution to Tribal Deprivation?" In Walter Fernandes (ed.) *National Development and Tribal Deprivation.*

18. Gadgil Madhav. "Forestry with a Social Purpose," in Walter Fernandes and Sharad Kulkarni (eds.) *Towards A New Forest Policy: People's Rights and Environment Needs* New Delhi: Indian Social Institute, 1983, pp. 111-133.

19. ---------. *Deforestation: Problems and Prospects* New Delhi: Society For Promotion of Wastelands Development, 1989.

20. ---------. *Environment and Development: Some Significant Issues Bangalore: Centre for Ecological Science, n.d. (Unpublished paper).*

21. Ganguly Thukral, Enakshi. "Dams: For Whose Development?" in Walter Fernandes and Enakshi Ganguly Thukral (eds.) *Development, Displacement and Rehabilitation* New Delhi: Indian Social Institute; 1989, pp. 39-61.

22. Gangwar, A.K. and P.S. Ramakrishnan. "Agriculture and Animal Husbandry among the Sulungs and Nishis of Arunachal Pradesh," *Social Action* 37 n. 4, Oct.-December, 1987, pp. 345-372.

23. Govt. of India. *Report of the Committee on Forests and Tribals in India* New Delhi: Ministry of Home Affairs, Tribal Development Division, Government of India, 1982.

24. --------. *Report of the Committee on Rehabilitation of Displaced Tribals*

Uue to Development Projects New Delhi: Ministry of Home Affairs, 1985.

25. Haimendorf, Christoph Von Furer. "Recent Developments in the Positon of Indian Tribal Populations," in S.G. Deogannkar *Problems of Development in Tribal Areas* Delhi: Leeladovi, 1980, pp. 1-15.
26. Hansda, Subotu. "Agricultural Development in Tribal Areas," in S.N. Mishra and Bhupinder Singh (eds.) *Tribal Area Development* New Delhi: Society for the Study of Regional Disparities, 1983, pp. 22-23.
27. Hoffmann, J. *Encyclopaedia Mundarica* Patma: Superintendent, Government Printing Press, 1950.
28. Iyengar, Sudarshan. "Issues in Agrucultural Development—A Study of Panchmahals District," in S.N. Mishra and Bhupinder Singh (eds.) *Tribal Area Development* New Delhi: Society for the Study of Regional Disparities, 1983, pp. 27-65.
29. Kabra, Govind Das. *Tribal Worker in an Industrial Setting* Allahabad: Vohra Publishers and Distributors, 1987.
30. Krishan, Raj. "The Centre And the Periphery: Inter-State Disparities In Economic Development," *Social Action* 31 n. 1, Jan-March, 1981, pp. 1-34.
31. Mankodi, Kashyap. "Disaplacement and Relocation: Problems and Prospects," in Walter Fernandes and Enakshi Ganguly Thukral (eds.) *Development, Displacement and Rehabilitation* New Delhi: Indian Social Institute, 1989, pp. 135-163.
32. Meher-Homji, V.M. "Deforestation, Ecological Destabilisation and Droughts," *Social Action* 38 n. 2, April-June, 1988, pp. 115-128.
33. Menon, Geeta. "Tribal Women" Victims of the Development Process," *Social Action* 37 n. 4, Oct.-December, 1987, pp. 373-390.
34. Mishra, Bani Prasanna. *Socio-economic adjustments of Tribals* New Delhi: People's Publishing House, 1976.
35. Nair, N.K. Sukumar. *Tribal Economy In Transition: A Study of Meghalaya* New Delhi: Inter-India Publications, 1987, pp. 27.
36. NCHSE. *Rehabilitation of Displaced Persons due to Construction of Major Dams Vol. I* New Delhi: National Center for Human Settlements and Environment, 1986.
37. NIUA. *Sardar Sarovar Human Settlement: a Strategy* New Delhi: National Institute of Urban Affairs, n.d.
38. Pars, H and C.S.K. Singh. "Rural Development Policies and Inequalities," *Social Action* 37 n. 1, Jan-March, 1987, pp. 28-44.
39. Paranjpye, Vijay, *The Narmada Valley Projects: A Holistic Evaluation of Sardar Sarovar and Indira (Narmada) Sagar Dams* New Delhi: The Indian National Trust For Art and Cultural Heritage, 1989.

40. Pathy. Jaganath. *Ethnic Minorities in the Process of Development* Jaipur: Rawat Publications, 1988.

41. Pati, S.N., B.K. Patnaik and P.C. Mohapatra. "Shifting Cultuvation-A Case Study of Koraput District," *Khadi Gramodyog* June 1984, pp. 384-390.

42. Planning Commission. *The First Five Year Plan* New Delhi: Planning Commission, 1951.

43. ---------. *The Second Five Year Plan: The Framework* New Delhi: The Publications Division, Govt. of India, 1955.

44. ---------. *The Secon Five Year Plan* New Delhi: Planning Commission, 1956.

45. Planning Commission. *Towards A Self-Reliant Economy: India's Third Five year Plan, 1901-06* New Delhi: Publications Devision, Govt. of India, 1961.

46. -----------. *Aspects of the Fourth Plan: Policy and Implementation* New Delhi: Directorate of Advertising and Audio-Visual Publicity, Govt. of India. 1969.

47. ----------. *Draft Fifth Five Year Plan 1974-79* New Delhi: Govt. of India, 1973.

48. ---------. *Draft Sizth Five-Year Plan* New Delhi: Planning Commission, 1980.

49. ---------. *Seventh Five Year Plan 1985-90 Vol. II* New Delhi: Govt. of India, 1985.

50. Prabhu, Pradeep and V. Suresh. "Transience and Transition In Social Institutions: The Warli Experience," in Walter Fernandes (ed.) *National Development and Tribal Deprivation* New Delhi: Indian Social Institute, forthcoming.

51. Ramkumar, Usha. "Progress of Compulsory Education Among Tribals in Karnataka," in S.N. Mishra and Bhupinder Singh (eds.) *Tribal Area Development* New Delhi: Society for the Study of Regional Disparities, 1983, pp. 183-193.

52. Reddy, Prakash G. *Politics of Tribal Exploitation: A Study of Tribal Unrest in Orissa* New Delhi: Mittal Publications, 1987.

53. Rothermund, Dietmar. "The Coalfield: An Enclave in a Backward Region," in D. Rothermund and D.C. Waddwa. *Zamindars, Mines and Peasants: Studies in the History of an Indian Coalfield and Its Rural Hinterland* New Delhi: Manohar, 1978, pp. 1-19.

54. Roy Burman, B.K. "Historical Process in Respect of Communal Land System and Poverty Alleviation among Tribals," *Social Action* 37 (n. 4, Oct.-December, 1987, pp. 391-420.

55. Sharma, B.D. *Tribal Development: The Concept and the Frame* New Delhi: Prachi Prakashan, 1978.

56. Singh. Bhupinder. "Industrialisation in Tribal Areas," in S.N. Mishra

and Bhupinder Singh. *Tribal Area Development* New Delhi: Society for the Study of Regional Disparities, 1983, pp. 97-109.

57. Singh. Chhatrapati. "Rehabilitation and the Right to Poverty," in Walter Fernandes and Enakshi Ganguly Thukral (eds). *Development, Displacement and Rehabilitation* New Delhi: Indian Social Institute, 1989, pp. 92-93.
58. Verma, S.C. *Human Resettlement in the Narmada Basin* Bhopal: Narmada Valley Development Authority, Govt. of Madhya Pradesh, 1985.
59. Viegas, Philip. "Land Control and Tribal Struggle For Survival," *Social Action* 37 n. 4, Oct.-December, 1987, pp. 325-344.
60. WCED. *Our Common Future: The World Commission on Environment and Development* New Delhi: Oxford University Press, 1987.

9

Internal Self-Determination and Tribal Sustainable Self-Development

Jagannath Pathy

The Context

The history of the tribes, especially from the time of colonial annexation to the present day, has been, in essence, the gruesome story of their enslavement, exploitation, expropriation and extermination. Despite tall claims, the post-colonial context failed to generate a qualitatively humane scenario. Consequently, the relationship of domination and subjugation persists; in fact many additional spheres have emerged and there are greater complexities than prevailed during colonial times. The notions of development, nation building and ironically human (individual) rights have been the chief contributing factors for the progressive destruction of the survival and reproduction of tribal peoples.

The superimposition of the capitalist conception of land as an object of permanent agriculture under the proprietorship of individual has consistently encroached the customary corporate rights of the tribal peoples over land and land-based endowments. Private property on land as the only recognizable right and *sine qua non* of social development has perilled the survival of the tribal peoples. In addition the outrageous technological deterministic modernization syndrome has played havoc with the tribal societies, depleted their resources, destroyed their political autonomy, displaced them in large numbers and devastated the ecological balance. Logging, mining, agribusiness, massive hydroelectric schemes and mega industrial project, often with multinational collaborations, have together institutionalized victimization of tribal peoples and irretrievably wrecked their survival basis, all in the name of development. The individual oriented paternalistic welfare system reaching to a small fraction of the populace sought not only to coopt and assimilate the few but also geared to facilitate the articulation of capitalist interests into an essentially pre-capitalist matrix.

The ambition to build a culturally homogenous political entity through elimination or absorption of other cultures into the "mainstream" culture, diminished the ability of the tribal peoples to reproduce themselves as socio-cultural collectivities. To put the issue succinctly, the emerging depressing scenario conveys the rise of significant pointers of an internal colonial situation created not simply by the ruling classes and the Indian state but is simultaneously linked to the ongoing onslaught of the predatory activities of the transnational corporations and the octopus like Bretton Woods institutional tentacles. The tribal peoples are, however, not leaving the atrocities and continuing ethnocide to their destiny.

Struggles for Internal Self-Determination :

During the heydays of anti-colonial struggles the right of self-determination was strongly asserted and pursued vigorously as a fundamental human right. But curiously enough soon after independence, the post colonial states are so aggressively protective of their territories that the very mention of the term self determination itself is somewhat paranoically denounced as secessionist and every tribal struggle even for cultural and administrative autonomy, is repressed. But why the States feel threatened by this ? After all self determination simply means recognition of the right of all people to rule themselves, *i.e.,* to make decisions freely about their own conditions of life, to protect and develop their own socio-cultural identity and the peaceful possession of time-honoured land and territorial resources without being expropriated. These are all expressions of universally acknowledged human rights (Brosted, 1987: 155). In other words, self-determination encompasses a set of combined rights to survival, enjoyment of culture and identity, and protection from external attacks and exploitations.

It may be recalled that following the Second World War, the application of the principle of self-determination was considered as the *sine qua non* of international peace as well as the pre-requisitie for the implementation of all other human rights and fundamental freedoms. Thus the right to self-determination which was originally enshrined as a fundamental political principle in the United Nations Charter (1948) and subsequently was made a binding legal principle by the two UN Human Rights Conventions, *i.e.* ICESCR & ICCPR of 1966. The very first Article of both the conventions establish in identical wording : "All peoples have the right of self-determination. By virtue of that right they freely determine their political status and freely pursue their economic, social and cultural development." But curiously this right is said to be applicable only to the specific case of political decolonization. Obviously, it is found wanting with respect to the rights of thousands of internal ethnic, linguistic and religious groups within the post-colonial and pluri-cultural States. Significantly, however, interpreting the said Article, the

International Court of Justice opined in 1975 that the nomadic tribes of Western Sahara, *i.e.* between Morocco and Mauretania did enjoy a right to claim full self-determination. This unique decision which implicitly rejected both the criteria of territorial contiguity and overseas colonization as a pre-condition for self-determination has hardly been pursued; instead there is now a major dispute on what constitutes a people, which alone has the right to self-determination. The restrictive application of the right to self-determination stands in contradiction to the universal principles proclaimed in the International Bill of Rights. Incidentally, though the tribals in India were popularly designated as *Adivasis,* the Indian Government has expressed to the U.N. Subcommission its reservations to treat tribals as the indigenous peoples and in fact in 1988 ILO Conference the Indian representatives strongly argued against the proposed shift of the term population to people in the convention No. 107.

The impasse, however, originates from the inability to comprehend the whole gamut of possibilities within the right of self-determination and without challenging the territorial integrity of the State structure. Exceptions apart, most of the tribal peoples' struggles are geared towards achieving some sort of local self-government and genuine democratic federalism within the existing State structures. Self-determination then implies a process of renegotiating their relationship to the State so as to defend and recuperate their rights to the traditional land and land-based resources and appropriate political institutions and powers to manage these for the tribal peoples, and to defend their rights to the maintenance of identity in the legitimate cultural, linguistic and social spheres and to cessation of abuses and discrimination, and equal participation in the development process within the embrace of the multi-ethnic federal system. Denouncing these struggles of greater regional and cultural autonomy as secessionists or mere manipulation of external powers and thereby legitimizing the repression and torture would continue to be counter productive as evident from the persistence and growth of tribal movements, despite decades of terrorization and cajoling.

This scenario brings us to the possibilities of outlining the forms of self-determination. To begin with, it may be divided into two broad categories, the "external" *i.e.,* secession and formation of independent States which would obviously be a matter of great worry for the modern States; and the other is "internal" which is limited to settle the legitimate grievances in accordance with the established international and national instruments of human rights and, of course, within the broad matrix of the State structure. The second option provides a mutual obligation, *i.e.,* the State is obliged to respect the right of tribal peoples to internal self determination while the tribal peoples are obliged to respect the territorial integrity of the State. To put simply, there are great possibilities for developing a wide ranging forms of self-determination without crossing the threshold of the principle of State sovereignty. Of course, if the democratic means to achieve the internal self-determination is absent or continuously thwarted with State violence, as a last resort, struggles for external self-determination cannot be faulted and in fact would be legitimate in the international law. As "non-self-governing people", they would form a category recognized by the United Nations as eligible for the right of self-determination, expressed through secession and consequent formation of an independent State.

Internal self-determination or "internal autonomy" is not intended to dismember the existing States but extends the rights to the tribal peoples to control their traditional territories and resources, the organization of their societies, decision making institutions, preservation and development of their own cultures and ways of life. And matters affecting them require their consent. Control is the major factor involved in the principle of internal self-determination covering rights to life, land, culture and self-development. There are many degrees and various levels of economic, social, linguistic and political autonomy. It may range from self-government in the areas of language, education and culture to "limited sovereignty" on a specified land base administered by the tribal councils, though ultimately subjected to national interests and regulations, and to "nation within a nation" on the model of American Indian nations of the USA where land based tribal collectivities form common elective councils within the mutually agreed upon spheres of influence. In other words, from regional autonomy to local self-government to federalism. The form would depend upon the specific regional contexts, peoples' aspirations and struggles.

Needless to reiterate that currently tribal peoples have no real decision-making rights. With the increasing centralization of economic and political power and incessant attempts to standardize the socio-cultural fabric, and of course, the ever expanding expropriation of territorial resources, several tribal peoples have been consciously expressing their desire for autonomy and identity fulfilment. The well-organized ones seek to establish territorial local self-government to satisfy their economic, social, cultural and political needs. They look forward to realise equal level of governments among the Union, State and territories, each with relative sovereignty within its own jurisdiction. Internal self-determination would increase their participation in the decision making process and thus have considerable influence on the present and future political, legal and administrative systems. And by strengthening and respecting the diverse social bases, it will contribute further to the richness and diversity of human civilization. Suffice to note that internal self-determintion is central in the struggles against colonialism, hegemony of welfare and development processes, including an overdue struggle against research paternalism, where most researchers continue to treat them as objects of professional interest. Unfortunately, any attempt for territorial autonomy and internal self-determination is simply dubbed as efforts at destabilisation and threat to national integrity of the Indian Union. This is myopic. Rather, recognition of such an autonomy could be a positive step towards social justice and emotional fulfilment, and, therefore, strengthen the Democratic Federal Republic.

It is worth emphasizing that the right to internal self-determination is very much within the constitutional framework of India. Though not explicitly, Nehru's five benevolent principles for the Indian tribes guaranteeing preservation and promotion of their rich identities and cultures and control over land based resources and the Fifth and Sixth Schedules plus Articles 29, 370 and 371 in the Constitution with provisions for regional councils, autonomous districts, and Scheduled Areas provide the contour of internal self-determination. Perhaps one coulld add the Anandpur Saheb Resolution, the West Bengal Cabinet's unanimous resolution on the subject in 1978 and the principle of regional autonomy applied in the case of Gorkhaland, the Rajamannar Committee Report and Karnataka Government's submissions to the Sarkaria Commission belong to the same genus.

The Sixth Schedule is the most powerful legal instrument towards tribal self-government and could form the essential structure for working out the contents and forms of internal self-determination. It authorizes the autonomous district and regional councils to legislate on management and use of land and land-based resources as per their customs, administration of justice, management of public welfare institutions, collections of revenues, taxes and royalties. It is, of course, true that over the years their law making powers and administration of justice has been curbed and in fact it has several problems and contradictions. Nevertheless, it must be acknowledged that only the Sixth Schedule respects customary corporate rights of the tribals and provides a scope for maintenance and development of cultural diversity, self-management, sustainable self-development and internal self-determination. It is beyond the traditional conception of individual civil rights of equality and non-discrimination. What is required is to strengthen the thrust of the Schedule and effectively implement its provisions in conformity with the tribal ethos and visions. The point is that there are already elementary provisions for internal self-determination and can easily be developed.

But curiously the concerned scholars often tend to deny this right to the tribal peoples by raising a number of objections to its impracticability. Given the constraints of the scope of the paper, let us deal briefly the most important objections. It is argued that the tribal peoples are neither the only indigenous peoples of the land nor there is proof that their ancestors were not immigrants from other parts of the globe in historical or pre-historical times. But the very fact that they are distinct peoples with identifiable separate cultural and linguistic identities and are so recognized by the State, should be sufficient for granting the relative autonomy for their survival and development, irrespective of the date of immigration. Secondly, it is held that the tribals are not only equal but also enjoy special Constitutional rights and therefore additional expansion of the support system is unwarranted. Suffice to state that despite the well intentional provisions, the ground reality vividly expresses their overall exploitation and marginalization. Mention may be made that special provisions are made at individual levels and not on tribal corporate level which is the crux of the matter. Thirdly, those who argue that the tribals are given a chance to participate in advanced culture and development of the State and, therefore, enjoy the privilege, should note that there is an inbuilt ethnocentrism of the ruling classes and nations in their proposition. Fourthly, the tribals allegedly lack essential elements of self-governing institutions and their population is small. But are they really smaller than the existing microstates of the world and what about the ongoing process of uniting diverse groups onto a single entity ? Besides they have a permanent population, a more or less defined territory and largely continue to have the traditional political institutions at local levels which are the essential features of the State. The major criticisms, however, are with respect to lack of autonomous and contiguous territory and non-viability of economic systems which would nullify the functioning of internal self-determination.

True that most tribal societies in India lack contiguous territories and they live interspersed amongst non-tribal populations and some are even spread over several countries. Moreover there are diversities of cultures, uneven distribution of wealth and class formations, geographical dispersion, linguistic fragmentation, articulation of capitalism and international division of labour, production and expropriation, many pursue the same occupations as those of neighbouring non-tribals, wide-ranging cultural interactions, and that some tribals even try to conceal their separate identities, may be formidable obstacles to the formation of regional or territorial governments. Each one of these appear true but only in isolation from the totality of the prevailing relationships. Despite differences in geography, culture and capital penetration, the tribal peoples across India share a common feature, *i.e.,* marginal lives, characterised by poverty and dependence. They face essentially similar problems like economic subjugation, socio-cultural stigmatization and lack of political power and make more or less similar demands all over, *i.e.*, greater self-control over their present and future status. Both historically and contextually, their relationship with the State is marked by fundamental assymetry, and is conditioned by economic and ideological considerations of the dominant classes and nations. Besides, it needs to be mentioned that most tribal peoples live in Scheduled Areas and they constitute a majority in nearly 800 blocks of the country and are in overwhelming majority in Meghalaya, Mizoram, Nagaland, Arunachal Pradesh, Dadra and Nagar Haveli and Minicoy and Amindii. Wherever their strength is limited in consultation with the people, the consociation model may be institutionalized, which would ensure each community the autonomy through community councils for education, language, healthcare, social policy, justice services, etc. On the other hand where regional autonomy movements have already created consciousness of territory based identities like Jharkhand, Bodoland, Ladakh, Telengana, etc. shall have their regional or territorial governments, largely based upon their own methods of decision-making with necessary changes to serve the current interests.

About economic non-viability, the issue appears to be rooted in the academic inability to tresspass the unilinear evolutionary model of development and the obsession for Western notions of development. Be that as it may, economic non-viability has never been accepted as an obstacle to the implementation of the right of self-determination. The Declaration of the Granting of Independence to colonial countries and peoples, states clearly in paragraph 3 that "inadequacy of political, economic, social or educational preparedness should never serve as a pretext for delaying independence". Most tribes still hold that their traditional way of life is still of practical importance and highly valued and given a chance it would continue so in the future. The requirement, however, is to restrict the coercive usurption of their resources by external powers. Natural resources provide substantial employment and income. Self-reliance and collective labour intensive and cooperative economic structures with necessary changes in institutions and values may meet the requirement of the modern times. Besides, all production systems are dynamic and innovative, protection of the resources and royalty from sub-surfaces itself could be in most cases substantial to build the necessary infrastructure for sustainable development. To maximize sustainable yields, the funds from taxes, rents and royalties and the government programmes can accommodate the required changes in technology and infrastructure. Additionally the criticism against granting the relative autonomy comes from the notion that given the overall domination of basic capitalist structure, dominated by world capitalism and consequent growth of a relatively heterogenous and conflictual population within and among the tribal societies, the traditional methods of consensus and decision-making process may not be appropriate and thus regional/territorial self-government with control on education, trade, taxation and regulation of exploitation of territorial resources, etc. may be dysfunctional. This implies that only parliamentary system of representative government and intermittant elections are suitable for all economic systems and not the face-to-face dialogue to resolve and arrive at decisions. Perhaps the right note should be that our understanding of the complex tribal epistemology is terribly weak and much more research is needed to comprehend the situation.

Ethnodevelopment and Sustainability

Having noted that internal self-determination is in essential conformity with the available avenues of the state and that the criticisms are largely vague and unsubstantiated, we turn to the pre-conditions for the successful implementation of the principle of internal self-determination. The crucial requirements include (i) legal recognition of tribal organizations, including their creations and development on the communal, inter-communal, regional and/or national levels with clear objectives of control over their traditional land resources, lives and culture; (ii) respect for traditional rights including soil, forest, sources of water, and sub-soil resources whose utilization requiring the consent of the people and then adequate royalty for their use in the country's interest; (iii) recognition of regional and local autonomy with respect to their own forms of authority, customary law, language, customs, values and identity as long as they do not clash with the internationally accepted standards of human rights; and (iv) working out appropriate strategies to counter the neo-colonial and other nascent capitalist forces, institutions and agents of State which prevent the realisation of the principle of internal self-determination. This should include subordination of bureaucracy to collective tribal authorities and forms of decision and official support for their own programmes of economic, social, educational and cultural development.

These preconditions to the internal self-determination lead us to the strategy of ethno or self-development. In a broad sense, ethnodevelopment is the practical manifestation of internal self-determination and without it the tribal peoples cannot put in practice self-determination. "Ethno" implies respect for the wishes and desires of other peoples, societies and cultures; and development in this context refers to a total phenomenon combining economics, politics and culture in an all encompassing whole, defined by the concerned people themselves. Ethnodevelopment then means control of the ethnic over its land, resources, social organization and culture. Additionally it implies that the tribal ethnics have the right to freely negotiate with the State the kind of relationship they individually wish to have (Stavenhagen, 1987). In other words, it conveys that basing upon the traditional institutions and values to confront the challenges posed by the modern world. This is not a self-imposed isolation on a political secession but redefining the notion of development and nation building on the basis of the legitimate aspirations of the culturally distinct groups. Afterall the U.N. General Assembly has adopted the right to development in 1986. What ethnodevelopment aims at is to elaborate their own cultural forms and knowledge systems so as to reaccommodate themselves to the new times, *i.e.,* in short, striving to change in order to conserve the essentials.

Ethnodevelopment should not be confused with the romantic tribalism which Indian anthropologists discussed under isolationism, built on the conservative, call fascist resonance, theory of cultural relativism. In contrast, the notion of ethnodevelopment does not intend to keep the tribal peoples outside the matrix of change or take refuge in the supposedly original unadulterated past. It recognizes that neither the history of the tribal peoples was ever frozen nor they can survive uncontaminated by the present and future events. The isolationist position is obviously paternalistic, anachronistic and discriminatory, for it denies the tribal peoples to elaborate and change, as a strategy of survival, their syncretic complexes. While both assimilation/"integration" and apartheid condemn the future of tribal peoples into a blind alley, ethnodevelopment pleads that they should have the right to choose what to conserve and what to change, what to adopt from the other cultures and what to reject, and all these in what pace and intensity in this fast changing world. In the process of reformulation it is likely that several aspects of their economy, culture, symbols and beliefs may lose their force and might have to be replaced but such a decision should come from them only. This is the alternative discourse or the "Third Way".

Moreover, it needs to be stressed that though class divisions have become all pervasive and therefore socially integrating category, tribal ethnic identity too persists as more or less equally significant principle of social integration. And therefore struggles for internal self-determination cannot underestimate the ethnic existence as a formidable force. In concrete contexts both the basis can be unified to achieve the common objectives. It is thus not a social class alone, but also a people, a culture, and a civilization. In any case for most tribes class and people are synonymous, despite the rise of limited internal differentiation. In other words their struggles demand multi-dimensional approach, including at the levels of ideology, culture and gender. Be that alone, the basic tenets of ethno/self-development would include the following elements or factors, namely, (i) self-sufficiency, *i.e.*, dependency should be progressively removed in the ethnodevelopment process. In order to achieve this, it is necessay to recuperate models of technology and systems of specific knowledge so as to make them integrate with the modern systems. Self-help housing cottage industries and the like with "appropriate technology" may be detailed out as components of self-government. (ii) Social justice, *i.e.*, development geared to resolve, not to create, the question of social and spatial inequality. This demands that they should be subjects of their present and future development. (iii) Control of their own development according to their own priorities, values and customs with full participation in the actual process of planning and implementation, and (iv) Ecological equilibrium or environmentally sensitive development which have been the cornerstone of the history of the tribal peoples across the world.

It is hightime to acknowledge that the traditional tribal cultures and knowledge systems have much to offer to our imperiled planet and thus internal self-determination and ethnodevelopment cannot be separated from the collective human rights of all human beings. The fact is that in the inhospitable regions, they have survived as viable societies for several centuries, may provide insights into the very survival of the planet itself. As the modern management systems are considered failures, it is important to understand the tribal responsible stewardship of the renewable resources and capacity to determine their own future and quality of life, it is time to look at the tribal holistic, futuristic ecologically sustainable and culturally specific modes of management and development as the "Third Way". The fundamental feature of tribal subsistence systems is their organization by community and a clear tendency for communal control and collective management of economic resources, with due respect to and balanced interaction with nature. It must be stressed that sustainability is not unchangeability, it refers to not only the needs of the present but also the future generations with appropriate technology and socio-cultural organization. Being based on highly cooperative local-self-development, it is suitable to local ecosystems and their safe reproduction. Moreover, it simultaneously refers to the sustainable cultural systems and calls for affirming and enhancing diverse cultural identities. Despite the changes, much of the tribal ontological status of integration of nature and human society have not been fully incorporated into the logic of world capitalism. This provides the basis to formulate appropriate designs for sustainable development.

In sum, the principle of internal self-determination and the strategy of sustainable self-development or ethnodevelopment would ensure the beginning of a porcess of emancipation of the tribal peoples. The detailed contours, however, are still to be worked out. Internal self-determination for autonomy over their economies, territories, culture and future could be a powerful tool for genuine democracy and federalism. It would provide a new physical and symbolic space. The Sixth Schedule, despite certain weaknesses, could be the basis for working out the principle of internal self-determination and ethnodevelopment.

In this complex, what role the conscientious tribal researchers can perform ? It must be acknowledged that as much as their knowledge is welcome by the *status-quoists,* several times more enthusiastic public ovation awaits them organized by the people studied by them; of course, with more or less equal conditions. Those who are concerned for the future of the people and the country, to me, should be allies in the liberation struggles of the tribal peoples in particular, and marginalised peoples in general. In the name of scientism and hypocritical objectivity, they cannot evade the responsibility to the people who contributed to their very professional existence. It is not a call to defend the tribal peoples' interests but also a complex responsibility of disseminating the relevant information and sorting out strategies to conscentize on their existence and potentiality for changing the structurally unjust social systems. Needless to state that production and dissemination of knowledge is central to their political struggles for realising internal self-determination. For those such roles are outside their professional integrity (Sic !) or difficult to perform, they can surely denounce all cases of ethnocide, ecocide and genocide and insist on the significance of respecting socio-cultural diversity, biodiversity and economic diversity of the peoples of not only India but everywhere. In case such a role is considered partisan, knowing pretty well that all the suggested strategies so far are either ignored or served the purpose of harming the tribal peoples, there is enough scope to develop the discipline of anthropology. There is an urgent need to locate the tribal approaches to historical and ethnological researches leading to rewriting their history and explaining their cultures themselves. Afterall, practical experience of the peoples should form the cornerstone of any research and thus contribute to the development of indigenous scientific approaches. Academic research should be presented from within rather than from above as a *fait accompli* and in terms of their intelligibility to the concerned people. There is also an urgent need to democratize information on human rights and development processes. Afterall, we have been benefited from their time, energy, love, hospitality and culture. Let us not forget that what we are today is because of them. Let me end here with the presumption that anthropologists too have some responsibility.

REFERENCES

1. Brosted, Jens. 1987. "Sami Rights and Self-Determination", *IWGIA Document No. 58*, Copenhagen, pp. 155-172.
2. Stavenhnagen, Rodolfo. 1987. "Ethnocide or Ethnodevelopment : the New Challenge", *Development, Journal of the Society for International Development*, I (i).

10

Ethnocide and Pauperisation Of the Tribal Oustees Of Large Dams

Lancy Lobo

The infrastructure upon which the edifice of Tribal Policy has evolved in India since Independence are supposedly the five fundamental principles for tribal development enunciated by Nehru (1957), mentioned in his foreword to the second edition of Elwin's book, *Philosophy of NEFA*. People should develop along the lines of their own genius and we should avoid imposing anything on them; tribal rights in land and forests should be respected; we should work through and not in rivalry to their own social and cultural institutions; we should judge results, not by statistics or the amount of money spent, but by the quality of human character that is evolved and so on.

Tribals were economically backward and so they needed 'development'. They were outside the 'national' mainstream and so they had to be brought back into it. Between the pious sentiments of Nehru soon after Independence and four decades later with 'development' and 'integration' of tribals into the 'national' mainsteam, there seems to be little or no relation at all.

The macro developmental model pursued by the State has gone against the interests of the tribals. It has further pauperised them economically and has caused cultural genocide or ethnocide. Ethnocide means that an ethnic group is denied the right to enjoy, develop and transmit its own culture whether collectively or individually. It implies the disintegration and destruction of cultural formation of an ethnic group. Large masses of tribals are reduced to being victim population of the development projects of the State and ethno-development has remained just a concept for the anthropologists.

One of the developmental projects has been large scale dams. By 1979, India had the distinction of holding nearly 15% of the world's large dams. The increasing lure of dams arose from their potential gains through production of cheap power, drinking water supply, control of floods, and increase in irrigation cover. While the benefits of the dams were highlighted, the costs and especially the hidden costs (socio-cultural and environmental) were underplayed. Most dams caused displacement of large number of people and their resettlement and rehabilitation have hardly been satisfactory. It is estimated that the number of oustees in India is 21.6 million, most of whom are tribals. Nearly 82% of the 38 million tribal population live in central and western parts of the country where three-fifth of the large dams are located. Some of the dams and the percentage of tribal population is given in Table 1.

Table 1 : Tribal Population in Selected Dams

Dam	*State*	*Tribal Population in the area as %*
Koel Karo	Bihar	88.0
Hirakud	Orissa	10.9
Sardar Sarovar	Gujarat	51.6
Inchampally	Andhra Pradesh + Maharashtra	20.0
Bhopalpatnam	Madhya Pradesh + Maharashtra	50.0

Source—People and Dams, Delhi: Society for Participatory Research in Asia, p. 25.

The oustees of the submerging villages undergo the following process when they are displaced: They are plucked out of isolation, from stable, low energy, sustained-yield systems of subsistence in a distinct socio-cultural milieu and flung into the deadly market-place of land with no protection against exploitation, cheating, avarice and hostility of outsiders belonging to another culture. There is no national policy for the oustee's relocation and rehabilitation. The half-hearted attempts and ad-hocism of the respective State governments have contributed to the ethnocide of the oustees.

We shall discuss below the latest large dam in the making, *viz.*, the Sardar Sarovar Project (SSP) and the rehabilitation policy and performance of the government of Gujarat. We select this case-study because the government of Gujarat has conceded, what is supposed to be, the best rehabilitation package for the oustees in the country. The following pages will reveal the inadequacy of the government's policy and performance which help us to guess the manner in which oustees of other dams have been rehabilitated.

Resettlement and Rehabilitation of Oustees—A Case Study

The Narmada River Valley Project is a colossal scheme of building 30 major dams*, 135 medium and 3000 minor irrigation schemes which is likely to cost Rs. 25,000 crores. A total of 219 villages are undergoing submergence, *viz.*, 19 from Gujarat, 27 from

*By large dam we mean a facility which has a Culturable Command Area (CCA) of more than 2,000 hectares. In Indian official terminology, a large dam would include the category 'major' having a CCA of 10,000 ha. or more as well as the 'medium' having a CCA ranging between 2,000 to 10,000 ha. In the case of a purely hydroelectric dam, a large dam would be generating five MW. of uninterrupted power. By implication, a small dam would be one with a CCA of less than 2,000 ha. and whose capacity to generate power does not exceed five MW. (*See* Chakraborty; no date of publication; p. 20).

Maharashtra and 173 from Madhya Pradesh and it is estimated that nearly 70,000 people will be displaced. Of the 19 villages of Gujarat, inhabited either by Tadvi or Bhil tribals, eight villages are relocated in the following manner. They are shifted to 100 new sites with as little as 8 kms. and as far as 150 kms. from the submerging villages. They are paid house and land compensation.

The tribal land comes under three Acts, *viz.*, (1) Preservation of Forest Act of 1965. The first one, classifies land into jungle and *kharabo*, waste; the second specifies the ceiling, and the third prohibits the sale and purchase of tribal land to both tribals and non-tribals without the Collector's permission. In other words, it is the government alone who can acquire the tribal land. The terms of acquisition are specified by the outdated Land Acquisition Act of 1894.

For the government bureaucrat, displacement has connotations of hydraulics...of mass being moved indifferently across space. But for the tribal oustees displacement has a wider meaning. For them, land is not just real estate or space over which people are moved like objects, but land is a memory, a map of one's world, a way of life for which they are willing to die (Viswanathan 1985: 41). No amount of compensation can make up for the loss of ancestral land. When Guyana's Akawaio Indians were asked to vacate their land, their headman wrote the following lines to the Prime Minister:

> "This land is where we belong. It is God's gift to us and has made us as we are. This land is where we are at home, we know its way; things that happen here are known and remembered, so that the stories the old people told are still alive here...This land is the place where we know where to find all that it provides for us—food from hunting and fishing, and farms, building and tools, materials, medi-

> cines. Also the spirits around us know us and are friendly and helpful.....If we had to move, we would be lost to those who remain in other villages. This would be a sadness to us all, like sadness of death" (*See* Vishwanathan 1985: 43).

One can appreciate the headman's sentiments from an anthropological point of view as man's relationship to nature is one of the four building blocks of culture. When it is altered, nothing short of cultural genocide ensues.

The principal government agencies involved in resettlement are the Departments of Irrigation and Power, Revenue and Forest. Though they hold joint meetings, they are hardly trained to handle rehabilitation as a human problem. As mentioned earlier, shifting of people appears to be the key responsibility for them. Scudder, an anthropologist on the World Bank Mission has noted that, "the strength of irrigation and revenue departments at Narmada Sarovar relates to land acquisition and compensation, but not rehabilitation. An approach to rehabilitation lays emphasis, not on the future welfare of oustees, but on their physical transference from the reservoir basin" (Chakraborty: 23). Underlying this is the assumption that tribals with weak economic and political strength can be easily sacrificed for the development project which is projected as good for the masses.

The tribal lands were not properly surveyed during the Re-settlement Survey especially in view of land acquisition for the SSP. Hence, many have no proper records of their lands. In other words, they become 'encroachers' in the eyes of the officials. Lately, the government has agreed to give two hectares of land to 'encroachers'. A male who has reached 18 years on 1.1.1987 is counted as a separate household. However, a female head with a major and other minor children are counted as one household and not two. The landless artisans and agricultural labourers, and those making a living on forest produce, get no compensation at all, except perhaps houseplots in few settlement sites*. The government has agreed to exchange land for land upto maximum five acres.

In a number of resettlement sites, good many oustees were palmed off encumbered land, *i.e.*, land with legal impediments. The nexus between the government officials and previous land sellers could not be ruled out. The illiterate oustees ignorant of land market became aware of encumbrance later when their applications for bank loans were rejected as they carried encumbrance of the previous owner.

In a few resettlement sites land given to the oustees was reacquired by the government for the construction of canals. Were the officials ignorant of the passage of the canal ? The government has paid compensation, however, it has withheld the same from those who had encumbered land. The government has not acquired a part of the oustee's land in the submerging villages, especially on hill-tops where waters are not expected to reach. How would they cultivate that land once the dam gets completed ?

The tribals lacked the know-how of the land market and the opportunist land sellers increased the price of land. Many oustees paid more than the rate of compensation given by the government. Not only could they buy less land then they owned previously, but they had to pool in the house compensation received previously.

The grazing land wnich was in plenty in submerging villages became an acute problem. Not only were the oustees forced to reduce the number of cattle, some of which died, they now had to engage a wage-earn-

---

* New GRs provide two hectares of land for landless. However, so far only one such oustee household has got the land.

ing adult to acquire fodder. Tensions have arisen between the oustees and the hosts as the former have 'encroached' on the latter's already depleted grazing land. Where the host villagers are poorer than the oustees, the former dislike the treatment meted by the government to oustees. In some places, the land given predominantly to share-croppers is now sold to oustees leaving the share-croppers in a precarious position.

Tribals who were on highlands are largely relocated on the plains, where the ecosystem is different and they have to adjust to the new cropping patterns.

By and large, governments of different States have given inadequate cash compensation to the oustees without, of course, considering the social and cultural costs of rehabilitation. Cash compensation to tribals, who are not conversant with the cash economy, has often resulted in their exploitation and immiseration. In the existing legal context, the displaced have no right except compensation for the acquired land. Most of the Ukai oustees in South Gujarat were given cash compensation which they spent within a year on alcohol, wrist watches and transistors. Today, these people are roaming in the streets of Surat or working as sugarcane cutters in the fields of *Patidar* landlords whose fields are irrigated by Ukai dam.

The concept of wage labour was absent in submerging villages, as tribals operated on exchange labour within kinship units. In the submerging villages, the forest provided a continuous source of economic activity. Now they have not only to hire in wage labour but also hire themselves out. Besides, there is little wage labour available to them.

Integration of oustees among the host villages has not been anticipated by the government. On social and cultural levels, the Tadvis who are highly sanskritized, have to live with least sanskritized Vasavas. The Tadvis say, "while we worship the cow, the Vasavas eat it".

According to the Gujarat Government's Resolution of 1985, the oustees are eligible for the following amenities: One primary school (3 rooms) for 100 families; one *panchayat* house, dispensary, seed store, village pond for every five hundred families; one children's park for every 5000 families; one drinking water well with trough and one tree platform for every 50 families, with each colony linked to the main road by roads of appropriate standard. In reality, none of the resettlement sites meets the above prescriptions, as the oustees are scattered in smaller number in all directions. However, the government has provided the oustees some amenities such as schools, drinking water wells, tree platforms, and in a few cases, electricity. But there is a litany of complaints regarding the broken-down wells, empty wells, broken handpumps, unusable tree platforms and roads, and blown-off school roofs left unrepaired for months. The government has initiated some developmental projects such as distributing bullock-carts, and badly-managed technical training courses to oustee youth. One of the stated concerns of government rehabilitation policy is not only to ensure the previous standard of life of oustees but to improve upon it. In the light of the story of rehabilitation we have described, it is anyone's guess if the oustees will retain their previous standard of life in new settlement sites.

The houseplots for oustees were given in a row in new sites amounting to three *gunthas* initially and now five. The living space concept of the tribal has not been taken into consideration by the bureaucrat with an urban background. A tribal uses his house more for housing cattle and storing agricultural produce than for himself. He spends more time outside than inside...under a tree or a platform. He has a separate place outside the house to store fodder and wood. In the resettlement sites, the tribal feels bottled up in a barrack-type existence which enforces on him a cheek-by-jowl existence.

The dismal record of rehabilitation of some selected dam oustees can be seen from Table 2.

Table 2 : Rehabilitation of Oustees of Some Selected Dams

Dam	*State*	*Year of impoundment*	*Displaced families No.*	*Rehabilitated families No.*	*%*
Hirakud	Orissa	1956	1,636	300	18
Bhakra	Himachal	1959	2,100	730	35
Ukai	Gujarat	1971	18,500	3,500	19
Pochampad	A.P.	1965	67 villages	39=land compensation 28=cash compensation	

The relation between tribal oustees and government officials can be summarised in the words of an oustee, "In the initial stages the government officals approached us with such respect and frequency only to entice us into agreeing to shift. Once we agreed to shift, their needs were over and ours began. We are now at the receiving end and they play the bosses" (*See* Lobo 1987: 34). One can imagine the hardships involved for the widely dispersed oustees (from eight villages to 100 villages) and the gap between them and the administrative centre (from 15-150 kms.). They have to walk miles to board a bus, pay the bus fare, suffer loss of wages, and finally confront a cold bureaucracy. Hence, there is a feeling of total helplessness among the oustees. It is the NGOs and social activists who at times intervene between the oustees and the officials.

Thus, one gets a picture of large-scale dams camouflaged as developmental projects in the interest of the nation, but in essence, assaulting the lives, culture, habitat, and more important, resources of the tribals

---

Source: People and Dams, p. 26

and converting them into cheap labour colonies. Tribals, it was claimed, have had no history; today, it is believed that they have no future.

Political Economy of Irrigation Projects/ Large Dams

The dismal picture of the rehabilitation of oustees cannot be understood except in the wider theoretical framework of the 'developmental model' operated by the State. The model of 'economic growth' which justifies the maximisation of profits by reckless exploitation of resources, imposes on the majority the views and ideology of the minority. The rhetoric of 'national interest' behind dam constructions masks the far-from-equal distribution of social benefits. The large dams are generally controlled by electricity generation authorities rather than by the Irrigation Departments. The former is more concerned with urban needs and industrial energy consumers rather than rural agriculturists. The Irrigation Department is more worried in providing water to lowland farmers who are already relatively better off than the displaced poor.

The large-scale dams have come under heavy criticism on displacement and resettlement and cost-benefit analysis. Repeatedly, the benefits are exaggerated and costs are lowered. Socio-cultural costs are ignored and environmental costs underestimated. Access to information is deliberately blocked. Media is used to orchestrate the benefits. The construction of large-scale dams appear to be more political than economic decisions. Apart from centralised control over a key resource like water, the State gets access to and control over peripheral populations through construction of roads. Resettlement of scattered population gives a high degree of control to State authorities over every aspect of the lives of those affected. The agriculture served by new irrigation schemes follow the Green Revolution Model and as such, rely on centralised technology, inputs and knowledge systems (Hirsch 14). For illustration let us examine the Ukai Dam case.

Ukai dam on Tapi river in South Gujarat was completed in 1972, a multi-purpose project visualized to generate 300 MW of electricity and irrigate 3.86 lakh hec. The area sought to be irrigated, *viz.*, the lower Tapi basin was one of assured rainfall—1200 mm average per year. The upper Tapi basin or the obey area (catchment area) consisted of highlands inhabited by tribals, and the lower basin or command area consisted of plains inhabited by Patidar caste, the dominant agriculturists. If production of food crops was the dominant motive of planners, it was belied as the cropping pattern suddenly changed from food crops like *jowar*, wheat and val to perennial crops like sugarcane, bananas and fruit trees. Thus, sugarcane increased from less than 3,000 hec. in 1958-59 to about 91,000 hec. in 1981-82 at the cost of food crops.

It must be pointed out that every project is either a benefit or a cost to particular groups in society. Prior to the construction of the dam, there was a vast difference in the development in the command and obey areas in terms of literacy, cropping intensity, ration of net irrigated area to gross cropped area, number of tractors, electric motors, etc. While the average score of development for the command area was 810, it was only 333 for obey area talukas (*See* Mankodi and Gangopadhyay 1983: 37). The dam submerged 200 sq. miles, *i.e.*, 100 villages totally and 70 partially, leaving 16,000 families affected. Those who cultivated the river banks with two crops without extra irrigation or fertilisers were ejected and given maximum 4 acres of land cleared of forests. Since large joint family holdings were in the name of the head of the household, only the title-holder received a small plot of land. The much-promised help in building wells, land improvement, building and removal of tree-stumps and supply of electricity were conveniently forgotten by the government. The inferior quality land could give the oustees just one crop. Mechanised irrigation in small plots became uneconomical and after the first crop the oustees had to fend for themselves as migrant labourers.

The high expectation of using the irrigation potential in the command area was belied, as only 50 per cent was actually used. How could such a costly project be justified in view of the miserable utilisation ? It must be said that the benefits of irrigation, electricity and flood control and the generation of employment favoured the command areas at the cost of obey areas. A decade after the completion of the project, there was nothing for the displaced, whereas the industrialists or agricultural capitalists in the command areas were favoured with everything including supply of unorganised cheap labour migrating from obey areas. Hence, both in terms of increasing food production and in achieving equitability the project has failed. The 'national interest' in this case was only the interest of the dominant caste of cultivators who had political clout. Those who paid for the national interest were uprooted from their traditional habitats, leaving behind the security of their land, houses, social relationships, customary occupations and faced the uncertainities of life in a strange land among strangers. The reward they received was a meagre sum of Rs. 450/- to Rs. 670/- for cooperating with the government. Prior to the construction of the dam, 64.9% families lived below the poverty line, whereas after rehabilitation 95% families were found to be living under the poverty line (Mankodi and Gangopadhyaya 1983: 99).

The condition of the migrant oustee workers of Ukai dam need some elaboration. In a paper in the Journal of Peasant Studies, titled 'Even Dogs are Better Off: The Ongoing Battle Between Labour in the Cane Fields of Gujarat', Breman (1990) has given a description of the physical or living conditions and economic conditions of migrant oustees (see also Interim Report 1987). An army of 150,000 cane-cutters come from the hinterland to the plains in October and remain for seven months, living in open-air camps in which they pitch their shelters. They drink the filthy water from fields and canals; have no medical facility, no school for their children and no protection from the raging malarial mosquitoes.

The basic work unit is the Koyta, (a sickle used for cutting cane), a cutting team consisting of two adults, and also a child, Koytas (the workers lose their identity and are called by the instrument they use) are organised in gangs supervised by *Mukadams,* with whom the sugar factories enter into a contract for recruitment. Koytas form an anonymous mass whose members do not appear in the factory's administration. There is no relation between the management and sugarcane workers. Each Koyta is given Rs. 30/- and 30 kg. of *Jowar* for every 15 days. This enables them to barely subsist and work as bonded labourers throughout the harvesting season. If they leave the work they lose everything as the accounts are settled only at the end of the season after substracting the advance paid. As the workers and "*Mukadams*" are uneducated, they have to rely on the accounting system of the factories and accept whatever payment is given. If they question the management they are threatened with dire consequences.

The rate of payment too has been very meagre, compared with the back-breaking nature of work. This rate has been revised from Rs. 18/- in 1987 to Rs. 22/- in 1988 and to Rs. 29/- in 1989 and Rs. 33/- per ton this year due to the litigation in the court by some activists. But there were incidents where the workers were paid Rs. 22/- per ton instead of Rs. 29/-. The workers' services were terminated even before the crop was not harvested in order to avoid implementation of the court order.

The factories are supposed to pay for the transport of the workers to-and-fro from their home-towns, but today the advance is deducted from the pay of the workers. Thus, all the provisions of the Inter-State Migrant Act of 1979 are violated.

The Bardoli Sugar Factory in South Gujarat is supposed to be the largest sugar co-operative in Asia, earning nearly a crore of profit. This profit is amassed greatly from the crushing of migrant labour and not the cane. It has been operating its diabolical designs by circumventing laws so that the migrant worker is totally helpless and the factory reaps the harvest of their helplessness. The farmers only provide the farm and grow the cane under the control and management of the sugar factories. The harvesting is entirely handled by the factory supervisors through *Mukadams.* The farmer does not have any direct relation with the workers or the Mukadams. In the final analysis, the factories deny that they are the principal employers, and pass the responsibility on to the farmers to escape the labour acts (*See* Report 1987).

Conclusion

As a critique of the present model of development Breman (1990) challenges the assumption of policy makers, planners and politicians that distribution is a natural consequence to growth and that although in the first instance development benefits the propertied classes, it subsequently improves the situation of those classes that are largely or wholly dependent on the sale of their labour. In his view, misery on a massive scale is a direct consequence of the way in which the development process has evolved in Gujarat and elsewhere in India. This development pauperises, subjugates and eventually eliminates the poor. It treats the tribals as objects rather than subjects of development. Through this model, the State, instead of integrating the different ethnic groups, especially the weaker ones, fragments them. The State has in-built violence and inequality and if people revolt, it supresses them through law and order keeping machinery. In other words, large dams submerge sub-nationalities in India.

The sentiments regarding tribals expressed by Nehru, mentioned earlier in this paper, have remained pious sentiments. Ecological degradation and control of resources of tribals by a minority ruling class caste, show that the concept of development is not a neutral one. Marx had said that in any society the ideas of the ruling class are the ruling ideas. The ruling ideas of development in our country are those of the ruling class and which protect their own class interests. The on-going battle between Narmada activists such as Amte, Patkar along with the oustees and the government of Gujarat is a living testimony to Marx's saying. The beneficiaries of SSP are once again largely well off districts. SSP is made out to be the life-line of Gujarat and the expectations of the people of drought affected districts have been heightened by well orchestrated media. It is a foregone conclusion that SSP will be any different from Ukai or most other dams in the country. If large dams are inevitable, the least the State could do is not only relocate the oustees but rehabilitate them.

REFERENCES AND BIBLIOGRAPHY

1. Acharya, S.K. 1988, "Ethnic Processes in North-Eastern India", *EPW* May 21,
2. Breman, J., 1990 "Even Dogs Are Better off: The Ongoing Battle Between Capital and Labour in the Cane Fields", *The Journal of Peasant Studies,* Vol. 17, No. 4, pp. 546-608.
3. Chakraborty, M., n.d. "Resettlement of Large Dam Oustees in India", in *People and Dams,* Delhi: Society for Participatory Research in Asia, pp. 20-33.
4. Gore, M.S., 1988 "Ethnicity and Nationhood in India Today", *New Quest,* March-April, Vol. 68.
5. Hirsch, P., n.d. "Dammed or Damned ?" in *People and Dams,* Delhi:

Society for Participatory Research in India, pp. 9-16.

6. Interim Report, 1987 "*Interim Report of the Committee to Inquire into the Condition of the Workmen Engaged in Sugar Factories in Valsad and Surat*", (*Mimeo*).
7. Kothari, R, 1988, *Rethinking Development*, Delhi: Ajanta Publications.
8. Kothari, S. and Bakshi, R., (Eds.), 1990 *Lokayan Bulletin*, March-April: 2.
9. Lobo, L., 1987, *Resettlement and Rehabilitation: Sardar Sarovar Project, Fifth Report*. Surat: Centre for Social Studies, (*Mimeo*).
10. Mankodi, K., and Gangopadhyay, T., 1983 *Rehabilitation, The Ecological and Economic Costs*, Surat: Centre for Social Studies, (Mimeographed).
11. Nehru, J., 1957 Forword to Verrier Elwin's *A Philosophy for NEFA*, Shillong: NEFA.
12. Reports 1985-1990 *Ressettlement & Rehabilitation of Sardar Sarovar Project on the Narmada*, Surat: Centre for Social Studies, (*Mimeo*).
13. Report 1987, *Report of the High Level Committee appointed by the Hon. The High Court of Gujarat by the Order Dated 1st May, 1987; Passed Special Civil Applicate*, (*Mimeo*).
14. Report 1987, *Report of the High Level Committee Appointed by the Hon. The High Court of Gujarat by the Order Dated 1st May, 1987; Passed Special Civil Applicate*, (*Mimeo*).
15. Shah, G. 1988, 'Congress and the Deprived Communities', in *Congress in Indian Policy: A Centenary Perspective*, Ram Joshi and Z.K. Hebsur (Eds.) Bombay: Popular Prakashan.
16. Singh, R. n.d. *Dams and Other Major Projects, Impact on and Response of Indigenous People*, Hong Kong: CCA-URM Daga.
17. Vishwanathan, S. 1985, 'From the Annals of the Laboratory State', *Loykayan Bulletin*, Special Double Issue: On Survival.

11

Direction Of Tribal Development: A Need For Social Audit And Participation By N.G.Os

M.L. Patel

In usage, Development has become a loaded word which implies welfare of the down trodden also. There cannot be an umbrella approach to foster the development of all Indian Tribes. There are as many as 427 types of Tribes and Sub-Tribes, which have been broadly classified into different class groups depending upon their present state of development and factors namely, mode of living in forest, shifting villages, forest village, community village and revenue villages. Therefore, policy prescription for each category of tribe also vary accordingly:

There are five main groups of Tribes divided according to mode of living and occupation. They are the following:

1. Food gatherer - Forest dwellers.
2. Pastoral and nomads - Living as cow herds, sheep/Goat Graziers.
3. Farmers -

(a) Shifting cultivators (Including 74 P.T.G.) given

in annexure-1 living in shifting villages, called forest villages and/or labour camps.

(b) Settled cultivators (Mainly the major tribes) living in permanent villages namely revenue villages, forest and community villages.

(c) Agricultural labourers (the landless tribals) living mainly in revenue villages.

4. Service sector employeess (weavers, iron smelters, etc.) living in mixed villages, towns and cities.

5. Producer (Non-agricultural Sector) including handicraft and dairy and poultry (Rural & Urban both). Cholanaikans and Chenchus the two main primitive tribes of Andhra Pradesh are examples of food gatherers. Lambada, Banjara and Sugalis of M.P., Maharashtra, Bihar and Orissa are nomads, who can be classified as persons belonging to production sector, also as they possess best skill of knitting and weaving. Among the primitive agriculturist, Baiga, Abujhmarias, Pahari Korbas are living examples of shifting cultivators of Madhya Pradesh and so are Nicobarese of Andaman, Jhumia of Tripura and Hill Mizos of North-Eastern Region. By and large, they are now adopting plough cultivation as settled farmers. Baigas now have developed awareness of advantages of plough cultivation; hence they demand lands on plains in vicinity of their villages, reveals a recent field research.

Raj Gond, Panika, Pradhan and Bhilala of M.P. and of many other States also are settled cultivators, who are nearly progressive farmers. Few of Oraons, Gonds, Meenas, Tangas and Ap Tani-Tribe peoples can easily be identified as I.A.S. and I.P.S. officers and or State civil servants, since quite many of them have availed of the constitutional provisions under schedule V and VI as the case could be.

Point at issue is that those tribes which have been included in top-class services should now come forward with the proposal to deschedule their tribes so that the limited quota in Govt. service sector may be availed by less progressive section of Scheduled Tribes. Similarly, income criterion could also be based to make revision of the schedule, as rationalisation of Scheduled Tribes.

There is need to receive feed back of curbing the policy of tribal development to suit the prevailing situations. Since tribes at large are very backward educationally and in other production and service matters too, it can be expected of them to feed back regarding success or failure of the development programmes which are being executed by Govt. agencies or non-Govt. organisations. If the functionaries themselves are asked to evaluate the schemes, under implementation at their command, the data of progress are bound to be inflationary of progress and achievements. This calls for change in Tribal Development and Evaluation Policy. Evaluation of tribal development programme should be entrusted to non-governmental agencies for unbiased assessment of the results of the work done.

A recapitulation of old policy, which traces its origin in British regime, does not make a pleasant story because isolation and seperation were the keywords of tribal policy, as spelled out by British administrators. The Direction of tribal development was to leave them as they were, quite undisturbed and unaware of the cross currents of fight for the freedom etc. The wholesale allowance to lead traditional life style, with minimum needs and their fulfilment with the bounty of nature, all together created a net-work for their survival without the external pull or pressure. Tribal chiefs, however, developed working equations with the Britishers and agreed to make payment of token fee to confirm their subordination of old traditions, stigmas, social sanction, taboos, etc., which were valued high by all the tribals. Even Dr. V. Elwin, the so-called friend, philosopher, and guide of tribals made the impact of his "Theory of Isolation" for tribal's survival. People of National status such as Gandhiji and A.V. Thakkar Bapa were the pioneer to promote N.G.O. for the welfare and reform works to be taken for the tribals and villagers at large.

Hence, Isolation Policy is out-dated for India after independence, because tribals have to be brought within the national framework not only culturally, politically but also economically and severally. No doubt the contributions of tribal sector in National Income by way of income tax, excise duty, vehicle tax, receipts are very meagre and do not measure well to capital investment for them, but their socio-economic upliftment is a need, under the constitutional directives.

Since tribals are mainly forest workers and cultivators, related schemes of contour bunding, field bunding, horticulture, dairy, piggery, goatry, small industry, carpentry, iron-smithy, rope making, cloth weaving, industrial training, education and other social sector schemes have to be given to tribals depending upon their stages of development. Intermediate technologies in production sector as well as in service sectors have to be preferably introduced among the tribals, who have limited capability to switch on to most sophisticated tools and machines for want of necessary training and knowledge.

Social Audit by Voluntary Organisations

Various development programmes have been implemented in tribal areas for the welfare of tribal people on family basis, community basis and on area basis too, almost on an uniform basis, without regard to their propensity to adopt them. Hence, many of them had bitterly failed on all fronts. Baiga could do better in bamboo work and carpentry but not in weaving and tailoring or iron-smithy by tradition. Area development approach has been adopted on the pretext that since the tribal areas have remained isolated for long due to inaccessibility, the tribal people living in such few areas have remained unaware of so many progressive programmes which could benefit them individually, family-wise and/or community-wise. They could not receive exposures of the developed societies. Hence, various State Govt., Central Govt. and Voluntary Organisation have undertaken so many development programmes of time bound nature. For want of awareness, family programmes do not make headway and neither do the community programmes for want of initiative and leadership. Voluntary organisation can come forward to create motivation among the tribal people by approaching them on social footing.

Since monitoring of the scheme/programme at the implementation stage is not done properly, the schemes get delayed and misdirected in many cases, where the benefits do not accrue to target groups. It is here, the voluntary organizations can come forward to feed back the progress of implementation and can carry out social audit with unbiased mind. They can assess the end-results in view of the proposed targets. For examples, people's representatives, *viz.,* M.L.A. and M.P. and/or Janpad Panchayat chairman can do well in this.

The area approach programme can be monitored after completing the projects taken at hand and may be by the joint authorities, where such projects are cutting across more than one district or State boundaries. For example, big dams, thermal plants, coal mines and rail line construction works cut across various boundaries. The monitoring can be done monthly or at mid-term plan period and evaluation can be done on their completion. However, when the projects continue as spill-over works for more period than orginally stipulated, their evaluation may be attempted on short frequencies so that impact of factors raising cost of the projects can as well be ascertained and delay may be avoided.

Generally, voluntary organizations, are neither implementing this big public programmes, nor are planning agencies. Therefore, they can make most unbiased evaluation of the Govt. schemes under implementation. But, they have their own constraints and lack in the technical staff and subject matter specialists. Therefore, it is feared that social audit can best be done by them provided the Govt. allows the voluntary organisations to go through the schemes and programmes as observers for rapid assessments on public utility fronts. For selecting the dam sites the voluntary organizations can also help in raising public opinion about its suitability on mass support.

Crux of Tribal Upsurgence

Land is the main stay of Tribal-Economy. Forest Products, however, supplement family incomes of tribals. Agrarian issues in tribal areas should be settled keeping in view of the inter-dependence of various other weak social groups and the need for evolving an integrated approach for solution of economic problems of the region. It is time to ask whether the blanket protection should continue to all sections of tribal community—advanced and the backward. It needs a second thought with all seriousness whether the poorest of poor in tribal communities should or should not deserve more and immediate attention of the Govt. and comparatively larger proportion of available capital subsidy, larger agrarian security and legal protection from exploitation and atrocities so as to help them to run in the race of resurgence.

Land alienation, indebtedness, slow growth of tribal economy, growing dissatisfaction among the tribals for land compensation are parts of the much larger problem of economic backwardness, which are now assuming a political overtone. Several programmes of educational development, health services and water resource development and industrialization at present suit best to high populous areas, possessing a minimum necessary population threshold. Whereas tribal areas having sparse population divided in small pockets at big distances, fail to satisfy population requirement of development strategy based on growth centre model for creating infrastructure to provide essential support services. This leads to evolving a system to transfer tribal population to centre of activities from low density areas. Madhya Pradesh Government has taken up development works on centrally located villages for the benefit of largest number of the tribals living in their vicinity.

Indebtedness of Tribals

Tribal society in general and primitive tribes, namely Baiga, Kharia, Nicobarese, Onge, Jarwa, etc., in particular are simple societies. However, the latter three have no practice of loaning and/or borrowing of economic goods. At best they can cooperate each other *engratis* without expecting interest or additional recovery in return. Therefore, these societies do not suffer from indebtedness. Also, land is not a saleable commodity generally among them, therefore, advancing of loan against the security of land also does not arise. Plots of shifting cultivation are not sold nor gifted or exchanged as land is the bounty of nature to them. Crop cycle of 7-5 years is followed by shifting cultivator's who again take-up the abandoned plots for shifting cultivation.

Indebtedness is the concept of a commercial society, which has developed an economic system of credit creations and investment of capital raised by obtaining loan on basis of payment of interest on its principal.

The loans can be advanced in cash and kind both. Tribal societies, which are settled at farming stage, suffer from this problem because they have to borrow loan from money lenders, traders, etc. who are professing this banking function as indigenous bankers. Problem of indebtedness become serious, if it perpetuates for long, despite payment of interest at a very high rate. 'Dam Dupat' concept is widely known as prevalent in tribal areas of Central India, which signifies practice of 100% interest rate per year on the principal amount advanced as loans. Tribal farmers have lost their lands and other properties including ornaments, animals, etc. on failure of timely repayment of loan to the money-lenders. This is more true of the Gonds, Korku, Kole, Panika, etc. who are major tribes. The minor tribes (*i.e.* the P.T.G.), however, have escaped from the indebtedness unless they come down to plain areas for settled cultivation.

Since various types of financial exploitation of tribes was taking place in very high proportion, to curb it 'Usurious Loans Act', 'Moneylenders Control Act' and Debt Redemption Act were passed by State Govt. from time to time during the British rule of M.P. (*i.e.* erstwhile C.P. & Berar). After independence 'Debt Relief Act' and 'Debt Reconciliation Act' were passed with a view to put a check on the exhorbitant rate of interest and set aside outstanding dues. Moneylenders had grabbed every wealth that this simple tribals possessed for recovery of never ending interests.

In M.P., special courts were opened to try out the cases of over recovery from tribals and after due investigations the debts were redempted/cancelled.

Need for Action Research

However, with all measures taken by the various governments to promote the quality of tribal life, much is needed to be enquired into by in-depth study of each programme under implementation in remote and near tribal sub-plan areas. It needs to be ensured, whether the development programmes have made any impact on improving the quality of life of tribal beneficiaries overall or the benefits have centered to few habitual beneficiaries, who could satisfy the development agencies and officials by allowing them to share a portion of total benefits. There is a strong feeling that selected team of well-off tribals have been bagging subsidies from so many programmes and this precipitated development did not allow the benefits to percolate to bottom comprising deprived and needy sections of poor tribals.

Dents of Tribal Development—It is absolutely an unpleasant task to reveal the malices of development dualism that the tribals suffer. Large scale depletion of resources, both natural and human from tribal areas, have frustrated the hopes of demagogs, whose dogmas were resting on hopes for bringing about the tribal people in the mainstream of economic development and social change. Not only the waters of rivers near Bailadila Iron-ores of Bastar have been polluted, but the Muria/Maria tribal societies have also suffered cultural shock by over interaction with the urban people and their culture. The natural consequences are that institutions of destitutes and prostitutes have appeared there due to premature social interactions. To escape this, they had to retreat to hill tops as earlier done by Abujhmaria Tribe. Alienations of tribal lands have widely increased due to concealed land transfers and tenancy system, developed as reaction to ban on transfer of tribal lands to non-tribals in tribal sub-Plan areas. This has led to the creation of artificial low market value of tribal lands, which disallows capitalistic gain on lands, when acquired by government or any company for use to construct irrigation dam, to work mine-ores or any other industrial use. The provisions of land Acts of State governments do not match with the provisions of Land Acquisition Act, 1894 and they offer all loss to tribals in getting fair compensation for their lands. This calls for necessary amendments in appropriate sections of Land Acquisition Act, 1894 and State Land Revenue Codes/Acts.

Discrimination against tribals in matters of their usufructuary rights in lands and forest and forest produces and ownership too, have been deep-rooted in tribal uprisings and rebellions, since Birsa Movement, Santhal Movement, Fituri Movement, to present day Jharkand Movement, etc. All these are dents of tribal development, which cannot be repaired beyond breakaway points and endurance limits. White-collar atrocities have escaped the purview of the SC, ST Prevention of Atrocities Act, 1989. Delay in justice leads to denial of justice in general practice and in land resumption to SC & ST equally.

Obviously, a well-set system of subsidy borne economic programmes for the "Habitual Beneficiaries" has come up, which has created a strong understanding between the programme executives and the beneficiaries to grab and share subsidy components. Soft bank loans are also availed by them as additive funding to subsidy to make the programme economically viable. However, they are out of bound to needy persons.

Heavy stress on family oriented development programmes has serious implications. Devastating effects of the inducement based development programmes have promoted national waste of costly agricultural inputs for want of awareness in the tribal target groups, who have more interest in the container than its contents. H.Y.V. seeds are consumed by the subsistence farmers, who under distress of poverty can not discount present for future. Hence, savings get eroded. May be, it is promoted by granting the alternate subsidy to them. Tensions have been created by changes brought about in political, social and economic structure of Indian society. On the one hand development programmes have promoted due and undue aspirations and expectations of the SC & ST and acute resentment among other classes of people, who have been denied similar privileges and favourable treatments from the government, and on the other hand, age old superiority assumed and exercised over the weaker sections and other social conflicts have risen to other heights, thereby changing nature of artrocities on SC & ST individuals to gang violence and arson. Thus, payment of compensation for the damages done to SC & ST has come up as a regular feature on non-plan expenditure, besides creation of permanent infrastructure to provide protection to weaker sections.

Legal Aid Cells

Tribal Welfare Department of Madhya Pradesh Govt. has created Legal Aid Cells, one each in all the tribal districts, which are assigned the duty to listen and examine the grivances of the tribals carefully and provide cost free all legal advices and services and to fight their causes. Lump-sum fees for such legal services are paid to specially appointed lawyer (advocate by the Govt. department). However, it is commonly experienced that most of the tribals suffer from common illicit approaches by the moneylenders and other exploitors, who want to alienate tribals' land and other property. This calls for Public Interest Litigation which can be taken up by NGOs.

Public Interest Litigation for Social Cause

Established lawyers are needed to form Legal Cells as a voluntary organisation to help the tribals and others in legal matters. Individuals fight for their cause with personal interest, but situation change when gang atrocities are committed on grand scale disregarding individual as target, then it becomes a case for protection of a social group from the social hazards emanating from anti-social elements. This calls for public Interest Litigation by non-individuals, but by voluntary agencies and NGOs. While addressing the august gathering on the occassion of 8th John Barnabas Memorial Lecture on Potential of Public Interest Litigation vis-a-vis Social Action Dimensions(1), V.R. Krishna Iyer, former Supreme Court Judge contended, unless we evolve remedies for ensuring realisation of Human Rights and relentlessly pursue them instead of merely talking about them from an elite platforms, Human Rights will remain merely a teasing illusion and a promise of unreality. Today, more than ever before, it is vitally more important to secure enforcement of Human Rights because there are millions in India, who are denied their rights rightly so, as long as this theme approach rests in the hands of the previledged class of people belonging to the Five-Star Culture, it will not be possible to make it action-oriented.

'The movement, so long it is getting surface treatment by those who hold some positions in such international platforms, it would remain as of ceremonial value for special occassions. The spotlight of Human Rights has to be turned on the half starving millions of our people for whom life is a long never ending vigil.'

It is a common experience that the advantages so far are being availed by those well-knit class of people, who are not only financially well off, better placed and highly aware of the redressal provided in such legal arrangement for their common cause and those who can seek social justice on the strength of collective approach. However, the situation is different when greivances of the pavement dwellers and others, or, for that matter tribals of the rural and forest areas are denied social justice simply because they are unorganised, resourceless and even unaware about their rights they possess belonging to human kingdom. His concern about pavement dwellers is, therefore, very apt and timely. Again to quote the Supreme Court Judge—"But how about the pavement dweller with no place to lay her bones or bear her baby just emerging from her womb asking for the human right to a shelter ? How about tens of thousands of tribal families in traumatic shock at the imminent prospect of displacement at gun point from ancestral habitat in the name of development and dams and Godavari canal which means to her homelessness today. How about thousands of humble bread winners dead and hundred thousand harrowing humans victimised by Bhopshima and Gassasination with life-giving justice nullified by the sophisticated legal rights of a mighty multinational ?"

Social justice has a big canvas to cover structurally and functionally both. How to prevent all sorts of atrocities on the helpless class of people, *viz.* the tribals, and other weaker sections of the society is a basic issue. It is not only the moneylenders, traders of the forest contractor(2), who are getting rich by grabbing income and properties from the exploited class of people, but even the government functionaries, big or small, all are no less than those others in this line. Even the white collar atrocities are nothing less than the wilful attempt to devastate the life of the have nots because they are insignificant in averting the potential atrocities. All sorts of malpractices prevalent in day-to-day life also add insult to injuries already sustained by the poorer section of the society. Even though the lands are restored to tribals by the decrees of the courts, their execution in practice is denied or delayed which practically means almost the same as justice delayed is justice denied. It is a very old and common-theory in vogue.

Social justice is the signature tune of Indian Constitution borne of right to equality, but it is time to examine objectively whether the same has been translated into practice by people at large[3]. It is the responsibility equally of the voluntary agencies to monitor, over which counts and in which situations, the entire purpose gets defeated when social justice is denied to people, who deserve that most. "The founding fathers of the Constitution stressed upon the delivery of social and economic justice to the most handicapped categories and to community generally. This had spawned Public Interest Litigation and Social Action Groups. But, in fact notwithstanding emphatic rhetoric in constitutional parchment, equal protection of laws and a just social order remained a paper project for the have not segments of the society.

"The rule of law is but a pleasing illusion, if the judicial process does not serve as delivery system of social justice in widest community spread. Litigation, the crucial modus-operandi for securing rights of citizens may well lose its curative potency vis-a-vis the indigents, agnostics and illiterates. For them it may survive for some time as the tantalising opium of remindial hope, if the court by its performance blesses the rich but betrays the poor."[4]

Role of Journalists in Arousing Awareness

Unlike the individual interest litigation, the applicant need not be the group of individuals or individual alone to file a writ petition for redressal in case of social grievances. For example, river waters of Shankhni and Dankni rivers of Dantewara *tehsil* of Bastar district of Madhya Pradesh were highly polluted with iron-ore-wash left-overs and were responsible to create health hazards to animal and man both. But the main damage was done to tribals who were drinking the polluted water without any alternate source of safe water. Due to lack of awareness, the tribals could not approach the court for redressal on the one hand, and being poor, they could not afford either. Here the offender was also a public undertaking, *i.e.*, Bailladila mine authorities. It could never occur to local people that a legal suit could be taken up to fight for the cause even against a public undertaking. Such situations can be cited in so many cases—Thanks to Nai Dunia, a Hindi daily of Indore city of Madhya Pradesh, which could take a lead in highlighting the ash-polluted waters by thermal power plant of Betul district of Madhya Pradesh, which helped in creating public consciousness against the big health hazards grown out of water pollution and air pollution. Once public opinion is aroused, it becomes easy to launch Public Interest Litigation against such social menace.

It is, therefore, very logical that social activists and Voluntary Organisations working among the deprived people and fighting for their amelioration, must challenge injustice on their behalf, both before the administration and the courts. Free legal aid plus Public Interest Litigations are aspects of people participation in the delivery of social justice. The courts have been overloaded with the routine type writ-petitions for longer periods. However, they can do a great deal in matters of Public Interest Litigations by taking their own initiative for the cause of the poor, the pariah, the protester, the *antyaja,* the rebel and the militant who seeks to fight the establishment because it destroys or damages our culture and our resources and very genetic justice to be borne in water and to eat food, which is not chemically contaminated but also must keep on pursuing the processes of securing actually the relief granted in decress and writs. The administration may demur, demonstrate, resist, thwart, even subvert. But the court must press on, invigilate, monitor, even mandate expenditure and infrastructure".[5]

The experience of free legal aid services, however are not very encouraging for the tribal people, who are approaching the concerned advocates. They get frustrated on their cold response, because they do not possess money, which could reinforce the sense of duty in the advocates connected with free legal aid programme. Reputed advocates can part with their income and can help the deprived people by wilful charity as social workers.

Atrocities on Tribals—A Growing Problem

Development of tribals without check on their exploitation and atrocities carries superfluous importance, because the tribals led the life of peace and happiness earlier, with limited wants and limited resources at their disposal. It is the civilized society that has bothered the down-trodden tribal society and the State and Union Government to develop the tribals in line with the so called civilized society, which is entirely dependent in the hands of the market economy and commercial production of agricultural and non-agricultural products. Settled farming on plough cultivation requires more land to feed the family and also calls for the transfer of tribal population from hill tops to the plains, where land is comparatively more in possession of settled farmers. Pressure on agricultural land has created land disputes on the higher side. Free gift of land to tribals has ingrained cut-throat competition, hence the stronger people have taken up the course of inflicting atrocities on tribal beneficiaries. As rightly held by Shri Murkot Rammunny (1992), "the atrocities on Scheduled Castes and Scheduled Tribes and other Backward classes are just the symptoms of a grave malaise that has afflicted them for centuries and which, instead of being alleviated since independence has been aggravated in many cases. The hopes and aspirations, which were aroused at the dawn of independence and not realized fully in four decades, seem to have made the wounds of injustice appear deeper than it was earlier". Annexure 2 & 3.

Voluntary Organizations to avert atrocities on ST, SC & OBC.

There are several voluntary organizations in India, working under the names of great man and top social workers of their days, namely Swami Vivekanand Asharam, Mata Rukamani Devi Ashram (Bastar), Bhartiya Adim Jati Sevak Sangh, New Delhi, Ramkrishna Mission, Harijan Sewak Sangh, Servants of India Society, etc., which were organized several decades back to create healthy awareness among the rural and down-trodden people of the urban areas with regard to social welfare activities, educational advancement and to promote healthy atmosphere to create a new egalitarian society where, equality and social justice have the rule and exploitation of the poor and helpless section of the society has to be eliminated. Public donations, collection of gifts and inheritance of the properties of the trusts, which sponsored such non-Govt. organizations are sources of their finances. These finances, however, remained below requirement of social works undertaken by these NGOs.

Role of Voluntary Organizations in Tribal Development (8th Plan)

Various evaluation reports of the Tribal Development Programmes implemented and their evaluation done by P.E.O. (Planning Commission) as well as the Commissioner for SC & ST of the past few years have depicted dismal picture of the performances of the governments, therefore, a sense of realization has been gathered to curb the ongoing mis-utilization of limited resources as well as the wrong direction of development.

The Working Group on Development and Welfare of the SC & ST during the 8th Plan (1990-95) has earmarked an outlay of Rs. 25 crores to finance the NGOs in the whole country under the centrally sponsored programmes (C.S.P.). Hitherto, under the Grant-in-Aid, programmes, such as running of *balwadis, chreches*, training-cum-production centres, functional literary centres, medical institutions, etc. have been covered, and the funds as per the norms determined earlier have been provided to organizations like Ramakrishna Mission, Bhartiya Adim Jati Sevak Sangh, Akhil Bhartiya Vikas Parishad and the Servants of India Society, etc. These are few of the well known NGOs of all India level engaged in the development and welfare work in remote tribal and rural areas.

New Vistas of the Tribal Development Works

It is attempted now to highlight some of the areas which need urgent attention of the NGOs' functions. Family oriented tribal development works have to be taken up in future by the NGOs which may raise the awareness of tribal farmers in improved agricultural practices, poultry farms, backyard poultry, goatry and piggery. The beneficiaries have to be selective from such tribal groups, who have no social stigma to adopt them.

Shifting cultivators mainly the 74 P.T.G. of India identified in 1989 have to be selected in each village, where the arable lands for these settled cultivator have to be identified with the Forest officials and the selected families of P.T.G. have to be rehabilitated in the nearest vicinity, so that their social fabric is not torn-out, as experienced in Machhalichhera Colony of shifting cultivator (Jhumias) of Tripura, and reported in a research report of Dr. Sarad Indu Bose, few decades back and Somany Housing and Colonization Programmes of Tribals taken up.

Bamboo ware-works have to be taken up among the Baiga P.T.G. of Madhya Pradesh, with adequate supply of Bamboo and necessary tools. The NGO will be required to collect the finished goods, transport and market it to the place where such products are demanded on commercial scale.

Small scale industries of the leaf plate and leaf bowls have be opened up in several village units in tribal areas, where the Baiga or other P.T.G. namely Birhor, Pahadi Korba, Saharia or Madia, Murla live in Madhya Pradesh. These production units will have to be managed by the NGO, who will distribute the profits to members of the unit—the P.T.G. will thus be involved directly. The MPCS or other cooperatives which were involved in such production programme and have failed to do so, will also be merged in such new units.

Rope making small units with manually operated machines have to be organised in remote village, where raw material such as Mowa-grass and/or Ketki plants are naturally available. The P.T.G. of particular locate will be involved in such units.

Local-handicraft, carpentry units need be organised by NGO invoking a set of given number of P.T.G., who will participate in the production work of handicrafts. NGO can organize trainer programme for the P.T.G. locally found and the trained tribals will then be required to join the production unit on a commercial scale. Marketing of the products has to managed by the NGO/Government.

Brick-klins have to be opened for the specific areas and villages where 'Indira Awas' Programme has to be taken up for the P.T.G. The deployment of locally available or migrated *kumhars* will be done to train the P.T.G. at the initial stage. The NGO will be held responsible to motivate the P.T.G. for the production unit.

Suggestions of Working Committee's on Development and Welfare of SC & ST during 8th Plan

Following suggestions have been made for implimentation during the 8th Five-Year Plan with my rejoinders for inclusion:

1. Identify voluntary agencies to work in tribal ar-

eas and to encourage them to operate in appropriate areas of activity.

Rejoinder—Here, it can be clarified that there should not be more than one NGO to take up the similar job in one locality to avoid unhealthy competition and leg pulling of each other, as commonly experienced.

2. Build up cadre of properly oriented trained voluntary workers and arrange orientation/training through organisations like-NIPCCID, New Delhi the Tribal Research Institute, etc.

Rejoinder—The NGOs themselves may be encouraged to arrange for the course of training as per the requirement for specific programme to be taken up in hand-tribal dialect-and its working knowledge will be an essential component of the training syllabus.

3. Include representation of the State Government as members of the Managing Committee of the voluntary organizations and of banks, if the project involves bank finances.

Rejoinder—For any development programme, earmarked for the P.T.G., it should be avoided to involve bank finances. P.T.G. does not understand banks rules and other legal formalities. The liability of bank loans would be ruinous to P.T.G. as they are much less monetized. They are almost illiterate and ignorant of bare facts of monetary dealings.

4. Determine the nature of participation of voluntary organization, give responsibility for implementing specific programmes and assure regular flow of financial assistance from the government.

Rejoinder—The NGO will be responsible to identify the local resource based programme, which should not be unfamiliar to local P.T.G. In the past, much of the attempts were to make fool of the legal provisions and take personal benefit. For example, in Udaipura village of Mandla tribal district which its located about 8-10km.

inside border, a Body Building (Bus & Trucks) workshop has been opened, where no tribal is employed in technical post. All workers are outsiders and vehicle chasis are being imported. Tax relief/subsidy was the reason for the selection of tribal area.

Here the industrialist is from U.P., raw material too is to be bought from outside, workers too are outsiders and local people/tribal hardly get employment as they are unqualified.

5. Review the scheme of grant-in-aid to voluntary organisation and further liberalise it so that new voluntary organisations working at State level may also be brought within the ambit of the scheme. This is necessary as there are several such organizations doing commendable work in the field and deserve encouragement.

Rejoinder—The newly organised voluntary organisation need not be encouraged, unless the old organization working there refuses to open its branch office and take up the work. This is important because new organisations may not only lack in necessary will and working experience, but will promote registration of superfluous NGO which may not have real motive to undertake social work and social services involved in new production unit/service units, etc. for the P.T.G. of that area/locality. It would be better to open more branches of the well established old voluntary organisations with capable network and manpower of social workers.

It is time, when major thrust has to be given to voluntary organization and pledge all hope in it, which have been frustrated with the bad experience gathered from the performances of joint and corporate sectors in the past. The grant-in-aid should be 100% of the cost of programme, fully auditable and subject to cross-checks. Provision of the 90% aid and 10% or 20% contribution from the NGO or public donations, promotes a malpractice of forced collection of donation/collection from lower functionaries and the petty social workers/employees of such voluntary organisation. This needs to be discouraged to ensure emancipation of tribals and encourage their participation.

REFERENCE

1. Organised by the National Institute of Public Cooperation and Child Development Sec-*NIPCCD News Letter* Vol. 10, No. 4, March-April 1990, coverage on Public Interest Litigation—A Potent Force for Achieving Human Rights.
2. M.L. Patel—Social Dimensions of Forest Development in *Vanyajati* Qly. Bharatiya Adimjati Sevak Sangh, New Delhi, April, 1968.
3. M.L. Patel—Social Justice and Economic Development, in *Research Journal of M.P. Economic Association,* Vol. III, No. 1, 1976, as shown in (1) above.
4. V.K. Krishna Iyer-Op. Cit. p.2.
5. Ibid. p.2.

Annexure-I

(As on 30th June, 1989)

Statewise Distribution of P.T.G. Households (In Decending Order)

S.No. State	Nos. P.T.G.	Nos. P.T.G. H.H.	Estimated Population	Name of P.T.G. 100 or less H.H.s
1. Madhya Pradesh	7	102362	511610	—
2. Maharashtra	3	40622	153010	—
3. Orissa	12	36144	180720	Birhor (20)
4. Bihar	9	33788	168940	—
5. Andhra Pradesh	12	21563	107815	—
6. Tripura	1	12935	64675	—
7. Gujarat	5	12101	60505	—
8. West Bengal	3	9378	46890	—
9. Rajasthan	1	7000	35000	—
10. Tamil Nadu	6	4000	20000	—
11. Karnataka	2	2652	13260	—
12. Uttar Pradesh	2	2074	10370	Raji (74)
13. Kerala	5	1624	8120	Cholanaikan (7) Kadar (66)
14. Manipur	1	908	4540	
15. A&N Islands	5	102	510	Great Andamanese-5, Jarwa (50) Sentenalese (10) Onge (19) Shompen (18)
15. All India	74	287253	About 15 lakhs @ 5 per H.H.	9 P.T.G.

Source : Based on Annexure V of Report of Working Group on Development and Welfare of SC & ST during 8th Plan 1990-95, Govt. of India etc.

Note : Table Nos. of P.T.G. identified now slightly exceeds 100 as per latest position of 1993.

Annexure-II

Table-A

(For Yrs. 1981-86)

Yearwise I.P.C. Crimes Against Tribals (National Level)

Year	Murder	Grievous hurt	Rape	Arson	Other offences	Total
1981	110	260	259	146	2,657	3,432
1982	133	320	256	132	3,761	4,102
1983	161	310	262	238	3,163	4,134
1984	171	348	312	132	3,327	5,190
1985	148	323	243	198	3,143	4,055
1986	160	311	285	232	2,957	3,945
Total	883	1,872	1,617	1,078	18,508	23,958

Source : Report of National Commission for SC & ST-Atrocities on SC & ST, Causes & Remedies, p. 55.

Annexure-III

Table-3

(For Year 1984)

Statewise and Comparative Statement of Atrocities on Tribals

No.	State	Murder	Violence	Rape	Arson	Other Offences
1.	Andhra	02	06	21	00	26
2.	Bihar	10	16	37	08	132
3.	Gujarat	08	28	09	01	68
4.	Karnataka	00	00	00	00	00
5.	Kerala	00	01	08	02	72
6.	M.P.	98	163	149	89	2218
7.	Maharashtra	09	17	24	04	105
8.	Orissa	03	05	15	02	03
9.	Rajasthan	14	60	11	10	299
10.	Tamil Nadu	00	00	01	00	03
11.	U.P.	00	00	00	00	00
12.	West Bengal	00	00	08	00	07
13.	A&N Island	00	00	00	00	03
14.	Arunachal Pradesh	00	00	00	01	29
15.	Dadara & Nagar Haveli	00	00	00	00	00
Total		144	296	283	123	2,965

Source : 7th Report of the Commission for SC & ST, 1984-85, G.O.I., p. 31.

Annexure-IV

LIST OF TRIBAL RESEARCH INSTITUTES

1. Tribal Cultural Research & Training Institute, Government of Andhra Pradesh, Telugu-Samkshema Bhavan, III Floor, Masab Tank, Hyderabad.

2. Dr. B.N. Bardoloi, Director, Assam Institute of Research for Tribal and Sch. Castes, Jawahar Nagar, N.H. 3 D. Guwahati-22.

3. Tribal Welfare Research Institute, Government of Bihar, Morabadi Road, Ranchi.

4. Tribal Research & Training Centre, Gujarat Vidyapith, Government of Gujarat, Ahmedabad.

5. Kerala Institute for Research, Training & Development, Studies of Scheduled Castes & Scheduled Tribes, Government of Kerala, Kozhikode.

6. M.P. Tribal Research and Development Institute, Government of Madhya Pradesh, 35, Shyamla Hills, Bhopal.

7. Tribal Research Institute, Government of Maharashtra, 28, Queens Road,Pune.

8. Tribal & Harijan Research-cum-Training Institute, Government of Orissa, Bhubaneshwar.

9. Tribal Research & Training Institute, Government of Rajasthan, Udaipur.

10. Tribal Research Centre, Tamil University, Missionary Hill, Uthagamandlam. Tamil Nadu.

11. Tribal Research Institute, Directorate of Harijan & Social Welfare, Government of Uttar Pradesh Lucknow.

12. Cultural Research Institute SC & ST Department, Govt. of West Bengal, PI/4, C.I.T. Scheme, VII, M.V.I.P. Road, Maniktala, Calcutta.

13. Tribal Research Institute, Govt. of Manipur, Imphal.

7. Tribal Research & Training [illegible], Bhopal.

12

The Subsistence Academics Of Indian Political Anthropology

A.C. Sinha

An anthropologist, whether a reluctant colonial or a radical activist, is intensely humanist and an explorer. He invariably follows a lonely trail, and in the process reaches isolated, archaic, exotic and at times a vanishing tribe. With the on-set of mass transportation and communication, discoveries, explorations and even adventures have become tamed affairs. However, anthropologists continue to be attracted to the unique institutions of the relatively small and isolated communities for their studies. And that is how a number of monographs are published on various institutions of such communities of the world. Among many others, anthropologists are interested in the political power and politics of the tribes and they have evolved a sub-discipline of their own, political anthropology. In this paper, firstly, we propose to comment on the nature of political anthropology as such. Secondly, we shall endeavour to examine the writings of political anthropologists in India. And lastly, we intend to explain the reasons for lack of a concerned and authentic political anthropology in India. Our limited exploration through the writings of Indian Anthropologists takes us to an unflattering conclusion that what is claimed as political anthropological research is something like a subsistence academics, which passes off unnoticed.

Political anthropology, a sub-division of social anthropology, is concerned with description and analysis of the political system proper in societies regarded as primitive or archaic. David Easton did not find it existent in 1959, though he found anthropologists working on political matters pertaining to simpler societies (Easton D., 1959). He hastened to add that political institutions and practices were viewed as independent variables for their effects on other institutions and practices of the society of which they were part. He took pains to examine the *African Political System* (Fortes, M. and E.E. Evans Pritchard, 1940) in which 'political activity has relevance only for the preservation of the social order whether for good or for ill'. For example, Radcliff-Brown's Weberian functional bias was reflected in formulation of political activity as 'the organised exercise of coersive authority through the use or the possibility of the use of physical force relating to order in a unique way'. Thus, in Radcliff-Brownian formulation politics is identified as a function of a society, and not as a structural mechanism.

Charging anthropology for its failure in transcending the ethnocentric limits of the post Western political conceptualization, Easton found its major pre-occupation with the collection of data about political systems to help in the development of a useful typology. For such an exercise, exploration of the conditions under which varying degrees of differentiation arise is desirable: "To what extent, for example, does differentiation vary with the size of the society with its ethnic composition; with its mode of subsistence; with the frequency, volume and types of demands made; with the nature of communication network; with the technical requirements for implementation of decisions; with the general attitudes towards authority, with social structure as evidenced in kinship and other kinds of relationships; with the types of personalities prevalent in the society; and with accessibility to the physical means for usurption, rebellion and the conquests. These variables add up to the physical, social and psychological setting in which a political system must operate and to which it will respond." (Easton, D. 1959 : 243).

A decade after Abner Cohen found Easton's verdict on political anthropology irresponsible and damaging and charged him of misunderstanding the nature of the chosen theme (Cohen, A. 1969). It was mainly because of the fact that Easton ignored the vital point that political anthropology happens to be a branch of social anthropology, whose traditional subject matter has been 'isolated small society' tackled through 'holistic' approach. As such societies are undergoing fundamental political change, social anthropology is re-examining its aims, methods and significant questions on the nature of relationship between political science and social (political) anthropology: What can they learn from each other ? And what kind of division of labour and cooperation can be developed between them ?

The major interest of social anthropologists is not in one-sided effect of politics or non-political institutions. They generally seek to explain these non-political institutions in terms of political relations, as these symbolic institutions are largely rooted in the unconscious mind. The social anthropologist, by analysing the symbols of power relationships in small scale, pre-industrial societies has gained a great deal of insight into the symbolism of power relationships generally. "Anthropological analysis of symbols involved in development, organization and maintenance of various types of kinship relationships, of marriage, friendship, patron-client relationships, corporate political groupings, ritual and of different systems of stratification, can give the political scientists working in industrial society significant concepts and hypotheses for analysing a whole range of informal political groupings and informal relationships" (Cohen, A. 1969: 228). These aspects have profound bearing on the term 'political culture' currently fashionable in political science. On the other hand, social anthropologists have ignored the importance of the modern state in the study of politics of small communities, a phenomenon besides concept of power, which has been a central theme for political scientists.

George Balandier, author of one of the earliest text books on political anthropology identified three principal claims of political anthropology: (i) a determination of the 'political' that limits it neither to 'historical' societies alone, nor to the existence of a State apparatus, (ii) an elucidation of the processes of the formation and transformation of political system by means of research parallel with that of historian; and (iii) comparative study, apprehending the different expressions of political reality, not within the limits of a particular history, but in its entire historical and geographical expression (Balandier, G. 1967 : 4-5). For him political anthropology led to decentralization and had broken the spell that state had long exerted on political theorists. It imposes a more dynamic conception favourable to consideration of history and conscious of strategies which any society (even an archaic one) must bear within itself. It also leads to a more critical consideration of the ideological systems by which traditional societies explain themselves and justify their specific order. It has collaborated widely in the critical work in dissociating political theory and the theory of the State. Such collaborations also reveal the by-ways of politics, which are present in the least organised societies and in situations least favourable to its emergence. "All human societies produce politics and none are resistant to the historical process", (Balandiers, G. 1967 : 196). Lucy Mair, looking back on the course of development in political anthropology since 1940, confidently asserts : "We have come a long way, so far that some anthropologists, particularly in America, salute the pioneers only to repudiate them. *African Political System* was a bench mark, but now-a-days we order things better." (Mair, L. 1975 : 8).

Coming to the Indian situation, way back in the aftermath of the revolt of 1857, some British officials made efforts to look into more closely at the structure of Indian society, to discover how it was being changed by imperial policy and to construct a theory of Indian social development based on the methods employed by the early anthropolgists (Oven, R. 1973 : 203). Alfred Lyall, one of the most influential men within the empire and in a position to make sure that his ideas did not go unregarded, used comparative method and anthropological concepts to project his notion of India. His efforts were aimed at maintaining differences rather than to attempting to create uniformity within the Indian society.

Anthropology, as such was introduced in the Indian academic establishment in 1920, but it remained inconsequential till 1950's. There were early individual Indian anthropologists such as S.C. Roy, L.K.A. Ayer, Hiralal, etc. who wrote under the patronage of the colonial administrators and even some of them were charged with pro-British leanings (Singh, K.S. 1984). Those of the few Indians, who went abroad for higher education in anthropology, went to the University of Cambridge. It was because among many, one of the reasons was that two British Indian administrators, T.C. Hodson and J.H. Hutton, were employed as senior faculty members after their superannuation in the department of Social Anthropology. We have shown elsewhere (Sinha, A.C. 1988) the prevalence of pre-functionalist academic trends up 1950 at the Cambridge, which were imbibed by the Indian anthropologists. Not for nothing that on the whole "anthropology was a suspect as nationalist opinion regarded it as an instrument of colonial policy, either to create divisions among Indians or to keep sections of them insulated from nationalist force" (Srinivas, M.N. *et al.* 1986 : 34). In such a situation no anthropologist thought it worthwhile to undertake the study of politics of an Indian tribe.

Tribes and tribal areas were treated as a special preserve of the colonial administrators in a typical paternalistic style. At times, they were accorded the special attention that a handicapped child in the family is often singled out for. It were the anthropologists besides the administrators and the missionaries, who diagnosed the uniqueness of the tribes with a view to, setting them apart from 'others'. Naturally, 'others' perceived the anthropologists as the hand in glove in the decisive designs of the British. Soon after the Independence, the anthropologists identified themselves once again with the new regime with all eagerness and expectation. It was but a natural response to which no one should impute any ulterior motives. And they were not disappointed in their expectations. They were offered positions in the Anthropological Survey of India, Tribal Research Institutes, Community Development Projects, Tribal Development Blocks and the Assam State Administration under the tutelage of the Anthropological Adviser to the Governor. That was also the time when the development administration was pushing its effective control to the tribal frontier areas in the North-East, which had remained relatively isolated in the past.

What came out of the above development was reflected idealistically as the *Tribal Panch Shila* (Five Fundamental Principles) in which the author of the Philosophy, (Elwin, V. 1957) called himself 'a missionary of the Prime Minister's gospel', who in return paid the compliments by acknowledging the influence of late Jawaharlal Nehru on him. These principles in course of time enlisted enthusiastic proponents and die-hard critics. This is not an appropriate occasion to review and assess them, but we would like to comment on the implications of the very first principle of the *Panch Shila*: 'People (tribes) should develop along the lines of their own genius and we should avoid imposing anything on them'. Have the administration, policy makers, tribals themselves and all the more—anthropologists—been able to identify the various facets of the special genius of the tribals—ideal for their development, which are distinctively 'tribal', setting them apart from 'others' ? Or is it a simple liberal platitude of an idealist humanist mind removed from the stark reality of practical life ? Or is it reflective of the political context exposing the ambiguity inherent in the Indian national approach to the ethnic minorities ?

A recent political analysis comes closest to the above scenario. "On the one hand, this frame (the Indian national approach to tribes) wants to preserve the uniqueness, distinctiveness and individuality of tribal systems. On the other hand, it wants them to come into the national stream. The assumption is that they can and want to transform themselves meaningfully because that would threaten the colonial order. The problem was simply reduced to one of law and order. If they left the colonial order undisturbed, let them be undisturbed. If they did threaten *Pax Brittanica,* then the system sent armed forces to handle the problem. The political ambiguities inherent in our outwardly humanitarian position have led to our inability to articulate clearly political frame. Thus, systematic study of the political structures and processes of the tribal societies has not come to be really seriously cultivated" (Rao, K.R.

Raghvendra, 19: 1986). Not for nothing that emerging tribal scholars find four decades old efforts of 'developing' them as actually leading to 'decay' in their social fabric (Aeir, L. 1986). This undoubtedly has to be attributed to the vagueness built in to our perspective on tribal societies and their political systems.

The African continent was the scene for the British social anthropologists for their major studies based on intensive field work between the two World Wars. Of the two leading lights of the structural-functional anthropology in Britain, Radcliffe-Brown taught briefly at Capetown, while Malinowski travelled to Africa pleading for an increasing role for anthropologists in the colonial set-up vis-a-vis the tribes (James, W. 1973 : 61). Their presence in Africa, though brief, did stimulate publication of a number of monographs on religion, kinship, marriage and family, customary laws, land tenure, barter and trade, political system and even social change. Their contributions were acknowledged in various ways, specially what came to be termed as political anthropology in course of time was decidedly African in its origin. With a possible exception of Edmund Leach, who worked on politics of Highland Burma, no other social anthropologist claimed to have studied the politics of a tribe by then. So far India was concerned, by the time Easton wrote his famous piece on political anthropology, no Indian anthropologist had claimed to have worked on the political system of an Indian tribe in the conventional 'holistic' manner.

It is not that no efforts were made to study the politics of the tribal communities. In fact, certain works reminiscent of the search for the origin and re-interpretation of the Hindu polity and the Indo-Aryan aspects were undertaken in 1920's by Beni Prasad, R.P. Chanda, and others. However, though efforts were made to study tribal economy (Pant, S.D. 1935), religion (Roy, S.C. 1921), culture, etc. no full length monograph was devoted to the study of tribal politics *per se.* It can also not be claimed that the tribes were restive. In fact, all over from the Burmese frontiers in the North-East, to the Afghan borders on the North-West and to Southern, tribes of the Deccan Peninsula had risen on the various forms of protests, uprising and revolts.

In all fairness though, it must be mentioned that politics of the tribes was not completely ignored by the anthropologists, who did write on various facets of the tribal politics since 1950's. Firstly, during the hey days of the village studies, factionalism at various levels was one of the dominant orientations in the study of tribes and castes. Secondly, political transformation of an ethnic group into a policy or formation of the State system was undertaken by a number of anthropologists (Sinha, S.C. 1962 : 1987, Mahapatra, L.K. 1970 : 1976, Sinha, A.C. 1985 and 1987). Recently, Surajit Sinha has edited a significant volume (Sinha, S.C. 1987) on the tribal politics and State systems in which historians and political scientists contributed besides the anthropologists. Thirdly, anthropologists along with historians, political scientists, sociologists and political activists wrote on various types of tribal movements (Singh, K.S. 1982; Goswami, B.B. 1979). Fourthly, studies on leadership, electoral participation and party politics among the tribals were also made. All these aspects were significant in their own ways, but not one of them could receive the treatment of a full length monograph on a tribe.

Among the studies of politics through holistic approach F.G. Bailey, though not an Indian anthropologist, stimulated a generation of anthropologists through his studies on Bisipara, a Khond village in Orissa (1956, 1957 and 1959). He not only provided an authentic ethnography on the Khonds of Phulbani district but also examined the changing economic frontiers of the village and the political interactions of the tribals in terms of various neighbouring castes extended to the province and ultimately to the national context. A second study in this context was that of the *Political System of Jats* (Pradhan, M.C. 1966) in which caste, clan and lineage of an important caste were examined in terms of politics of Uttar Pradesh. A third study in this tradition is that of the A. Beteille's on caste, class and politics of Sripuram, a Tamil village (Beteille, A. 1966). A fourth one is that of Richard Fox's analysis on State hinterland relations in pre-industrial eastern Uttar Pradesh (Fox, R.G. 1971). And lastly, Sinha's study of elite and political development in terms of nation-building efforts in theocratic Sikkim (Sinha, A.C. 1975).

Among the studies mentioned above, only Bailey's works on Bisipara fall strictly in the typical anthropological tradition of micro study through holistic approach on an 'isolated' tribe. Beteille's study comes just next to Bailey's approximation in terms of the above criteria, but it is not the study of a tribe. Pradhan, Fox and Sinha's studies are not strictly microscopic in the typical anthropologist tradition. Moreover, they addressed themselves to more evolved non-tribal political systems at the regional levels. In this context, even Bailey's analysis and linkage of Bisipara extends beyond the village, region, and the province to the nation.

Nobody can possibly prescribe a fixed agenda for the future researches on the basis of the past models for all the time. In fact, it is desirable that anthropologists should choose their subject matter keeping in mind the changing times in a vast country like ours. They may innovate their strategy on research method depending on the demands of their chosen themes; and they may also evolve a complex conceptual model to analyse their data. The point is not that every anthropologist must replicate an *'African Political System'* for his chosen study. The issue to be examined is that of carrying studies on the politics of tribes in anthropological tradition by trained anthropologists. And in this context, one fails to understand why there is not a single monograph on the politics of an Indian tribe during the last eight decades. And one need not have to go very far to look for the reasons.

With the coming of the Independence the handful of available anthropolgists came handy to the new regime for their expertise on the tribal affairs. Besides their authentic, intensive and microscopic field work, the intense humanism of the discipline in terms of applied and action anthropologies attracted attention of the State. And thus, some anthropologists got engaged in the formulation of tribal welfare and development policies as well as in the implementation of programmes. In between the monographs were being published on the classical synchronic model and in 1950's non-tribal villages were studied through the 'holistic' approach as if they were tribal 'isolates'. Meanwhile, the discipline was expanding; new departments in the newly established Universities were opened; new research institutions were started. Consequently, demands for anthropologists' expertise were on increase steadily.

The craft of social anthropology in India has to address itself to certain relevant issues. In case the discipline insists, which it should do, that simpler (tribal) societies continue to be its central object of study, it must analyse the various aspects of tribal political dimension that have hitherto received attention. Naturally, anthropologists should be aware of the status of the tribals in the Indian political system as a marginal entity, who rarely influence the course of national politics in a decisive and meaningful way. Another important issue may be that anthropologists should ponder over nature of their discipline. In their humanistic concern for doing good to the 'tribes' through their expertise of action and applied anthropology, they are bound to strike liaison between the State and the tribe, which invariably ends in favour of the State. Not necessarily one has to take up the cause of the tribes in extreme political situation as suggested by Kathaeen Gough (Gough, K. 1968). However, no one would deny the possibility of conflicting situations between the State sponsored nation building programmes and tribal techno-economic requirements. In such a situation, the anthropologists have to ask themselves: Have they analysed the political economy of the tribal developments enunciated by the Central Government ? In what ways their special constitutional status is being affected by their sheltered course of development prescribed by the existing mixed economy ? Is it going on the prescribed criteria of the genius of the individual tribes ? In the changed dominant values of 'development' and 'modernization' what specific contributions are they going to make in the nation-building of the emergent Indian plural polity ?

Anthropological writings in India, by and large, present a situation which is far from satisfactory. Political anthropology is rarely taught as an independent paper in Indian Universities. Not many anthropologists claim to have specialized in this branch and those who claim to have some interests in the politics of the tribes, write stray articles. Very limited concerned efforts have been made in this regard. Anthropology continues to be a marginal discipline among the established disciplines as its thrust and, thus, identity is counted in humanities, social sciences and natural sciences. The anthropologist, who studies the exotic, primitive, distant and marginal communities himself remains marginal in the national academic establishment. The students who offer to join the course are not among the better than an average stock. In such a situation what comes out in the name of anthropology rarely leads to a national debate; rarely influences the national course of academic thinking and much less determines the national policies even relating to its own claimed preserve—the tribes. A few of the anthropologists, who were associated with formulation and implementation of tribal policies in 1950's, appear to be exceptions. It seems anthropologists carefully avoided uncovering the political aspects of tribal scenario. Thus, what is claimed and known as political anthropology in India is an apology for a serious academic exercise. In fact, what we do in the name of political anthropology, and to a lesser extent even for anthropology in general, is a type of subsistence academics, which passes off unnoticed.

REFERENCES

1. Aier, L. 1986. "Naga Social Formation: A Case of Development or Decay", Ph. D. Thesis, Department of Sociology, NEHU, Shillong. MSS
2. Bailey, F.G. 1956. *Caste, Tribe and Nation,* Manchester University Press.
3. Bailey, F.G. 1957. *Caste and Economic Frontier,* Manchester University Press.
4. Bailey, F.G. 1959. *Politics of Social Change: Orissa in 1959,* Berkeley, Los Angeles, University of California Press.
5. Beteille, A. 1966. *Caste, Class and Power,* OUP, Bombay.
6. Balandier, G. 1967. *Anthropologie Politique,* Presses Universities de France, Paris.
7. Cohen, A. 1969. "Political Anthropology: The Analysis of the Symbolism of Power Relations", *Man,* New Series, Vol. 4.
8. Easton, D. 1959. "Political Anthropology:" *Biennial Review of Anthropology,* (ed.) B.J. Siegel, Stanford University Press.
9. Elwin, V. 1957. *A Philosophy for NEFA,* Adviser to the Governor of Assam, Shillong.
10. Fortes, M. and E.E. Evans Pritchard, 1940. *African Political System,* OUP.
11. Fox, R.G. 1971. *Kin, Clan, Raja and Rule,* University of California Press and OUP, Bombay.
12. Gough, K. 1968. *Current Anthropology,* Vol. 9.
13. James, W. 1973. "Anthropologist as Reluctant Imperialist" in *Anthropology and Colonial Encounter* (ed.), T. Asad, Ithaca Press.
14. Goswami, B.B. 1979. *Mizo Unrest,* Aalekh Publications, Jaipur.

15. Mair, L. 1975. "How Far Have We Got in the Study of Politics ?" in *Studies in African Social Anthropology* (ed.) Fortes, M. Academic Press, London.
16. Mahapatra, L.K. 1970. Transformation of Tribal Society, UGC National Lectures, MSS.
17. Mahapatra, L.K. 1976. "Gods, Kings and Caste System in India" in, A. Bharati (ed.) *Realm of the Extra-Human Agents and Audience*, Mouton & Co., Paris.
18. Oven, R. 1973. "Imperial Policy and Theories of Social Change" in *Anthropology and Colonial Encounter* (ed.) T. Asad, Ithaca Press.
19. Pant, S.D. 1935. *Social Economy of Polyandry*, Allen & Unwin.
20. Pradhan, M.C. 1966. *Political System of Jats of Northern India*, OUP, Bombay.
21. Rao, K.R. 1986. "Political Anthropology in India", MSS Seminar on "Relevance of Anthropology Today", Department of Anthropology, Karnatak University, Dharwar.
22. Ray, S.C. 1921. "Oraon Religion and Customs", *Man in India*, Ranchi.
23. Singh, K.S. 1982. *Tribal Movements in India*, Manohar, New Delhi.
24. Singh, K.S. 1984. "Colonialism, Anthropology and Primitive Society: The Indian Scenario", *Man in India*, Vol. 64 (4).
25. Sinha, A.C. 1975. *Politics of Sikkim*, Thompson Press, Faridabad.
26. Sinha, A.C. 1987. "Frontier Feudalism and State Formation in Sikkim", in *Tribal Politics and State Systems* (ed.) S. Sinha.
27. Sinha, A.C. 1988. "Indian Social Anthropology and its Cambridge Connections in 1940's", MSS.
28. Sinha, S.C 1962. "State Formation and Rajput Myth in Tribal Central India", *Man in India*, Vol. 42 (i).
29. Sinha, S.C. 1987 (ed.) *Tribal Polities and State Systems in Pre-Colonial: Eastern and North-Eastern India*. K.P. Bagchi & Co., Calcutta.
30. Srinivas, M.N. *et al*. 1986. "Development of Sociology and Social Anthropology in India" in *Indian Sociology: Reflections and Introspections* (ed.) Oomann, T.K. *et al*., Popular Prakashan, Bombay.

13

Land Alienation : Causes and Consequences Among the Tribals Of South Bastar

A.R.N. Srivastava

This paper is an anthropological investigation into the phenomenon of land problem in a tribal region in Dantewara *tehsil* of the district of Bastar in Madhya Pradesh against a background which is changing fast under the pressures generated by a large public undertaking mining project, the Bailadila Iron Ore Project (BIOP). The study is primarily based on on-the-spot studies of the tribal life in its socio-economic aspect and takes note of the impact of the new forces generated by the BIOP on the natives of the region in general and on their land alienation in particular.

The methology of the present paper includes "the case-study approach". This approach as prevalent in anthropological inquiry entails in-depth analysis of the phenomenon under investigation. The field work was

* The present paper was presented in the Seminar on Agrarian Structure and Land Reforms in India organized in Nov. 1987 by G.B. Pant Social Science Institute, Allahabad. In a revised form it was published in *The Eastern Anthropologist*, Vol. 41, No. 4 (1988).

directed in ten non-randomly selected villages of Dantewara *tehsil* over a period of nine months between 1982 and 1984 as a part of research assignment sponsored by the Ministry of Home Affairs, Govt. of India. The tools employed were mainly informal interviews, participant observation and schedule-filling in the sample villages. In addition, available informations on land and people of the area under study were also a major sources of data collection.

Bailadila Mining Project

The National Mineral Development Corporation of India (NMDC) acting on behalf of the Government of India signed an agreement with the Japan Steel Mills for assistance to explore the Bailadila iron-ore reserves and to export iron-ore to Japan via Vishakhapatnam. The activities started in 1961 included the construction of road, building up of two townships, construction of crushing and screening plants needed to prepare iron-ore of requisite size, tunnel to run loading belt, erection of machines and other items required for the fully mechanized mining. Side by side, S.E. Railway began constructing a railway line, 470 km. long, in order to run ore-cargo for its onward shipment to Japan. The entire project cost was around Rs. 500 crores. Finally, in November, 1968 the plant was put into action first at Kirandul (known as Deposit No. 14), and second at Bacheli (Deposit No. 5) which is only 8 kms. from the first site.

This project is Asia's largest mechanized system and it brought the Bastar district, which before 1965 had remained almost isolate, on the economic map of the country. Bailadila has the best quality of iron-ore. Currently over 25 lakh tonnes iron-ore is produced at Kirandul alone and the project is the largest single foreign exchange earning unit in the country.

Unlike Bihar and Orissa where heavy industrial

mining complexes are at work in the tribal areas, the Bailadila project did not cause the uprooting of native and local population except for some land for laying rail-road. The entire project area comes under the jurisdiction of 'Reserve Forests'. It was taken for granted, as seen elsewhere in India, that the local problems will be minimized and tackled in course of project activities. With availability of skilled workers and electric power and in the name of National Economic Development, *i.e.* regional development, the Central Government with the assistance of State Govenment took responsibility of entreprenual skills.

Land Alienation in Tribal Regions

The alienation of lands, both in rural and tribal regions of the country, has been continuing for a long time, though it has been considerably checked by the promulgation of the Scheduled Areas Regulations in various States from time to time. There is, however, divergence of views regarding the extent of land alienation in the tribal areas. Some are inclined to believe that it has taken place on an extensive scale, especially in those regions where large scale industrial-mining complexes are at work. The real situation in this respect may be ascertained only after a comprehensive survey by the State Government. It is a well known fact that surveys and settlement operations are a time consuming job. For the present we may have some idea from the isolated studies completed by individual researchers and organizations.

In order to know the dimension of the problem in some details, the present author made efforts to examine the impact of the Bailadila project on the land-based economy of the tribals of Dantewara, one of the six *tehsils* of the district Bastar. Bastar occupies a very important place not only on the economic map of the country but also the tribal map. Spread over 39,000 sq.

km., it is located in the extreme south of the State. About 42 per cent of its area is under forest. The tribals contitute 72 per cent of the total population of the district which was 1.84 million in the 1981 count. The density of population is 47 per square km. The total labour force for the tribal population in the district in 1971 was 5,56, 212 (about 37 per cent) of which 67 per cent are cultivators, 22 per cent agricultural labourers and the rest, a very small number, are engaged in other occupations.

Pattern of Landholdings in Bastar

Among the tribals of Bastar the percentage of landholdings by size is presented in Table 1. It is evident there from that the total landholdings in the district is 1,58,063 hectares out of which 1,10,502 or 70 per cent belong to the tribals. Analysis of data in this respect reveals that 67 per cent of the holdings are below 5 hectares. Further, about 50 per cent of the tribal households have less than 3 hectares, 3 per cent between 20 and 30 hectares and hardly 2 per cent have holdings larger than 30 hectares.

We may now examine the situation in Dantewara *tehsil*, spread over 2,0203 sq. kms. including an area of 43.8 sq. kms. classified in 1971 as urban. Before 1971 the entire *tehsil* was hundred per cent rural-tribal dominated area. Urban population emerged because of the creation of townships at two places, *viz.* Kirandul and Bacheli near the project sites. Bastar is famous for rich stock of natural resources and Dantewara contributes a lot to this. Bailadila hills alone contain over 36,000 million tonnes of iron-ore (NCAER 1960).

The total population of the *tehsil* in the 1981 count was 194,977 as compared to 172, 174 in 1971 showing a growth rate of 13.23 per cent over the decade. Before the opening of the BIOP there were, as per 1961 census, 1,34,148 people in Dantewara of which 82.45 per cent were tribals. In 1971, the percentage of tribals came down to 73 per cent. Density of population in rural Dantewara has increased from 62 (1961) to 82 (1981). In urban area it is 204 to 352 (1971-81). The sex ratio for 1971, rural and urban population are 998 and 653 respectively. Literacy rate is extremely poor in Dantewar: just 1.24 per cent tribals were literates as compared to 4.23 per cent tribals in Bastar and 17.2 per cent in M.P. The literacy rate for rural Dantewara was 5.84. Among the tribals, Dandami Maria (a section of the large Gond tribe), Halba, Bhattra, Kawar and Dorla are the main tribes.

The bases of subsistence of tribal population are agriculture, forest produce and occasional agro-labour. In 1961 about 50 per cent of the tribal population was classified as workers: of these 82 per cent were agriculturist, 8.42 per cent agricultural labourer, 2.36 per cent forestry, and 4 per cent were involved in mining and quarrying. In 1971, the working tribal population came down to 43 per cent. Of these, 77 per cent were agriculturalist, 9.80 per cent were agriculture labourer and 11 per cent were engaged in mining and quarrying. In other words, economically dependent population in Dantewara increased from 41 per cent to 57 per cent; also there was decrease in the percentage of workers following cultivation.

Besides the internal growth of population, the increase in growth rate, change in the patterns of livelihood, sex-ratio and density of population can be safely attributed to the opening of the project.

Table 1
Distribution of Landholdings in Bastar

Size of holdings in Hectares	% of total number of holdings (N=110,502)
2-0.5	12.6
0.5-1.0	10.0
1.0-2.0	14.0

Size of holdings in Hectares	% of total number of holdings (N=110,502)
2.0-3.0	12.4
3.0-4.0	9.1
4.0-5.0	8.1
5.0-10.0	17.6
10.0-20.0	10.5
20.0-30.0	2.7
Above 30	2.2
Total 1,58,063	100

Source: Deptt. of Statistics Land Records, M.P. (Bhopal).

Causes of Land Alienation

The general causes of alienation of lands are well known. Most of the lands, particularly uplands are not very fertile; therefore, the tribals find them no longer useful for livelihood. Besides, addiction to drink quite often leads the tribals into hardship. He has to alienate more and more land to maintain his family. Indebtedness, lured by the moneylenders who have eyes on tribal lands is another major cause. Tribals are simple people; their ignorance of complicated laws and other operations have been instrumental in accelerating the process of land alienation. Finally, some of the developmental schemes also had adverse effects on the tribals, because people from outside infiltrated into the tribal areas in search of job etc.

Methods of Land-Alienation

Let us briefly examine the process through which land alienation has been going on among tribals under investigation. First, there are some legal methods, *viz.* the provision in the State laws of M.P. relating to tribal lands, Section 165(6) of the M.P. Land Revenue Code of 1959 disallows transfers of lands between tribals and non-tribals. But the available data (cases) that we shall examine here brings out a large number of valid and invalid transfers. Similar is the law noted under section 250(1) of the M.P. Land Revenue Code of 1952.

Briefly stated the provision under section 165(6) of the 1959 Code is that "notwithstanding anything in sub-section (1), the right of a *Bhumiswami* belonging to a tribe...shall not be transferred to a person not belonging to such a tribe without the permission of a Revenue Officer, not below the rank of a Collector, for reasons to be recorded in writing".

Section 170(1) of the M.P. Land Revenue Code, 1959 further states: "Where possession is transferred by a *Bhumiswami* in pursuance of a transfer which is in contravention of sub-section (6) of section 165, any person who, if he survives the *Bhumiswami* without nearer heirs, would inherit the holding, may, within two years of such transfer of possession, apply to the S.D.O. to be placed in possession so far as the S.D.O. may determine, subject to his acceptance of the liabilities, far arrears of land revenue or any other dues which form a charge on the holding."

The above clause appears to be defective since the provision gives an enormous scope to non-tribals to grab the lands of tribals.

Similarly, sections 168(1) and 169 of the Code are also defective for non-tribals are in a position to circumvent the relevant sections by stalling the presentation of an application by a tribal within two years of his dispossession.

In order to examine the results of the operation of above code, in the present study efforts were directed to analyze the available cases recorded in the official files over a period of 10 years. The categorized cases are indicated in Table-2. This table shows that Collectors granted permissions to a little less than 50 per cent of the applicants. The rate of legal transfer of land, in above cases, during the period 1966-1975 was 52.78 per cent while during 1975-80 it was 21.14 per cent. A total of over 1700 hectres of land passed into the hands of non-tribals.

Table 2

Disposal of Applications Related to Transfer of Lands from Tribals to Non-tribals

Year	*Total number of applications received*	*No. of cases granted by Collector*	*Total Area sold*
1966-70	554 (28%)	274	347 hect.
1970-75	1107 (56%)	574	901 "
1975-80	299 (15%)	101	520 "
Total	1960 (100)	949	1768 "

Note: During the year 1979-80 about 29 cases were under consideration.

Source : Dantewara Tehsil Records.

The second mode of valid transfer is the sale of a tribal's holding in order to recover cooperative dues. Data on this could not be collected, but according to a rough estimate by this author from different sources including cooperative banks, it was found that during the period 1972-76 about 70 defaulter tribals paid the dues by disposing of their land to the banks. A sum of Rs. 65,000 was realized out of 18 such holdings. In all these cases the land was purchased by the non-tribals. It is to be noted that only about half of this amount was actually due from the defaulters.

According to a study completed in Dantewara *tehsil* by a government organization the average annual rate of transfers from the tribals to non-tribals is 127 hectares with the Collector's permission and 10 hectares by way of sale for recovery of dues.

The above picture is that of legally transferred lands from tribals to non-tribals. It does not present a true picture of the size of land alienation because in many cases the transfers to non-tribuls take place illegally and are unidentified by the existing legal codes.

Illegal Modes of Land Alienation

In order to understand the extent of illegal transaction of tribal land, its cause and consequences, the author directed his efforts to Dantewara tehsil in which the situation is most alarming primarily due to opening of BIOP complex.

Before the related data are presented, let us first see some of the modalities of illegal transfers in Dantewara. It may be noted that these ingenious and fraudulent modes are also prevalent in other parts of Bastar district. The modalities and their extent as reported by the villagers occasionally recorded in the First Information Reports lodged with the local police as well as in the files of Patwari (recorder of land details) of the area are :

		Cases	
		No.	Percentage
1.	Non-tribals in possession of land as the tribals had taken a loan from them	11	14
2.	Sale in the name of non-tribals' servants who are tribals	9	11
3.	Forcible occupation	17	21
4.	Occupation by non-tribals after desertion by the tribals	4	6
5.	Purchases falsely showing the caste of purchasers as tribal	4	5
6.	Unauthorized sales	30	38
7.	Oral transactions	3	4
	Total	179	100

It is crucial to note that these 179 cases were reported from ten sample villages alone. This indicates the alarming situation of landloot phenomenon. An attempt was made to classify the cases into two phases : before the opening the BIOP in 1962, and after 1962. Because of the unavailability of past records in govt. files, the position during pre-BIOP days could not be ascertained. Certainly, some cases did exist earlier because some outsiders have been living in Dantewara since the fifties. But the recent cases in large numbers do show that illegal transactions were made during

1962-82. During the initial phase of BIOP, many tribals came in contact with outsiders (contractors, labourers from other areas, govt. and project employees, merchants, shopkeepers, etc.), who took advantage of both the existing laws and, in many cases, the illegal modes detailed above.

In the survey conducted by Pradeep Baijal, the then Collector of Bastar district and his senior staff members it was found that apart from legal transfers, about 80 per cent land has been alienated from tribals to non-tribals through illegal practices (Baijal & Joshi 1977). In Dantewara tehsil, according to this study, transaction of 25 holdings or 12 per cent out of a total of 210, was declared illegal. Joshi, in his survey made during 1970-72, noted how a Halba male tribal committed suicide because he was upset due to an illegal land transaction. This incident had taken place on 19th June, 1970 (Joshi 1978).

Crimes Related to Land, Cattle and Crops

The present author, in his attempt to relate data on land alienation to the reported crime incidence over the period of three years in the sample villages, found that out of 326 crimes a large number of cases were of 'urban-oriented crimes', *viz.*, dacoity, highway robbery, theft, gambling, burglary and sexual offences. These are the new phenomenon for the tribal society in this region and tribals were involved in a very few cases reported in police stations of Bacheli and Kirandul. What is of interest to us are the crimes in which tribals and non-tribals were involved over the factors relating to land transfers. In 86 cases, it was found that land and crops were two major factors which inspired tribals and non-tribals to have serious fights with each other. Surely, in earlier times there such crimes were fewer (Elwin 1943). Thus, one can safely conclude that industrial-urbanization in the BIOP complex in Dantewara is responsible for the spurt in urban-oriented crimes and land-related crimes among the tribals of Dantewara.

There is no doubt that there are a few positive aspects of the impact of the BIOP complex on the economic life of the tribals. The tribals are on the threshold of a money-oriented market, selling vegetables and dairy products in the township markets, earning cash income from wage-involving tasks, but, by and large, due to the project activities, tribals are being exploited by the non-tribals. Both mentally and materially the tribals have become upset due to the landloot phenomenon.

Prevention of Land Alienation and Restoration of Alienated Land

How to put checks on the process of land alienation has been a subject of serious debate among the scholars and administrators. One thing is, however, clear that there is no permanent solution to the problem as alienation of land is more a symptom than a disease.

The Commissioner for the Scheduled Castes and Scheduled Tribes in his 28th report has discussed the issues related to land alienation among the tribals of the country at length. The following paragraphs are worth quoting :

The issue of alienation of tribal lands were discussed in the conferences of State Revenue Ministers in May 1985 and November 1986. In persuance of the decisions taken in these conferences, the Government of India advised the provisions to make adequate administrative arrangements for speedy and effective implementation thereof and to create sufficient awareness among the tribals to enable them to take advantage of these legal provisions. The following recommendations were made by the above conference held in May 1985 :

(i) A scrutiny of the existing provisions regarding banning of transfer of land belonging to tribals to non-tribals and its implementation be completed by December 1985 and necessary legislation for these and to plug holes be enacted by December 1986.

(ii) Survey may be undertaken to detect old cases which could be taken up under the law.

(iii) Continuous review of legislative and executive measures be undertaken.

(iv) Updating of land records of the Scheduled areas be completed in a phased manner by the end of the Seventh Plan.

(v) Complete reports on the recommendations of the Commission for Scheduled Castes and Scheduled Tribes be sent by the concerned State and UT administrations so as to reach the Union Government of Rural Development by June 1985.

The Revenue Minister's conference again met in November, 1986 and made the following recommendations :

(i) If not already done, suggestions made in 1985 (see above) in respect of giving protection to tribals concerning their rights on land should be implemented without delay.

(ii) Administrative and judicial machinery should be strengthened to detect cases of alienation under the existing laws and for speedy disposal of these cases.

(iii) Effective arrangements including deterrent legal provisions should be made for ensuring that tribals were not evicted from land restored to them in the context of the concerns expressed about growing alienation of tribal land; in spite of the existence of protective provisions, sufficient awareness must be created among the tribals about the legal rights.

(iv) While taking action to restore land to tribals from which they have been dispossessed, the law of limitation and any other law seeking to nulify protective provisions should not apply. Suitable legislative proposals must be undertaken by the States for such enabling provisions.

(v) All steps should be taken for speedy disposal of cases arising out of alienation of tribal lands so that such lands can be restored to them under the existing legal provisions and the possession of tribals over the restored land can be effectively protected. Most of the States did not consider the setting up of special courts necessary because of disposal of such cases is done by Revenue Courts. However, where such arrangements do not exist and the cases are triable by Judicial Courts, special courts may be set up. Appelate and revisionary forum should be curtailed to ensure speedy implementation of protective laws in favour of tribals.

It may be pointed out that prevention of land alienation and restoration of alienated lands through legal ways will not be enough but certainly deterrent action against the exploiters in the tribal regions can lower its incidence. It is a happy feature that the Govt. of M.P. has issued several remedial directions to cope with the situations, and in some cases the tribals have got their lands back from the non-tribals.

Since the problem in question has a direct bearing on the tribal economy, efforts should be made to improve the productivity of lands in tribal regions. It has been found that where agricultural conditions have improved, the incidence of land alienation has gone down.

Spread of non-formal education in the regions will

help tribals in knowing their rights and priviledges. I am of the view that the Gandhian approach can be followed in this direction. Voluntary organizations, youth clubs, adult-education centres, cooperative banks and societies in the tribal areas can play a significant role in overcoming the situation.

REFERENCES

1. Baijal, P. and S.M. Deo 1977 "Land Alienation in Baster, A Trend Report'. *Land Alienation and Restoration in Tribal Communites In India.* Editor : S.N. Dubey and Ratna Murdia. Himalaya Publishing House, Bombay; p.p. 100-111
2. Census Of India, 1961, 1971, 1981, Relevant Volumes on Bastar District, Bhopal
3. Commissioner For Scheduled Castes and Scheduled Tribes. 1990 *Twenty-eight Report.*, New Delhi, Chapter VI, relevant paragraphs.
4. Elwin, V 1943, *Maria Murder and Suicide;* Oxford University Press, London.
5. Joshi, R.S. 1978 'Report on Baster', *National Labour Bulletin.* Vol. 4, No. 8, p.p. 299-312.
6. National Council of Applied Economics (NCAER) 1960, *Socio-economic Conditions of Primitive Tribes of M.P.*, New Delhi.
7. Srivastava, A.R.N. 1990, *Tribal Encounter with Industry* (A case study of the Dandami Maria of South Baster, Central India); Reliance Publishing House, New Delhi.

14

Tribals And Forests Of North-Eastern India– Strategies For Sustainable Development

A.K. Gangwar

Introduction

North-Eastern region of India is very rich in flora and fauna. The region favours luxuriant growth of a variety of forests in the form of tropical moist evergreen, semi-deciduous and wet temperate conifer forests. The region is considered to be the original home of many *Citrus,* cereals and orchid species. The rare insect eating plant, the pitcher plant *(Nepenthes khasiana),* and one of the rarest and endangered orchid, blue vanda, are found in Meghalaya. *Abies delavari, Coptis teeta, Pinus mercussi* and *Quercus rex* are the species found in Arunachal Pradesh and nowhere else in India. More than 50% of the total mammalian fauna of the Indian sub-continent is represented in this region. All kinds of cats from Royal Bengal Tiger to Clouded Leopard, Leopard Cat, Wild Cat, etc., inhabit this region. It is the home of Binturong *(Arcticitis binturong),* a rare animal, so also the hoolock *(Hylobats hoolock),* the only true ape found in India. Meghalaya has the highest concentration of elephants per sq. km. of habitat in the country, having 29 numbers per 100 sq. km. of forests. The region bears above distinction despite our incomplete knowledge of its flora and fauna.

Alas ! the forests in the region have started dwindling at a very rapid rate. Many species have become extinct and many more are on the verge of extinction even before they could be catalogued. Forests in the North-Eastern region are under dark clouds due to increase in human population pressure, reduced acreage, slash and burn agriculture and timber extraction.

Repurcussions of Jhum and the Concept of Sacred Groves

The North-Eastern region is inhabited by a large number of tribal communities which are markedly different in their socio-economy and socio-culture. Slash and burn agriculture, locally called as Jhum, is the predominant land use and provides livelihood to a majority of population of the region (NEC, 1982; Ramakrishnan, 1985). This agriculture is characterised by clearing of a forested area, burning of the dried slash to add fertility to the soil, cultivating the land for a year or two and then abandoning it for natural regeneration to restore fertility in the soil, shifting to a fresh site and subsequently coming back to the previous one (Gangwar, 1987). The lapse of time between two successive croppings over the same site, called one jhum cycle, in the past in the region was as long as 20-30 years or even more. The longer jhum cycles allowed adequate build-up of soil fertility and also at the same time regeneration of a thick forest cover. As a result, jhum in the past, under longer cycles, was in harmony with the nature both in terms of soil fertility maintenance and forest regeneration (Gangwar & Ramakrishnan, 1987a). But during recent past due to increased human population and reduced acreage, the jhum cycle has shortened considerably. The present average length of the jhum cycle in most parts of the North-Eastern region varies between 2-5 years (Gangwar & Ramakrishnan, 1987 b). This brief fallow period is considerably insufficient both for soil fertility, regeneration and appearance of a forest cover. As a result, jhum during recent past has resulted into severe environmental degradation. The succession is arrested at the pioneer stage. There has been biological invasion of exotic weeds and over large areas, these exotics have eliminated the native species (Kushwaha et al., 1983; Saxena & Ramakrishnan, 1984a, b; Swamy & Ramakrishnan, 1987). The jhum infested areas in the region have lost even the germplasm of the late successional species. To take an example is the case in Meghalaya where climax vegetation of the area, species such as *Bauhinia, Castanopsis, Eugenia, Myrica, Quercus, Rhododendron, Schima,* etc., grow no more in jhum fallows and are spared only in the sacred groves and protected forests (Gangwar & Ramakrishnan 1986). Throughtout at the higher elevations of Meghalaya, Khasi pine *(Pinus Kesiya)* imposes to be the climax species of the area, which infact is an early disturbance, it had got a gain over the native species (Das & Ramakrishnan, 1985, 1986). The local practice of maintaining sacred groves has contributed a great deal in conserving the local biological diversity (Khiewtam, 1986), as they are maintained undisturbed; not even the litter or a dead twig is removed. Sacred groves are considered to be the abode of deities and spirits of the passed away people and thus any removal from such a forest is considered to be an offence. But recently, due to the weakening of faith in such religious practices, the very survival of these sacred groves is also threatened. A large sacred grove at Shillong peak, which was in existence undamaged till 1980, exists no more now.

In many parts of the North-Eastern India, desertification has reached to an alarming extent. Original forest stands of 50 years age or more are rare in existence in the region. Most of the forests are degraded jhum fallows of 10-12 years. Cherrapunji which receives world's highest rainfall (1150 cms. an annual average and 2250 cms. or more in an exceptional year 1974) till recent past had a thick forest cover but now the extent of desertification there has reached to an extreme. Most of the areas are converted into degraded grasslands (Ram & Ramakrishnan, 1988 a, b, c; Ramakrishnan & Ram, 1988). Presence of a lush green forest in the past in the area, is clearly revealed by the existence of a nearby sacred grove at Mawsmai. As we noted, the grasslands in the vicinity of sacred grove do receive the propagules of forest species after their dessimination from the sacred grove. Germination of these seeds also takes place, but as soon as the reserve food stored in the seeds is exhausted and the seedlings shift to depend on soil for mineral nutrition, they die off soon. This happens due to poor soil characteristics. A few seedlings being fortunately located at a rich site, pass off this stage and could establish themselves, but are toppled down by biotic perturbations. Forests from this area will be irreparably damaged if an extensive afforestation programme is not taken up immediately. Delay in this context will deteriorate the situation.

Forests are Vital for Tribal Existence

Forests are an integral part of tribal life (Gangwar & Ramakrishnan, 1990). Most of the tribals sustain largely on forests. If they are taken away from the forests they cannot survive, not the least. They make their household entirely of forest produce of which bamboo and cane are the chief constituents. Floor and walls of houses and graineries are made of bamboo after cutting them open and making flat. For skeleton and to raise the houses on stilts, timber is used. For thatching, banana, palm and other broad leaves and grasses like thatch grass *(Thysanolaena maxima)* and *Imperata cylindrica* are used. Bark of some trees and thin peels of bamboo and cane are used for tying. For vegetables, fruits, medicine, meat, honey and a variety of other food products forests meet the basic demands of the tribal people.

Tribals living in the interior parts largely depend on forests only. The Sulung tribe of Arunachal Pradesh still leads a semi-nomadic life, depending for their food requirements more on forests than on their agriculture and animal husbandry. They extract sago, a starchy food locally called *tashe,* from a wild palm *(Metroxylon sagu)* and use it as staple food. The sago is cooked as porridge and is consumed upto about 750 g. (dry wt. basis) per capita per day. From the pith of *Cyathea gigantea* (a tree fern) a pulp is obtained. This pulp, locally called *tachee,* is cooked as pancakes. Besides *Metroxylon* and *Cyathea,* a number of tubers from species of *Dioscorea* and *Ipomoea* are obtained from the wild. A variety of seasonal fruits are consumed. A number of species are eaten in large quantities, while many others have lesser value. A variety of seeds are collected from the wild when traditional food is scarce. Seeds of *Coix lacryma-jobi, Echinochloa colonum, Fagopyrum esculentum, F. tataricum, Panicum miliaceum, P. miliare,* etc., are cooked like rice or made into pancakes. Seeds of *Atylosia goensis* makes soup. Flour of *Coix lacryma-jobi* seeds and *Dioscorea* tubers are fermented to make liquor. *Calamus erectus, C. Floribundus, Elaeagnus* spp., *Ficus* spp., *Cordia myxa, Morus, Pyrus, Rubus, Solanum* and *Vitis* are the important fruit species. Bamboo shoots are used as chief vegetable. They are consumed fresh when available in nature. For out of season use, fresh shoots are processed in many ways, dried up and stored. Water from fermented shoots is squeezed and stored in bottles till the next season. This water serves as an important mix for all vegetables and meat preparations. Wild animals are hunted for meat. For all the tribal communities of North-Eastern India, meat is the chief source of protein. Even common salt is extracted from rocks. The Sulungs continue to live at a place till the natural resources become limiting. Afterwards, they shift to a fresh site rich in natural resources. Of course, now nomadic tribes are being rehabilitated by the Government by providing them built houses, subsidy for doing agriculture, animal husbandry and other enterprises.

The Nishi and the Hill Miri tribes make permanent settlements and largely practise jhum. The agricultural produce they harvest, lasts only for 6-8 months. For the rest of period of the year, they survive on forests. The Apatani tribe of Ziro plateau of Arunachal Pradesh makes a salt from the ash of a variety of plants. This salt called *'tapio'* in the past, was used as a susbtitute of common salt when the latter was not available readily. Now-a-days also, *'tapio'* is made but is usually eaten by itself or with home brewed liquor. *'Tapio'* is a rich source of iodine and therefore prevents goitre.

A variety of plants are used as fish and animal poisons (Gangwar & Ramakrishnan, 1990). Tubers of *Aconitum lethale,* seeds of *Croton caudatus* and the plant juice of *Forrestia Mollissima* are used as poisons on tips of arrows for hunting. The latex of *Arisaema freturnum* and *Pegia nitida* is used as adhesive to fix these poisons on the arrow tip. Household goods are made largely of plant products. Ornaments, traditional body coverings and items of daily use such as ropes, baskets, containers and utensils are all made of bamboo. A variety of plant-based dyes are used for colouring yarn and clothes.

Most of the States of North-Eastern India either have lost or have rapidly been losing their forest cover. There is needed a massive afforestation programme besides an immediate conservation of the forests left over to have a rational forest cover and ecological balance in the region and also in the country. Arunachal Pradesh, which has mininum human population density in the country, 7 persons per sq sm., so far has plenty of original forests, but the depletion is taking place at a vary rapid rate. If care is not taken, no doubt, in very near future the entire area will turn into a barren landscape like Cherrapunji. Along the road sides near the cities and towns, due to dense population jhum practice is intense leading to forest and site degradation. To a road traveller between Ziro and Yazali (in the lower Subansiri district of Arunachal Pradesh) and also at many places elsewhere, the nude hills with a thin soil layer and covered with only grass cover clearly depicts the picture of deforestation and desertification. Original forests are spared only far off from human habitations. To collect forest produce, now tribals have to go a long distance, as older forests are spared no more in the vicinity. Even collection of fuelwood requires long trecking by the women folk.

Original forests are worst hit by their encroachment for jhum. We have noticed numerous cases of original forest stands being clear felled for jhum (Gangwar, 1987). A jhum field made after a primary forert clearing is also cultivated only for a year or two. Getting agricultural produce of one or two croppings after removing a virgin forest in a situation when we are left with only 14% forest cover in the country (NRSA, 1983), (that too much overestimated), will it not be an irrecoverable loss? For making one jhum plot of 2-2½hec, the average size of a jhum plot a family owns to a minimum of 200-250 tall trees besides a rich undergrowth are removed.

Ecosystem Functioning of a Tropical Rainforest

Tropical rainforests constitute a very fragile ecosystem. In North-Eastern region, owing to high rainfall, loose and porous soil, nutrient losses from the soil are very high. Tropical forests (most of the North-Eastern India forests fall under this category) contain 80% of their total mineral nutrient capital locked-up in the biomass. To short circulate the nutrients between ground and vegetation, a surface root mat is present just below the litter layer. Nutrients released through the decomposition of litter are directly absorbed without their ever entering into the soil. Once such a fragile forest is removed the nutrients left out in the soil, only about 20% of the total mineral nutrient capital, that too under a highly leached soil, leads to a very slow growth of vegetation. Under a high rainfall conditions of North-Eastern India where rainy season prolongs for more than six months and the rains are very intense, if the soil is exposed once, followed by short cycled disturbances, as happens in jhum, it becomes difficult to restore a tree cover except some grasses. The world's wettest spot Cherrapunji being a prominent spot has received much attention but otherwise situation in many other areas is even more grave. If the forests in region are not saved, the survival of tribal communities will be adversely affected besides the immense loss of biological diversity, germplasm of many valuable species and degradation of environmental quality.

To what extent are the tribal people responsible for the depletion of forests ? In the local situation where there in no infrastructure for developmental activities, forests cannot be used as a source of income in any other way other than forest farming. The locals have been practising and surviving on jhum since ages. The time tested system developed after empirical knowledge accumulated through centuries is deeply interwoven into tribal societal organization and can not be discarded till we suggest some alternatives as good as jhum, if not better than it. But if jhum has survived till recent past it ought too have valid reasons for it. If we compare jhum with other land use systems, jhum under sufficiently longer cycles (the length of the fallow period between two successive croppings over the same site is termed as one jhum cycle) stands out to be one of the best land use, even better than the modernized agriculture of many western countries. Let us have a look at the scientific principles on which jhum system is organized.

Jhum a Scientific Land Use

Mixed cropping is a characteristic feature of jhum. A mixture of 20-30 crops or even more is sown together in one single jhum plot which yields an all crop diet and makes an isolated family independent. The system is self-regulating and is based upon low level technology. Labour and seeds are the only input into the jhum system. Seeds are obtained from the previous crop stock and the labour is contributed by the family itself. For the strenuous tasks, such as clearing of the forest, weeding and harvesting, community labour is involved. In any case, labour is free of cost. There is no input of imported technology and any petro-based energy. The yield is on a sustainable basis though at a subsistence level making the system dependable. The system incorporates a tight recycling of nutrients and resources within it. Mixed cropping yields a high leaf area index (ratio of leaf area to the corresponding land area) through the stratification of the leaf canopy of different crops, allowing optimum photosynthesis and thus the yield. Similarly, the stratified root system taps the mineral nutrients to an optimum, avoiding intercrop competition. Sequential harvesting, another characteristic of jhum, besides reducing competition, exposes the crops left over in the field to more sunlight at the peak of their growth. Jhum system involves 'non-weed' concept of the weeds (Chacon & Gliessman, 1982;

Altieri, 1983; Swamy & Ramakrishnan, 1988). Weeds alongwith other large non-edible crop biomass are recycled into the system itself. The system has a high energy efficiency (upto about 50 units of energy output for every unit of energy input) (Steinhart & Steinhart, 1974; Leach, 1976; Mitchell, 1979), and stands out to be a viable land use if the jhum cycle is maintained to 10 years or longer. A 10-year jhum cycle has been proved both ecologically and economically viable (Mishra & Ramakrishnan, 1981; Ramakrishnan & Toky, 1981; Toky & Ramakrishnan, 1981; Mishra & Ramakrishnan, 1982; Toky & Ramakrishnan, 1983).

Strategie for Integrated Development

What remedial measures can we have to cambat the situation. Attempts made so far are merely to discard jhum. The first and foremost step should be to improve jhum itself which is possible to a considerable extent. The emphasis should be on not stopping jhum but to take pressure off the land for jhum by making a partial shift towards plantation and horticultural crops and agro-forestry measures (Gangwar & Ramakrishnan, 1989 a; Kumar & Ramakrishnan, 1989). Besides giving yield on a sustainable basis, it will help in checking soil erosion and maintaining bio-geochemical cycle by providing a permanent vegetation cover to the soil. Banana, pears, peach, plum, jackfruit, mango, guava and citrus fruits, and crops like chilly, cardamom, cotton, ginger, mustard, pineapple, potato, etc. grow well in the region. Citronella, grass, tea, coffee and rubber cultivation should be encouraged and small scale industries should be set up to process or semi-process the produce locally.

Growing cereals should be confined only to the valley lands which are sinks of mineral nutrients washed off from the hill slopes. In the entire North-Eastern region except parts of Assam, only one crop is taken from valley lands in a year. If attempts are made, two or even three crops can be harvested in a year. Introducing fast growing nitrogen fixing species in fallows, such as alder tree, *Alnus Nepalensis* (*SCERT*, 1984) and crops such as *Flemingia vestita* (Gangwar & Ramakrishnan, 1989b) in the cropping phase will help in quick recovery of fertility in the soil besides giving economic returns to the farmer. There is scope for manipulating the crop mixture/cropping pattern to yield higher. A viable export/import oriented economy should be developed in the region. Cereals should be imported into the region as cultivating them in short cycle jhum is untenable and in return, local produce should be exported out. To make this possible, adequate network of roads and the related developmental infrastructure should be developed in the region.

Poulty and piggery are sustained on waste food and crop residue. With improved varieties, better management practices and diet these two animal husbandry practices may prove highly economical. Sericulture and bee-keeping also have bright future in the region. Even if practised on small scale, these will help augment family income substantially. Handloom, handicraft, blacksmithy, carpentry should be encouraged and locally available market facility should be provided. This will give employment to the people not only in the lean season but throughout the year.

Locals need to be educated on the importance of forests to the very existence of human beings and about their systematic, scientific and rational utilization and proper management. Input of low level science and technology will help a lot. Only by using the energy efficient *chullahs,* fuelwood consumption in the region can be curtailed to half. North-Eastern region has a good scope for hydro-electric projects. Making electricity, cooking gas, solar cooker, wind mills available, forest conservation in the region can be accentuated. In most parts of the North-Eastern India cowdung is used in no way. Cowdung and other biomass can be used for biogas production. The left over forests should immediately be protected and prevented from their removal for jhum. This may even need a change in land tenure system. Afforestation programme should be geared up giving priority to the native species rather than going for the exotics. Emphasis should be laid on mixed forestry rather than creating pure strands.

The role of forest department in the region has not been satisfactory. There is felt a lack of understanding of the real problem and so the forest and other departments in the region have not been able to achieve the desired success. Choice of species for afforestation does not include suitable species. Erecting pure strands neither homes wild life nor meets the local needs except yielding plantation area figures to the forest department. A monoculture also does not help in maintaining the ecological balance of the area. Planting Khasi pine *(Pinus Kesiya)* and *Eucalyptus* is underway on a large scale in many parts of the North-Eastern region and the programme is an utter failure. Pine deteriorates the soil quality and makes it acidic.

The huge amount of money Government allocates to bring up the tribal areas is not being utilized properly merely due to the lack of knowledge of the local authorities of the appropriate developmental strategies for the region and also because of the faulty implementation of the schemes. North-Eastern region being peculiar in climate and inhabited by a large number of tribal communities, markedly different in their socio-economy and socio-cultural background, cannot have the developmental programmes conveniently adopted for the plain areas. Owing to marked differences amongst the tribal communities living within a short distance the entire region cannot have just one single developmental strategy. To operate the plan effectively, area should be divided into functional units. All activities have to be designed considering the village as the unit of development within a cluster of villages, and the tribal family as the focal point. This would ensure peoples' participation and would also ensure a development that is accepted to the people it is supposed to serve. Local potential should be worked out; an inventory should be made of the local resources, and local problems should be identified as perceived by the locals themselves. It will also be desirable to understand tribal village organization and the processes operating in the local village ecosystem function.

REFERENCES

1. Altieri, M.A. 1983. *Agroecology: The Scientific Basis of Alternative Agriculture.* Division of Biological Control, University of California, Barkeley.
2. Chacon, J.C. and Gliessman, S.R. 1982. Use of the 'Non-weed' Concept in Traditional Tropical Agro-ecosystems of South-Eastern Mexico. *Agro-Ecosystems* 8: 1-10.
3. Das, A.K. and Ramakrishnan, P.S. 1985. Litter dynamics in Khasi pine (*Pinus kesiya* Royle ex. Gordon). *Forest Ecol. Manage.* 10: 135-153.
4. Das, A.K. and Ramakrishnan, P.S. 1986. Adaptive Growth Strategy of Khasi Pine (*Pinus kesiya* ex. Gordon). *Proc. Indian Acad. Sci. (Plant Sci.)* 96: 25-36.
5. Gangwar, A.K. 1987. *Cropping and Yield Patterns Under the Slash and Burn Agriculture (Jhum) in North-East India and Related Ethnobiological Studies.* Ph.D. Thesis. North-Eastern Hill University, Shillong, India.
6. Gangwar, A.K. and Ramakrishnan, P.S. 1986. The Sacred Groves. *Science Reporter,* January: 54-57
7. Gangwar, A.K. and Ramakrishnan, P.S. 1987 a. Cropping and Yield Patterns under Different Land Use Systems of the Khasis at Higher Elevations of Meghalaya in North-Eastern India. *Int. J. Ecol. Environ. Sci.* 13: 73-86.
8. Gangwar, A.K. and Ramakrishnan, P.S. 1987b. Agriculture and Animal Husbandry among the Sulungs and Nishis of Arunachal Pradesh. *Social Action* 37: 345-372
9. Gangwar, A.K. and Ramakrishnan, P.S. 1989a. Ecosystem function in a Khasi Village of the Desertified Cherrapunji Area in North-

East India. *Proc. Indian Acad. Sci. (Plant Sci.)* 99: 199-210

10. Gangwar, A.K. and Ramakrishnan, P.S. 1989b. Cultivation and Use of Lesser-Known Plants of Food Value by Tribals of North-East India. *Agric.Ecosys. Environ* 25: 253-267.
11. Gangwar, A.K. and Ramakrishnan, P.S. 1990. Ethnobiological Notes on some Tribes of North-East India. *Econ. Bot.* 44: 94-105
12. Khiewtam, R.S. 1986. *Ecosystem Function of Protected Forests of Cherrapunji and Adjoining Areas.* Ph.D. Thesis. North-Eastern Hill University, Shillong, India.
13. Kumar, A. and Ramakrishnan, P.S. 1989. Ecological implications of some Cash Crop Ecosystems in North-Eastern India. *Proc. Indian Acad. Sci. (Plant Sci.).* 99: 211-221.
14. Kushwaha, S.P.S. Ramakrishnan, P.S. and Tripathi, R.S. 1983. Population Dynamics of *Eupatorium odoratum* in Successional Environ-ments Following Slash and Burn Agriculture. *J. App. Ecol.* 18: 529-535.
15. Leach, G. 1976. *Energy and Food Production.* IPC Science and Technology Press, Guildford.
16. Mishra, B.K. and Ramakrishnan, P.S. 1981. The Economic Yield and Energy Efficiency of Hill Agro-Ecosystems at Higher Elevations of Meghalaya in North-Eastern India. *Acta Oecol/Oecol. Appl.* 2: 369-389.
17. Mishra, B.K. and Ramakrishnan, P.S. 1982. Energy Flow through a Village Ecosystem with Slash and Burn Agriculture in North-Eastern India. *Agric. Systems* 9: 57-72.
18. Mitchell, R. 1979. *An Analysis of Indian Agro-ecosystems.* Interprint, New Delhi, India.
19. NEC. 1982. *Shifting Cultivation in North-Eastern Region.* North Eastern Council Publication No. 17, Shillong, India.
20. NRSA. 1983 *Mapping of Forest Cover in India by Satellite Imagery.* 1972-1975 and 1980-1982. Summary Report, N.E. States and Union Territories, National Remote Sensing Agency, Hyderabad.
21. Ram, S.C. and Ramakrishnan, P.S. 1988a. Growth and Allocation Strategy of some Important Species of Seral Grasslands at Cherrapunji in North-Eastern India. *Proc. Indian Acad. Sci. (Plant Sci.)* 98: 13-23.
22. Ram, S.C. and Ramakrishnan, P.S. 1988b. Hydrology and Soil Fertility of Degraded Grasslands at Cherrapunji in North-Eastern India. *Environ Conserv.* 15: 29-35.
23. Ram, S.C. and Ramakrishnan, P.S. 1988c. Litter Production and Decomposition Patterns in Seral Grasslands of Cherrapunji in North-Eastern India. *Pedobiologia* 32: 65-76
24. Ramakishnan, P.S. 1985. Jhum Cultivation-Prospects for Developing

Countries. *Sci Technol. Dev. ISCU COSTED* 9: 1-5

25. Ramakrishnan, P.S. and Ram, S.C. 1988. Vegetation, Biomass and Productivity of Seral Grasslands of Cherrapunji in North-East India. *Vegetatio* 74: 47-53.
26. Ramakrishnan, P.S. and Toky, O.P. 1981. Soil Nutrient Status of Hill Agro-ecosystems and Recovery Pattern after Slash and Burn Agriculture (Jhum) in North-Eastern India. *Plant and Soil* 60: 41-64.
27. Saxena, K.G. and Ramakrishnan, P.S. 1984 a. Herbaceous Vegetation Development and Weed Potential in Slash and Burn Agriculture (Jhum) in N-E India. *Weed Res.* 24: 127-134.
28. Saxena, K.G. and Ramakrishnan, P.S. 1984b. C_3/C_4 Species Distribution among Successional Herbs following Slash and Burn in North-Eastern India. *Acta Oecol/Oecol. Plant.* 5: 335-346.
29. Scert. 1984. *The Use of Alder Tree.* State Council of Educational Research and Training, Nagaland, Kohima, India.
30. Steinhart, J.S. and Steinhart, C.E. 1974. Energy use in the U.S. Food System. *Science* 184: 307-316.
31. Swamy, P.S. and Ramakrishnan, P.S. 1987. Weed potential of *Mikania micrantha* H.B.K., and its control in Fallows after Shifting Agriculture (Jhum) in North-East India. *Agric. Ecosyst. Environ.* 18: 195-204
32. Swamy, P.S. and Ramakrishnan, P.S. 1988. Ecological Implications of Traditional weeding and other Imposed Weeding Regimes under Slash and Burn Agriculture (Jhum) in North-East India. *Weed Res.* 28: 127-136.
33. Toky, O.P. and Ramakrishnan, P.S. 1981. Cropping and Yields in Agricultural Systems of the North-Eastern Hill Region of India. *Agro-Ecosystems* 2: 127-132.

[illegible]

25. Ramakrishnan, P.S. and Ram, S.C. 1988. Vegetation, Biomass and Productivity of Seral Grasslands of Cherrapunji in North-east India. *Vegetatio* 74: [illegible].

26. Ramakrishnan, P.S. and Toky, O.P. 1981. Soil Nutrient Status of Hill Agro-ecosystems and Recovery Pattern after Slash and Burn Agriculture (Jhum) in North-eastern India. *Plant and Soil* 60: 41-64.

27. Saxena, K.G. and Ramakrishnan, P.S. 1984. Herbaceous Vegetation Development and Weed Potential in Slash and Burn Agriculture (Jhum) in N.E. India. *Weed Res.* [illegible].

28. Saxena, K.G. and Ramakrishnan, P.S. 1984. C_3/C_4 Species Distribution among Successional Herbs following Slash and Burn in North-eastern India. *Acta Oecol. Oecol. Plant.* 5: 335-346.

29. [illegible] 1984. *Practical* [illegible]. [illegible] Research and Training [illegible], India.

30. Steinhart, J.S. and Steinhart, C.E. 1974. Energy use in the U.S. Food System. *Science* 184: 307-316.

31. Swamy, P.S. and Ramakrishnan, P.S. 1987. Weed Potential of *Mikania micrantha* H.B.K. and its Control in Fallows after Shifting Agriculture (Jhum) in North-East India. *Agric. Ecosyst. Environ.* 18: 195-204.

32. Swamy, P.S. and Ramakrishnan, P.S. 1988. Ecological Implications of Traditional Weeding and Other Imposed Weeding Regimes under Slash and Burn Agriculture (Jhum) in North-East India. *Weed Res.* 28: 127-136.

33. Toky, O.P. and Ramakrishnan, P.S. 1981. Cropping and Yields in Agricultural Systems of the North-Eastern Hill Region of India. *Agro-Ecosystems* 7: 11-25.

15

Some Reflections On Culture, Development and Politics Among Tribes in India

Tiplut Nongbri

There is perhaps no other primordial category in India which has evoked as much concern for the preservation of their distinctive cultural identity as the tribes. Their simple qualities and nature-based life styles prompted the colonial rulers to adopt a policy of exclusion and protectionism towards them. Yet, their simplicity notwithstanding, tribal social organisations exhibited a high standard of orderliness and political sophistication based on such democratic principles as equality and cooperation.

India boasts of over 400 known tribes spread over almost the entire length and breadth of the country. While many of them tend to concentrate in some hilly terrain, geographically isolated from the mainstream society, some are found interspersed among the general population. Although, by and large, tribes have existed within their own social and political framework, their varied cultures and distinctive styles of life lend colour and richness to India's cultural hertiage. However, the process of acculturation and modernization have taken their toll of our vast tribal culture. Many scholars, administrators and political leaders have expressed their concern at the erosion of tribal cultures as they come into contact with external elements. In the post-Independence period this concern finds expression in Pandit Jawaharlal Nehru's famous *Panchsheel* or five fundamental principles for tribal development.

These steps, directed at maintaining India's cultural plurality, not only reflected Pandit Nehru's lofty ideals and aesthetic value, at the same time, they revealed that under his cloak of sophistication and humanism lay an astute political mind. India is a large country populated by people of different ethnic, linguistic, religious and cultural background. If India is to survive as a single political entity it would be prudent to ensure that the primordial categories and symbols that make up the core of a people's culture are not made light of. Further, to expedite the goal of nation building the State should give priority to economic development so as to bring the entire sovereign State within one economic base. Although, development itself is a product of and connotes a particular culture, development policies should be couched in such terms and their programmes designed in such a manner, that they do not become instruments of cultural domination.

India's draft Five-year plans on tribal development loudly proclaimed Nehru's policy of cultural pluralism and the preservation of tribal cultures and their distinctive identity. In reality, however, Nehru's vision of a self-sufficient and functionally independent tribe existing against their pristine cultural backdrop remains a distant dream.

This paper attempts to understand the social dynamics of tribal development and the processes which emerge when a small scale primitive society interacts with a large scale modernising one. This perspective is necessary because we can better appreciate the dynamics of tribal development if we look at it as a contact of cultures, where each is rooted in its specific socio-structural and institutional framework.

But, what precisely do we mean by culture ? Given the fact that Indian tribes are a heterogeneous category with diverse ethnic, religious and linguistic background, can we speak of a universal tribal culture ? To fully grasp the social dynamics arising from the interaction between culture and development among the tribes, it would be necessary to have conceptual clarity of the categories used and the structural framework within which the process operates.

In ordinary parlance, culture is often thought of as something which is associated with the aesthetic and refinement, the end product of human behaviour transmitted by tradition. Looked at in this manner, cultural activities are those which enhance the quality of life by endowing it with meaning of beauty, truth and goodness. In Sociology, however, culture is used in a broader sense, not restricted to things of aesthetic value only, but also includes various aspects of the people's life.

Culture constitutes the essence of a people. It reflects both the ideological base and material level of the society. This means that while culture may be perceived as an abstract quality characterising a people, it is tangibly related to the social structure. Thus, while culture refers to the totality of behaviour and modes of thought of a people who make up a particular society, it may express itself in various forms. Art, craft, folklore, music, religion, literature and symbols serve as important idiom through which the culture of a people finds expression.

As a conceptual level, tribal cultures stand apart from the elite and folk tradition of pan-Indian culture. Both in content and the level of spread, tribal cultures are distinct from the two. While the elite and folk traditions cannot be conceived of in isolation from the other, tribal cultures are essentially wholes in themselves (Unnithan, 1965 : 19). But this does not mean to say that there are no common elements between them. Historical evidence shows that tribal cultures have borrowed many elements from other cultures, and *vice versa*. But this does not make them a part of the other. It is only when a whole culture assimilates itself with the other and loses its own distinctive characteristics that it ceases to retain its original identity. There have been instances of tribal cultures becoming a part of the pan-Indian culture in this manner. But when this happens they cease to be tribes.

To be sure, one cannot speak of a universal tribal culture. Tribal societies exhibit vast differences in the external respresentation of their art, craft, belief or language. Yet, in contrast to caste, one can discern common principles of cooperation, egalitarianism and value-based behaviour running through their different cultures. It is this common value held by the people which is manifested in their well organized social structures and philosophical world views—firmly rooted in the mysteries of nature and super nature—that distinguishes tribal cultures from the cultural traditions of the mainstream society.

Paradoxically, the process of tribal development has created contradictory conditions in their cultural continuity. While on the one hand the process of development has uprooted the tribes from their cultural moorings, on the other hand it indirectly reinforces their cultural identities. To understand his contradiction we will have to examine the process of tribal development in the context of nation building envisaged by the State.

Development in India has been conceived as an instrument of political reconstruction. The long years of colonial rule have not only mutilated the country but have also depleted its economy and reduced India to a dependency status in the international economic order. The task of economic development is, therefore, not only to fully exploit its natural and human resources and attain a level of productivity that would give it a respectable position in the community of nations, but also to achieve political stability. Keeping in view India's cultural diversity and its socio-economic hierarchical structure, translating this approach into action would require political expediency and distributive justice. To the extent that development is directed at bringing about change in the conditions of existence, it would be naive to disregard the socio-cultural framework within which development is to take place.

Several questions arise in this regard. Should tribes develop along the lines of their own genius or in terms of global industrial societies ? Considering that development is a process directed at achieving the desired state of material and social well-being through the optimum utilization of capital, labour and natural resources, what standards do we use to measure the desired state of well being ? And, if development is directed at a particular people, how do we perceive that the course we take is the desired goal of that people ? Development cannot be measured exclusively in material terms. Nor can we use the yardsticks of one society to gauge the needs and expectations of another. These questions are not only of ethical value but are of practical consequences to the success of development.

The plethora of studies on tribes generated in recent years have not only highlighted the failure of development paradigms to take these questions into consideration but that development itself has become an instrument of their economic exploitation and cultural subjugation. This may be due to the fact that our ideas of what constitute a tribe, and their social and material need, have been defined by using yardsticks alien to their culture. That is why, the motto 'growth with equity', strongly emphasised in our development planning, has failed to realize its objective in tribal development. In academic discourse it has become fashionable to lay the blame for our failure to solve the problems of tribes on our colonial masters. Not that, the latter were entirely blameless in this regard but an examination of the Indian academic tradition shows that Indian scholars themselves are no less free from ethnocentricism than the colonial administrators and scholars were.

In recent years increasing attempts have been made to highlight the Indianess of tribes, Vidyarthi in particular made a strong plea that Indian Social Science should not overlook what he termed its 'Indianess'. To quote him,

> This Indianess in the field of Social Science refers to our distinct cultural milieu and value-attitude system as well as a body of ideas of Indian thinkers reflected in Indian scriptures, which are full of social facts and should be used in the understanding of the cultural process and civilization history of India (1985, 5).

The 'synthetic approach' became an important analytical frame in the study of Indian tribes. And, as if to undo the 'damage' caused by the colonial policy of 'exclusion' and 'partial exclusion' the years following Independence saw a number of publications (Majumdar, 1961; N.K. Bose, 1967; Ghurye, 1959; Surjit Sinha, 1957, 1965; K.S. Singh, 1985) which highlight the position of tribes in the Indian civilization.

The historical reconstruction of ancient Indian civilization revealed that tribes were an integral part of the Indian society. Some historians are of the opinion that Indian society itself was founded on a tribal base. According to D.D. Kosambi. '*The Entire Course of Indian History shows Tribal Elements being Fused into a General Society*' (1956, 25, emphasis in original; also quoted in Beteille, 1986). Tribes (*jana*), however, were distinguishable from castes (*jati*) though the boundaries separating them were not rigid; the former could easily pass into the latter by the adoption of their behaviour and normative standards. Another historian, Nihar Ranjan Ray, elaborates the relationship between the two. According to Ray, *jana* means community of people while *jati* refers to the socio-religious-cum-economic system that are supposed to sustain the *jana* the keep the given community of people together. Over the millenial *janas* which adopted the *jati* system of socio-economic organisation merged into the *jati* complex of Hindu society; the *janas* which have not been drawn into the mainstream society remained a separate category, constituting what today are defined as tribes (1972, 9-15).

This new cognitive map informs the study of tribes is not restricted to historians alone. Social anthropologists and sociologists too are increasingly turning towards the past to gain an insight into the present. It is an acknowledged fact that history provides an important frame of reference, but for history to be useful the approach would have to be a holistic and integrated one, covering all dimensions of the problem. In the study of tribes it is important to take note of this fact if we are to have a correct picture of the reality. While it is truè that tribes constitute an important element of the general society, we cannot ignore the processes which have resulted in their isolation from the mainstream population. Some literature on tribes have illustrated the push-back effect of the dominant social structure which has resulted in a withdrawing syndrome among Indian tribes. When faced with economic and socio-political pressure from the dominant population, tribes withdrew into the interior of hills and forests so as to be able to maintain their cultural identity and practice their life-ways undisturbed (Haimendorf, 1985, 34-35; Ray, op. cit.11; Dube, 1987). The hierarchical structure of the Hindu caste system and the exploitative character of their production relations added in no small measure in driving tribes away into remote areas. Yet this insight provided by history in understanding the problems of tribes, remains lost on our planners and policy makers whose development programmes have perpetuated the exploiter-exploited relations between castes and tribes.

Commenting on the contemporary tribal situation in India, S.C. Dube notes with concern the social tensions between tribes and castes, which tend to get further aggravated with the process of economic and political modernisation. In his words-

> The confrontation between tribals and non-tribals is not a phenomenon of recent origin. The long history of their interaction has been one of tension and conflict. To begin with, the tribal way of life contended for a position of dominance, but in the unequal fight it had to reformulate its goals and to struggle first for co-existence (on a basis of equality) and later for bare survival. In the process there was considerable adjustment and accommodation.....But the fusion of the two ways of life was never complete.....In the plural society that emerged, many tribal societies retained a measure of cultural autonomy, but accepted in different degrees—the "broker institutions" (such as national administrative, political and economic institutions).....The acceptance of these institutions, however, was not without resistance. Time healed some of the wounds caused to tribal self-respect and their cultural autonomy, but some of them turned into festering sores partly because of the unyielding tribal pride and partly because of the newcomer's arrogance that made them insensitive and unresponsive to tribal sentiments. Changing social, political and economic contexts continued to alter prevailing tribal

> non-tribal equations. In many predominantly tribal areas the situation could never really stabilize itself. When India became free, the bonds between the tribals and non-tribals were tenous and fragile.....Suspicion and distrust prevented them from forging lasting bonds of cooperation and independence. An uneasy co-existence prevailed (1972, 28-29).

To students of tribal society such observations could not but cause deep concern at the direction in which the tribe non-tribe relations appeared to be taking. As Dube has rightly pointed out, the conflict and tension between them has deep historical roots. Underlying this tension was the variation in the socio-economic organisation which characterised the two systems. The *jati* system of production with its superior technological base attracted tribes to it but when this happened they were accorded an inferior position within the social structure. The Brahminic model with its emphasis on the specialization of occupations while it encouraged the absorbtion of tribes into its productive system maintained a strict rigidity on the monopolization of occupations. Associated as it were with an equally rigid normative structure, tribes who entered their productive system did so at the risk of being placed at the bottom of the caste structure and losing their socio-cultural autonomy. N.K. Bose defines this process as the 'Hindu method of tribal absorbtion' and sees it as an on going mechanism by which tribes are integrated into the larger society (1941, 188-94). More recently, K. Suresh Singh came up with an alternative to the Brahminic model in the diffusion of Hindu culture. In this model, although the acts of acculturation were carried out by the peasants and the artisans through their economic interactions with the tribes, the end results were the same, transfer of technology was associated with the transmission of culture (*op cit*, 53-69).

Due to the dearth of historical material on the early period it is difficult to know the exact reactions of tribes to this domination. Interestingly, sociological accounts were too concerned with highlighting the integrative mechanism of Indian society to pay any attention to signs of fission. In addition, the theoretical-methodological framework of structural-functionalism, which was then in fashion, were not only equipped to deal with conflict but the ethno-frame within which most Indian sociological studies were conducted could only provide us with an external view of the sociological implications of tribe-caste interaction. As a result, many tribal studies placed undue emphasis on the so called symbiosis, perceived to exist between tribes and non-tribes, and ignored the exploitative and assymetrical character of their relationship.

If one were to reconstruct the past on the basis of evidence available in recent times, we can say that tribes could not have been passive subjects of cultural domination. The storm of protests which erupted during the colonial period were indicative of their love for freedom and indomitable spirits. It is important to note that these protests were directed not so much at the white rulers as towards the non-tribal (*diku*) businessmen, and petty officials of the *Raj* who, in the course of carrying out their duties, unleashed a reign of terror over tribes in furtherence of their own selfish interests. The extension of the colonial system of administration into the tribal areas facilitated the entry of the more advanced population who exploited the ignorance of tribes and siphoned off their economic resources. The impoverization process and the cultural subjugation caused by this development were the main factors which triggered large scale tribal unrests from the nineteenth to the early part of the twentieth century. During this period the entire tribal belt reverberated with echoes of the tribes' demand for independence and freedom from exploitation (cf. Haimedorf, *op cit;* Singh, 1982; 1983).

Colonialism increased the vulnerability of tribes in that it not only made them easy victims of the non-tribals' greed, it also threw them open to capitalist forces which exploited their rich natural resources and subjected them to the mercy of the market economy. The specificity of the tribal socio-economic formation with their subsistence level of production suffered heavily at the hands of capitalism. Although there was wide variation in the degree of economic backwardness suffered by a tribe, given the socio-structural milieu within which tribes had to strive for their existence, the struggle was indeed heavily weighed against their favour.

It is this specificity of the tribe-caste equation that has to be taken into consideration while planning for tribes. The penetration of the macro-economic forces into tribal areas has not only affected the viability of the tribal productive system and the erosion of their rich natural resources, it has also brought them directly in contact with the normative structure of Brahminic Hinduism with its rigid hierarchical order and strict notions of purity and pollution. It is instructive to note that Indian academic discourse has rarely touched upon the effects of caste repressions upon the tribes. Caste repressions are not restricted to the Dalits or the Harijans. In the highly materialistic world of today caste repressions are as common among tribes and other backward communities. The almost daily report on atrocities perpetrated by high caste Hindus on the Scheduled Castes and Scheduled tribes in the electronic media and the Press are indicative of the growing strength of caste prejudice. What are often termed as class-wars or class-conflict infact masks an inherent cultural disequilibrium.

A lot has been written on the adverse effect of development upon tribes. It is not our intention to produce another thesis on it here. But what we would like to emphasize is that economic deprivation and cultural subjugation go hand in hand. Historical evidence suggests that so long tribes remained outside the Hindu system of production they could retain their cultural distinctiveness and respect in their status. Writing on the Gonds, Haimendorf stated that aboriginals who retained their tribal identity and resisted inclusion within the Hindu fold fared better than the assimilated groups and were not treated as untouchables even though they indulged in the eating of beef, which Hindus considered polluting.

This respect for the tribal way of life prevailed as long as contact between the two communities were of a casual nature. Frictionless coexistence was also possible, since there was no population pressure, the incentive to deprive tribes of their land was lacking (*op cit*, 33-35).

Today the demographic and economic structures have undergone tremendous transformations from conditions prevalent in the past. The extension of the centralized system of administration and population explosions could no longer insulate tribes from the mainstream society. But a proper planning strategy could surely minimize the problems of adjustment when a micro-economy merges with the national macro-economy. It is a measure of our failure to take the qualitative aspect of economic development into consideration that development, far from improving the standards of life of the tribes has, on the other hand, resulted in the degradation of their culture and further economic deprivation. Perhaps, it is sheer coincidence that the tribal belts of the country are coterminous with the natural resource map of our industries. Practically all the natural resources utilized by the industries, such as land, water, forest products, oil and minerals are located in tribal areas. Planning for tribal development would, therefore, be incomplete unless we take into consideration the consequences of the industrial policies and national economic objectives on the tribal economy. An integrated approach linking the micro-economic systems with the macro-economic perspectives would have to be undertaken if every section of the population are to benefit from economic development. But the four decades of experience behind us has only left trials of miseries for the simple and ignorant tribes. Land alienation, ecological destruction, isolation from their traditional economic base, cultural degradation and dehumanization of their person are the vicious circles within which economic development has ensnared tribes.

Dislocated from their traditional moorings and deprived of their age-old support system, many tribes from in and around the industrial centres are forced to struggle for their survival as landless wage labourers. To quote Bhupinder Singh, an official tribal-activist and social anthropologist :

> Such is the picture of a section of the Indian people who only a century ago regarded themselves as lords and masters of land and forest in their territory, who had total control over their economic needs and who normally were self-sufficient.....Yet today there is manpower glut and unemployment is rife. The migrant tribal labour is subjected to physical excesses and mental torture, notwithstanding the laws to safeguard him (1989, 16).

The pangs of transition from a closed-circuit tribal economy and isolated social system to a highly monetised macro-economy and complex social system are indeed severe for tribes. The severity of the distress cannot be measured solely in instrumental terms. More painful are the cultural degradation and marginalization from their existential and mystical world, the hills and forests from which they derived their basic needs, and the abode of their gods and deities. Forests are the second life-line of tribes and the source of their spiritual strength and comfort. Hence to deprive a tribe the use of forests is to take away the one element which gives meaning to their existence. Yet the large destruction of forests by the industries and the stringent forest laws which restricted the access of tribes to forests reflect an utter lack of concern for the economic and spiritual needs of tribes.

While at the micro-level, tribes have to come to terms with these practical exigencies of existence, at the macro-level they have yet to counter another face of development, the bureaucracy with its internal and external networks. It is in their contact with the bureaucracy that tribes discovered the power of the State and the corruption of its officials. As the main implementing agency of the government policies and programmes, the success of tribal development would depend upon the sincerity and efficiency of the people who manned the various organs of the bureaucracy. The experience of the tribes with the bureaucracy, however, has been far from happy. On the other hand, the problems of tribes have often been multiplied manifold by an unresponsive and corrupt bureaucracy. It has often been alleged that tribal development suffers because of the simplicity and ignorance of tribes who could not absorb the benefits specially worked out for their welfare. It is a fact that many tribal economies could hardly ingest the development inputs earmarked for them due to the dearth of infrastructural facilities and the low cost structure of their traditional economic system. But we could hardly blame tribes for these factors. Even with regards to the allegation pointed above, empirical evidence suggests that more often than not it is the failure of the implementing agencies in taking development to the tribes rather than the latter's ignorance that has resulted in stagnation in the implementation of development programmes. It is the government's duty to protect the tribes' interests and create awareness in them about their rights and privileges. In actuality, this is far from being the case. On the contrary, many government officials acted on behalf of local influentials and other non-tribals.

Leslie Calman in his recent study on the Naxalite movement, in which the tribes of Srikakulam district of Andhra Pradesh were involved in the 1960s, has highlighted in sharp detail the role of the government in the impoverization of tribes. According to him the violent movement launched by the tribes of Srikakulam against the State had its roots in the apathy of the government officials towards their abject condition. The movement was motivated no so much by the idea of capturing State power as it was an act of helplessness when all efforts to obtain redressal for their sufferings by peaceful means failed. Calman cites the plethora of rules and legislations passed by the State, since colonial times, to protect the interests of tribes but were hardly being implemented. Some of the chronic problems which have resulted in the dehumanization of tribes such as the loss of land, indebtedness and inaccessibility to forests, all came under the purview of State laws but tribes could not derive any protection from them because of the official-businessman-landlord nexus.

Calman observed that to the extent that the government at all operated in the tribal districts it did so in ways that favoured the powerful ruling elite of traders and rich farmers who monopolised the policies as well as the economy of the tribes. Although government itself did not directly oppress the tribes, but through its failure to implement the laws it gave full reign to those who exploited them (1985, 21-43).

The picture presented by Calman is not a single instance of official indifference to the problems of tribes.

All over the country, in Bihar, Madhya Pradesh, Orissa, Rajasthan, Maharashtra, West Bengal and even in the North-Eastern region, which have a predominantly tribal population, official attitude tilted towards the powerful section of the society. Considering the social and cultural background to which most of these officials belong, it is perhaps understandable that they are inclined towards the interests of their own section of the population. Haimendorf once took note of the fact that it is inherent in any plan for the protection and support of tribes that whenever benefits are envisaged for them must adversely affect the interests of the more advanced sections of the population (*op cit.* 48). This does not imply that there are no honest and committed officials in the bureaucracy. There are, but they are rare and far between. What is more, the system within which they are located hardly allows a sincere and dedicated officer to function without external interference and pressure. In most governmental activities, political interference is the rule rather than the exception. This is so, because the system of electoral politics by which government is formed demands that the government of the day sheds off (covertly at least) some of its socialist orientations, if it is to survive through successive elections.

Although the large majority of tribes still lie below the poverty line, the struggle for survival has assumed a new dimension. Faced as they were with an ineffectual government machinery and culturally-biased society, tribes turned towards politics to find solutions to their problems. In their search for internal solidarity they appealed to the bonds of ethnicity. The use of ethnicity for political mobilization came easy to tribes. The degradation of their culture and the loss of control over their territory instilled a strong sense of protonationalism in them which propelled the tribal leadership towards attempts to reclaim their lost rights.

However, in their efforts to retrieve their position, tribes may not necessarily be willing to return to their original state but may negotiate with the new political structure for a political settlement acceptable to their thinking. It seems that tribes have come to realize that if they are to survive in the milieu within which they are located, the best way to do so is through the national political process. In addition, the political aspirations of tribes have sharply been accentuated by the rise of a new middle class, with a western oriented education and new inventory of social needs, the fulfilment of which has brought them into open competition with the non-tribes. Characterised as they were by a dearth of economic and political power tribes were at a serious disadvantage in this new situation. The policy of protective discrimination enshrined in the Constitution helped them in some ways but the disequilibrium was too enormous to be restored without their own active involvement in the various decision-making arenas. Cultural prejudices are not easy to erase, and given the history of tribe-caste equation as directly dependent upon their economic relations, politics was considered as the most viable means by which tribes could ensure of a more equitable share in the national resources.

It is against this background of economic deprivation and cultural subjugation that we can understand the spate of tribal movements in different parts of the country. The move to secure political autonomy by various tribal groups, illustrates the depth of their dissatisfaction. The entire North-Eastern region has been fragmented beyond measure. What was previously a single State, dominated by the highly sanskritised Assamese has given rise to seven political units, four of which, Nagaland, Meghalaya, Mizoram and Arunachal Pradesh, are predominently tribal States. Today, the smaller tribes located in the plain districts of Assam have also intensified their demand for political autonomy of their respective homeland. In many pockets of the central tribal belt, tribes had launched mass movements for the restoration of their political rights. In all these movements, it was the educated middle class who initiated the process of political bargaining. While the educated tribal elite may lack organisation and cohesiveness among them, they share a common goal in their strive towards social liberation. There is a new awakening among them that the only way to maintain their distinct identity and retain their social dignity is through the acquisition of political power.

While the politicization of tribes appeared to be a logical outcome of the socio-economic processes operating in the society, their political consolidation would not have been possible without the democratic ethos which characterise the Indian State. With the attainment of Independence, the new political arrangements in the country provided for equal opportunities in the participation of all sections of the population in the national political process. To protect the interests of tribes in this regard, some areas with predominantly tribal population were reserved for them in political representation. Thus the post-independence period saw a sharp rise in the political participation of tribes both at the regional and national levels. Some scholars, however, expressed concern at the nature of tribal politics. Dube, in particular notes :

> The emerging political culture is disturbing in several aspects.....it is oriented more to sub-national-tribal-identities than to a broader national identity. Where interests of the smaller unit and the larger unit clash, the tendency is to ignore or sacrifice the latter. This constriction of perspectives, resulting in exclusive or excessive focus on purely regional, local, or tribal interests and on their solution un-

linked with broader national interests, imparts parochial overtones to the emerging political culture (1972, *op cit*, 31).

Twenty years have passed since Dube penned down these lines and much water has flowed down the Yamuna since then. Today tribal politics could no longer be adequately defined in these terms. Tribal politics had become an aspect of national politics; it symbolises the rising aspirations, needs and perspectives of tribes. Except for a few secessionist elements, the mainstream tribal politics could be seen as sub-national in its articulation and national in disposition.

The characterisation of tribal politics presented by Dube perhaps corresponds to what Roy-Burman terms as a phase of 'infra-nationalism'. According to Roy-Burman, this is the initial phase of tribal politics which symbolises the explosion of an unformulated urge, rather than a systematically and consciously built-up approach. This is followed by a phase of 'proto-nationalism' in which a conscious elite comes into existence to promote the process of expansion of identity and other interests of tribes. In this phase the tribes are aware, if somewhat unclearly, of the goals, symbols and ethos of the nation-State (1988 : 39).

Sixteen years separated the observation of Roy-Burman from that of Dube, during which period significant changes have come about in the pattern of political participation of tribes. In fact, the 1970s could be defined as a watershed decade in the history of tribal politics. It was in the 70s that the reorganisation of Assam took place, which gave legitimate recognition to ethnicity and marked the coming of age of tribal politics in the country. Considering the plural character of the Indian society, the articulation of tribal and regional interests cannot be termed as parochial.

Today, tribal politics is no less national than the politics of the Bengali, Tamil, Gujarati or Marathi, each of whom obtained their statehood because of the linguistic basis in the reorganisation of States in 1950s. But this is not to suggest that all tribal groups in India deserved to be given separate States. The viability of State-formation is dependent upon a complex set of factors than ethnicity alone.

In a way the dynamics of tribal politics can be seen as an interplay between class, status and power. Although in the Weberian sense these are analytically separable concepts (see Gerth and Mills, 1974, 180-195 and Beteille, 1977) to some extent one can lead to the other. While class is rooted in economic terms, in the Indian society status is defined on the basis of caste purity. As we have seen, economic deprivation condemned tribes to poor social status by being relegated to the bottom of the social structure. However, there are evidence which shows that not all tribes were assigned an inferior position within the caste structure. Among chiefly clans and aristocratic families, admittance into the higher echelons of Hinduism could be carried out through the process of 'Kshatriyaization'. By tracing their genealogical links to some Hindu families, real or mythological, and adopting the values and standards of Brahminic Hinduism, the tribal rulers could claim for themselves a Kshatriya status (Singh, 1985 : 77-80). Although we cannot strictly characterise the political aspirations of tribes today as a quest for status, this evidence from the past suggests that possession of power could ensure tribes of a better position within the larger society.

The educated tribal middle class saw political power as the only instrument by which tribes, long submerged under the forces of cultural domination and economic backwardness, could undo the injustice perpetrated against them and restore their self-esteem. This is so because Indian society, being basically caste dominated, is a closed-system where members falling outside its orbit could find no way of penetrating into its fold save at the cost of losing their cultural identity. But power, unlike status is a property which could be acquired through the monopolisation of material resources and control over the decision-making processes. Within the narrower level of the political domain, possession of power also means the right to weild one's influence over policy matters. In at least areas involving one's interests this right could be put to much effective use. The prestige of power in itself brings numerous glories not associated with instrumental factors. In all political systems power has been seen to create its own sychophants and favour seekers which boosts the image of the power holder. And in sychophancy, there is but little barrier of caste, creed or culture.

It would, however, be erroneous to assume that tribal politics has resulted in equal benefits for all sections of tribes. The emerging socio-economic and political processes gave rise to sharp patterns of stratifications. Within each tribe there emerged a new stratum of well-to-do class of people who cornered the benefits ushered by the new political order. Apart from constituting the political leadership in their respective society, a sprinkling of these tribes could be found in almost all levels of the government bureaucracy, government controlled undertakings and professions like education, health, engineering and law. Tribes who constitute this category differ widely in their attitudes and life styles from their less fortunate counterparts. Although they constitute but a handful of the total tribal population, they are the visible members of their society. A significant trend discernible in recent years is the close political and economic alignment which exists between this class of tribes and the exploitative class of non-tribes in cornering the benefits of development.

It is not enough to decry the existence of this nexus; what needs to be done is to unravel the causal factor which contributed to its existence. A careful analysis of the problem points to the political system itself as the inherent cause. The federal structure of the Indian polity and the centrist character of its political parties made it difficult for tribes to enter the system without the support of non-tribes.

This situation attains a more serious dimension by the centralized nature of the administration and the nationalist-orientation of development programmes and schemes. At the empirical level this has generated conflicting trends with the tribal society. While tribes nearer the centres of power and administration could identify themselves with the goals of the Nation-State, those at the periphery nursed a sense of deprivation against the system. When the perception of their deprivation becomes acute, the conflict expressed often assumed cultural overtones.

The rise of tribal politics speaks of the danger of cultural domination. To the extent that culture gives meaning to a people's life, any tendency to belittle that culture, either by word or action, would be inimical to peaceful co-existence. Today, however, it would be more appropriate to speak of 'tribal identity' than of tribal culture. Although as we have argued, tribal culture stood apart from pan-Hindu culture, it lacked a definite boundary between the two. But with the promulgation of the Indian Constitution and the designation of certain communities as 'Scheduled Tribes', tribal culture has achieved a kind of concreteness it lacked in the past. Although in content and form it may share several elements with the pan-Indian culture, it has acquired a definite legal personality.

It is this new political identity within which tribal culture is clothed that assumes significance in development. Whatever be a tribe's cultural orientation, there is now a definite political advantage in maintaining and strengthening their tribal identity. That development is a powerful cultural weapon cannot be denied. But how best development can be used as an effective tool to achieve the goal of economic advancement, without injuring the symbolic and material interests of any particular section of the society, is the task that planners would have to carefully consider.

REFERENCES

1. Beteille, Andre. 1977, *Inequality among Men*, Delhi, Oxford University Press.
2. ———1986, 'The Concept of Tribe with Special Reference to India' in *European Journal of Sociology*, vol. 27.
3. Bose, N.K. 1941, 'Hindu Method of Tribal Absorption', Proceedings of Social Science Congress, Reprinted in *Cultural Anthropology*, Bombay, Asia Publishing House, 1961.
4. ———1967, *Culture and Society in India*, Bombay, Asia Publishing House.
5. Calman, Leslie, 1985, *Protests in Democratic India : Authority's Response to Change*, London, Westview Press.
6. Dube, S.C. 'Inaugural Address' in *Tribal Situation in India*, K.S. Singh (Ed.), Simla, Indian Institute of Advanced Study.
7. ———1987, *Cultural Heritage of India*, Bhopal, Madhya Pradesh Uchch Shiksha Anudan Ayog.
8. Gerth, H.H. and Mills, C. Wright, 1974, *From Max Weber : Essays in Sociology*, London, Routledge and Kegan Paul.
9. Ghurye, G.S. 1959, *The Scheduled Tribes*, Bombay, Popular Book Depot.
10. Furer-Haimendorf, C.Von, 1985, *Tribes of India : The Struggle for Survival*, Delhi, Oxford University Press.
11. Kosambi D.D. 1956, *An Introduction to the Study of Indian History*, Bombay, Popular Prakashan.
12. Majumdar, D.N. 1961, *Races and Culture of India*, Bombay, Asia Publishing House.
13. Ray, Niharranjan, 1972, 'Introductory Address' in *Tribal Situation in India*, K.S. Singh (Ed.), Simla, Indian Institute of Advanced Study.
14. Roy-Burman B.K., 1988, 'The Naga Upsurge, Ethnic Identity and Social Change, in *Social Action*, Vol. 38, Jan-March.
15. Sinha, Surajit, 1957 'Tribal Culture of Peninsular India: Dimension of Little Tradition in Study of Indian Civilization', in *Man in India*. Vol. 37.
16. ———1965, 'Tribe-Caste and Tribe-Peasant Continuum in Central India', *Man in India*, Vol. 45, No.1.

17. Singh, Bhupinder, 1989, 'Tribal India Economy' in *Report of National Seminar on Contemporary Tribal Economy in India,* Delhi, Jigyansha Tribal Research Centre.

18. Singh, K. Suresh 1982, *Tribal Movements in India,* Vol. I. Delhi, Manohar Publications.

19. ——1983, *Tribal Movements in India,* Vol. II, Delhi, Manohar Publications.

20. ———1985, *Tribal Society in India.* Delhi, Manohar Publications.

21. Unnithan, TKN *et al,* 1965, *Towards a Sociology of Culture in India,* New Delhi, Prentice-Hall of India (Private) Ltd.

22. Vidyarthi, L.P. 1985, *The Tribal Culture of India.* New Delhi, Concept Publishing House.

16

International Tribal Policies—An Appraisal

J.S. Bhandari and Subhadra Mitra Channa

A discussion of Tribal policies is intrinsically linked to the concept 'Tribe' itself. For an indepth discussion of the concept we shall have to go into historical and philosophical issues which are at present beyond the scope of this paper. Roy Burman (1983 : 1172) has given a comprehensive definition saying, "Tribe refers to a stage of social formation in an evolutionary scheme of development of technology, knowledge and capacity for control of the forces of nature, method of transmission of the same, perception of man's relationship with man and with nature and scale of organisation of social group". Further, "...A tribe can outgrow its primitiveness and maintain its social boundary and essential features of identity".

The important thing about the concept tribe is that, more than an objective reality, it is an identification that is constantly being made by the people. It has a subjective content which is expressed by cultural symbolism and renewed with culturally meaningful acts.

As Eickelman (1981 : 87) puts it, "Such patterns of meaning change with historical situations. It makes great deal of difference whether they occur in the context of strong or weak State organization or a colonial society". 'Tribe' is thus not an objectively uniform category.

The word 'tribal policy", itself envisages a dichotomy between the policy-makers and the recipients and more frequently than not this dichotomy has also been that between non-tribal and tribal. The very historical process of formation of tribes has been the progressive advancement towards complexity of entities we call Nation-States. The classic dichotomy of Morgan between *societas* and *civitas,* of Tonnies between *Gemeinschaft* and *Gesselschaft* is the fundamental basis of the divergence between tribal and non-tribal. More than a technology or occupation, it is a world view, an identification and a scale of organization, as rightly put forward by Roy-Burman, that is the concept of tribal. The non-tribal identification has been formed by those groups that have evolved to a level of complexity and cosmology which has expansionist and universalistic tendencies. Such non-tribal groups have established dominance in the creation of most Nation-States except perhaps Saudi Arabia which is known as the only tribal Nation-State.

Many Nation-States today are composed of a multiplicity of ethnic groups. The tribals have not historically formed the dominant ethnic group in any Nation State—culturally and politically they have been peripheral.

In our discussion of International Tribal policies we have taken two types of Nation-States into account. The ones like Russia, China and Iran, which have developed out of an amalgamation of indigenous populations-whom we can visualize as orthogenetically evolved and those Nations that have been formed out of a colonization and domination of the native populations by an outside population such as Australia, Africa and America. In the latter case the colonizing population has finally claimed the Nation-State as its own after overrunning the indigenous population.

As we shall presently see,, the nature of tribal policies have been influenced and shaped by the nature of the historical contact between the State or policy makers and the tribals.

Karklins (1986 : 6) while discussing ethnic relations in USSR has talked of two types of ethnic groups, "E.K. Francis has used the terms primary and secondary ethnic groups to differentiate between minority nationalities which become such in the case of territorial annexation and those resulting from large scale migrations".

The term "tribe" has always been used in the context of primary ethnic groups; those which are the native inhabitants of a territory. The large scale migratory or colonizing groups are those which have established ethnic dominance inspite of their non-indigeneous nature. As tribe is no longer synonymous with "primitiveness" but only with identity, it is difficult to distinguish between the term "ethnic group" and tribe. The term ethnic group has been extended to include all groups "those who conceive of themselves as being alike by virtue of their common ancestory, real or fictitious, and who are so regarded by others" (Burkey 1978 : 5). Hence "tribe" will be those ethnic groups who regard themselves as such and are also regarded as such by others—these 'others' include both administrators and anthropologists, the view of all the three need not always tally.

In picking up our examples, we have chosen those Nation-States that are influenced by different types of political ideologies as well as different historical circumstances of their formation.

In the earliest times the various ethnic groups, especially the tribals who occupied the more inhospitable and marginal areas away from civilization were largely ignored. The two factors that have pushed the tribals and non-tribals in active interaction have been, the spread of European colonization and the emergence of modern Nation-States. Under the feudal structure in Russia, China, India and Middle East, the State maintained various types of policies regarding their tribal populations, depending upon their own interests, which under feudal conditions did not go beyond collection of revenues and maintenance of some semblance of order. Since the income from tribal economies was not visualized as lucrative to the State, in China, India Russia and Iran, the State and tribal interactions were not integrative.

The tribal groups were maintained as separate ethnic identities and political order was sustained by the divide and rule policy of playing one group against the other, if they had any political autonomy worth the name. Otherwise marginal groups were completely ignored. The tribes, being by definition ethnically distinct and politically autonomous, were never integrated into any consolidated State machinery.

The regions inhabited by the tribals became important only when in the course of industrial development and in the political context of the Nation-State, their populations and the resources under their control became important for adding to the political and economic strength of the dominant ethnic group. As we shall see presently, the extent of domination was almost directly proportional to the value of the coveted resources and this domination was exerted through both brute force and ideology. In China, the term minorities have been used for all the Non-Han populations including the 40 million Chinese Muslims who form 1/10th of Chinese population and are known as Hui. The total minority population comprises 55 identified groups with a population of over 67 million and covering over 62% of the country's total land area including much of China's borders like Mongolia, Tibet, Yunnah and Kwangsi.

The Chinese State dictated by the Communist ideology professed complete political and social equality of all groups, reinforced by the National self-determination policy of Lenin. What is interesting in the Communist situation is the recognition of the minority regional and ethnic groups as Nations. The communists, both Chinese and Russians, have deliberatly stayed away from the ideological hierarchy of the word "tribal". The Chinese Communists were committed to the maintenance of ethnic/cultural identities and also towards an upgrading of social and economic status of all groups to the National level. On the other hand, the integrated interests of the Nation were directed towards maintenance of border security and an access to the vast amount of resources that existed on the land under the control of minorities. The ideologically desired self-maintenance of the minorities would in real terms deprive the Nation of resources such as the 40% of national coal deposits and 52% of the nation's water deposits and nearly half of the country's timber resources which all lie in the minority areas. These areas also raise large amounts of livestock and cash crops such as sugar, tea, tobacco, rubber plants and coffee.

It becomes obvious that an increase in regional autonomy will endanger both the security and the National identity as well as deprive the State of extremely valuable resources. This conflict is expressed in the compromise in the policies formulated by the State.

The State policy towards the minorities comprises the following elements[1] :

1. Improved medical and economic care which the State claims has led to a marked increase in

1. This information is based on 'Questions and answers about China's minority nationalities. Compiled by the National Minorities Questions Editorial Panel. 1985 New World Press, Beijing, China.

the rate of growth of the minority population.

2. An input of industry in minority areas which has increased these rate of urbanization. Today, the rural/urban ratio is the same all over China.
3. The government has adopted a policy of regional national autonomy in areas where the minority people live in compact communities. China currently has 116 autonomous areas including five autonomous regions, 31 autonomous prefectures and 80 autonomous counties. A very significant fact mentioned here is that the total population of these areas is **120 million of which 50 million are minorities.** This means that in population size, the minorities are outnumbered by the Hans even in their own autonomous regions. Secondly, the Law on Regional Autonomy clearly mentions that, "The verified leadership of the Central People's Government must be guaranteed and its general principles, policies and plans must be implemented".

The national autonomous regions are given rights of self-govenment, of adopting special policies and flexible measures, but only as long as they do not, **"contravene the Constitution & the Law"**. Further, they can make their own local economic constructions but **under the guidance of State plans.** They can also have locally administered projects for **(education, science, culture, health and sports) (emphasis mine).**

While giving a number of conditions for independent use and exploitation of local resources, it is stipulated that, "self-government organizations may independently arrange for utilization of industrial, agricultural and other local products after **fulfilling the planned quotas for State purchase of those products".**

It would seem from all this that Communist China

has compromised its ideology in favour of a Nation-State dominated by the Hans. The minorities are given only enough concessions to pay lip service to equality but in real terms they are subordinated and their resources usurped for the State or the dominant population. Even in setting up industries in minorities areas, the dominance of Han population in these areas, makes one apprehend that in the manning of these industries it is the Hans who play a major role.

The situation comes out even more clear in case of Communist Russia where the struggle for the ethnic minorities to independence from Russian domination lends credence to the hypothesis that the idealism of creating a Federal State, where all have equal role is more of a myth than reality. The entry of Russian armed forces in Lithuania to suppress the local people is a poignantly real example.

The Russian model was to have been a glowing example of the successful solution of multi-racial and multi-ethnic statehood. The Russians claimed to have successfully delivered their people into an utopian co-existance where each group is maintaining its regional, political and social autonomy under the guidance of the benevolent Russian "Big Brother". What happened after *Prestroika* is history. Today U.S.S.R. is non-existant on the map of the world, but let us examine some of its erstwhile policies under the Soviet regime.

The Russians, unlike other White races did not have the kind of racial prejudice that led them to segregate themselves from non-White populations. From the earliest time of contact in the middle of the sixteenth century, racial inter-marriage was a perceived solution of integration and largely practiced. Even today such marriages are highly favoured except that the tussle remains as to who, out of the two partners, should give up their ethnic and cultural identity. White Russians wanted that such marriages should assimilate more and more people into the Soviet communist fold but folk ideology and popular folklores of the ethnic minorities stress otherwise. The strong Russian Nationalism had favoured integration much before the advent of Communism as evident in works of writers such as Chekhov.

Communism, with its strong political indoctrination viewed race relations in a less idealist sense than that visualised by earlier Russian thinkers. The erstwhile Soviet constitution provided for fifteen fully fledged Soviet Republics, Sixteen Autonomous Republics, nine Autonomous Provinces and ten National Areas. In reality, as has been historically demonstrated, these provinces could be disbanded at the stroke of a pen if they anyway violate the "narrowly defined interests of Soviet State as a whole" (Kolarez 1955 : 191).

Another strategy on the part of the dominant Russian state was to isolate the ethnic minorities by making each ethnic province directly linked with the centre. Any attempt at joining together of ethnic minorities to form sub-National level federations was strongly discouraged. There have been conscious attempts to break down larger ethnic areas into smaller ones in order to make them weaker. Turkestan, for example, was cut into six republics in spite of being culturally and racially homogenous.

The economic policy of the Soviet Union was directed towards homogenising economic disparities which was to be done through "industrialisation and general economic development" of previously neglected minority areas. A very rapid and intensified programme of industrialization was initiated for this purpose. For example coal production in Kazakhistan went upto 16,000,000 tons in 1950 from 90,000 in 1913 and the same occured in many other places. In reality this implied a virtual colonisation of these areas by the White Russians. Between 1926 and 1939, 1,700,000 Europeans entered Soviet Central Asia alone. These persons have moved into manning of industries in high statuses and monopolising all strategic positions. This is also a result of the purging out of local intelligentsia by the Soviet Communist Party. The picture clearly emerges that the minorities are to be tolerated only if they bow down to the paternalistic attitude of the Soviets. Ultimateley it was the Russian culture, ideology and the Communist Party which for all practical purposes were equated with the European ethnic stock, that is, to form dominant Soviet Nationalism.

In none of the indigenous areas was the local ethnic population even sufficiently represented in the industries. The more resources were exploited in their areas, the more marginalised the local populations became.

The Shorians of Southern Siberia had the unfortunate position of sitting on vast natural resources of iron-ore, gold and timber. Phenomenal increase in the exploitation of these resources made the Shorians a minority in their own area and put them in danger of disappearing as a "national and cultural entity".

The only real concession made to the minorities was the tolerance towards the Islamic religion followed by most of them. But this may be to maintain the divide as "to the less educated sections of the native populations of Soviet Asia, "Russian", "non-Muslim" and "Communist" even appeared for quite a time to be identical notions" (Kolarez 1955 : 199).

The important fact remains that the decisions regarding these minorities were always taken with National interest, equated with Russian and Communist interests without ever considering the minorities themselves. "Big Brother" in this context was not always benevolent as Burkey explicities states as to what happened in 1920 as a result of Govt. decision for economic reform. "In Central Asia thousands a decision as to whether nomads should first be collectivized and then settled into agricultural communities or whether they should be settled before being collectivized".

Lenin's ideology was to make the nationalities feel the benefit of staying within the Soviet Union and hence voluntarily form a part of the Federal Republic. Karklins (1986 : 6) has referred to E.R. Francis who divided the minority ethnic groups in USSR into two types. The primary ethnic groups are those that historically belong to the territory on which they live and which are named after them, and secondary ethnic groups are migrant populations, such as Soviet jews, Soviet Germans and Crimean Tartars. The primary ethnic groups alone can be considered under a tribal State.

All Soviet citizens have a dual identification on their official passports. One is, the citizen of a State and another an ethnic identity of belonging to a people. The latter is self-determined and hence open to a person's own subjective interpretation. However, Soviet official practice percieved ethnic identification as inherited and children have to choose the ethnic identity of one of the parents. Usually in case of mixed parents, children chose the more advantageous identity—preferably 'Russian' or one of the National States.

Although USSR recognized the identity of other ethnic groups, a Russian predominance, which was both demographic (52% of total population) and political and cultural as a result of official policies existed. Russian language overran all other native languages. As Karklins (1986: 61) has enumerated, "the central policy on languages stresses the use of Russian and regards the study and use of republic languages as unjusified in the interests of nationalism".

The ideological conflict of the Soviets of maintaining political dominance and on the other hand subscribing to the Leninist policy of pluralism has led to interesting development of key concepts in Soviet philosophy. The most important is the development of the concept of 'ethnos'. As Bromley 1980 writes, "In Russian ethnography the term 'ethnos' was used from the very beginning to denote people...ethnoses belong to that variety of communities which emerge as a result of the natural historical process and not as a result of the given people's will. These are complex formations, each possesses not only a certain internal unit but also specific features which distinguish it from all other formations of the same type".

The 'ethnos' was concieved as a distinctiveness, an identity which come to be associated with a particular population and which is not bound to any particular social structure; like French as people remain French, whether in a monarchy or in a democracy. "An ethnos is a useful analytical device, being a unit which can be traced vertically through history" (Dragadze 1980: 163), unlike societies which dissolve in one form and reorganize in another. Thus societies tend to form horizontal strata, while ethnoses move vertically up through these various strata without losing their essential identity or essence. The identities of the ethnos are comprised a common language, self-awareness and self-appointed name or ethnonym.

Thus, in retaining plurality of their society, the Soviets emphasized on the 'ethnos' and not on forms of structural relations. The self-identification of ethnicity, the multi-language formulas and retention of ethnic names for particular nationality regions was directed towards this end. However, in terms of structural relations it is assumed that ethnos will retain its identity in any social formation including a communist one. Since the ethnic identity is taken to be a subjective and not an objective reality, the Soviet social sciences emphasize the study of ethnopsychology to a great extent.

Lenin's ideology was to make the nationalities feel the benefit of staying within the Soviet Union and hence voluntarily form a part of the Federal Republic. Obviously, such an ideology did not materialize and in desperate attempts the Soviets stopped at nothing including genocide to subdue the minorities. However, one may concede that political and economic subjugation did in its wake also lead to cultural protection. A major contribution was the development of the minority languages and a large number of dialects without alphabets were provided with one.

Stalin's glorification of Russian language and culture had a further aim, to make Russian, the language of Socialism all over the world. To the great dismay of the Soviets, the replacement of Nationalism by Communism did not take place as a natural process. The ultimate aim of the Russians had been to inculcate in the minorities a sense of dependence upon the benevolent "Big Brother". But the minoritie's perception was quite different. Ultimately, the simmering dissension led to the dissolution of the Soviet-Socialist Republic in 1991; the political entity of Soviet Russia dissolved.

To take the example of the evolution of another Nation-State as a result of merger of indigenous populations is that of Iran. The ethnically diverse people of Iran are constituted by a number of very large nomadic pastoral groups who confirm to the ideal definition of tribe as given by Sahlins. The most dominant character of these groups is their acephalous nature which refuses to bow down to any centralized authorities. In discussing Iran we shall take as a specific case, the Qashqai from the excellent source material provided by Lois Beck (1986). Iran itself has evolved through several historical regimes from its early consolidation under Islamic rule to the present day regime established by Ayatollah Khomeini intervened by a long period of dynastic rule by the Pahlavis.

The dominant ethnic majority who have formed the State here are the Persians. The nomadic and semi-nomadic people of the vast deserts were earlier rarely attempted to be brought under rigid State control, till about the mid twenties they were ruled indirectly through their indigenous leaders. The State took advantage of their inter-tribal warfares to keep them divided and under control. However, Qashqai federations arose whenever attempt was made by the State to exert direct political control over them.

Tribes like the Qashqai and Bakhhtiari were made targets of States intervention only when they came in competition over strategic resources. One reason for this was their large populations, control over vital trade routes and national resources like oil wells and well organized tribal leadership. The Qashqai Khans were wealthy and articulate leaders. Other tribals like the Lurs were completely ignored as they occupied fairly remote and unimportant areas resource-wise. They also had smaller and more dispersed populations. In the 19th century the tribals exerted considerable political pressure. Their population equaled the dominant, settled Persian population and each tribe had its representation in the army.

The Qajar rule followed the policy of divide and rule working through the intervention of tribal leaders. They assessed taxes an land and flocks but the State control was otherwise minimal. During the reign of Mohammed Shah (1834-1848), the Qashqai selected their own pastures which indicates considerable political autonomy. The political intervention over the Qashqai increased enormously due to development of trade routes by the British though the rugged mountaineous road between Shiraz and the Persian Gulf, part of Bushire.

The Qajas rulers onwards till the present regime, the relationship between the Qashqai and the State has been one of constant confrontation. The first consolidated attempt to exert political control over the Qashqai was at the instance of the British who found them a constant interference in their trade and communication links. The game of power between the Germans and the British in which each tried to play up these tribes against the others made the Qashqai powerful enough to be perceived as a real threat to the State.

Strong State retaliation directed against the tribes attempted to disarm them. Concentrated effort was made to breakdown the ethnic identity of the tribes. The attempts of Shah Pahlavi' was to assimilate the entire Iran, tribal and non-tribal, into a single Western Culture in order to create a strong modern Nation-State. Attempts by the tribes to retaliate against the loss of ethnic identity led to fierce oppression which included aerial bombing of migratory routes, removal of tribal leaders and a concentrated effort was made to destroy their nomadic pastoral subsistance base.

The British accused the Qashqai of intervening in their trade routes and disrupting vital telegraph lines. This began in 1865 and continued well into the 20th century. The only way in which the Iranian State, under pressure from the British could deal with the matter was to make the Qashqai leaders (The Ilkhani) personally responsible for safety of roads passing through, what was regarded as his domain. Such a role was not traditionally granted to the Ilkhani even within the tribe. The precipitation of the Ilkhani's role served to organize the Qashqai identity further. The Qashqai, earlier divided into individual egalitarian tribes, was regarded as one taxable unit and one person held responsible. But the Iranian State itself, because of its own weak power structure, was unable to exert any real influence in the first twenty years of the twentieth century.

It was the British and the Germans who used the Southern Iranian Tribes as pawns in their own game of power. The British armed them against German factions. As a result Germans played up the tribes against the British in order to block their trade routes and communications. The tribes beccame locally autonomous and powerful. The European interference and their own military and capitalist interests made the tribals ultimately appear as powerful enemies of their own State. Out of fear of the tribes becoming totally anarchical, Reza Khan in 1925 made an attempt to destroy the threatening military power of the Qashqai, to disarm them and place them under military governership. Other ways to break down the tribal autonomy was to conscript tribal youth and place them under Persian command far away from their home regions. By removing them from their cultural region and placing them under Persian commanders, they were forced to learn Persian and became detribalized. During this period, for the first time, a concentrated effort was made to breakdown the ethnic identity of the tribals and to impose western dress on them. The attempts of Shah Pahlavi was to assimilate the entire Iran, tribal and non-tribal, into a single western prototype in order to create a strong modern Nation-State. At the same time all important indigenous leaders or the Ilkhani were removed from power and held as prisoners in Iran. The Qashqai, by no means weak people to be so easily subjugated, rose in an uprising in 1929.

This led Raza Shah to undertake fierce retaliation in 1933 to finish them off. Military campaigns were directed against the Qashqai, their migratory routes were subjected to aerial bombings, large number of leaders were imprisoned and killed and the nomadic tribals were forced into settlement in inhospitable areas with no means of subsistance. Against all this the Qashqai defended their ethnic and cultural identity and in the process evolved even more strongly as a political unit.

In Iran, because of the nearly balanced equation in the power structure between the State and the tribals, we find strategies of direct confrontation rather than the veiled domination couched in paternalism which is found where the State is considerably stronger than its tribes.

The Iranian tribes have suffered more because of foreign intervention where they have been used as strategic political resource. During World War II the Germans wanted to build up the Qashqai to rebel against the Iranian State and the Qashqai Khans managed their own tribal affairs without any interference from the State. The Government at this period did not impose any policies.

The real suffering of the Qashqai came with the realization by American capitalism of the vitality of resources such as communication links, rich agricultural land and oil fields under their control. As in the history of all other tribals, here again we find that it is not the poor but the 'wealthy' tribal who perceived by the spreading capitalism to be controlling valuable resources, is subjected to the maximum domination. In the early 1950's the American Government set out on its mission to help Mohamed Raza Shah to subjugate the Qashqai tribes, obviously with an eye over their resources. American officials offered the then ruling Khans five million dollars and posts as ministers in the Shah Cabinet, if they supported the Shah. They declined.

In order to bring them politically under control in 1956, the Shah made an unsuccessful attempt to settle these nomadic pastorals. The government officers were notably unsuccessful in unarming the Qashqai and to bring them under settlements. The government passed land reform laws which made no provisions for the seasonal use of pastures by these people. These policies encouraged the widespread expansion of settled cultivation at the expense of grazing land in all Qashqai areas. In a matter of few years, land rents and new regulations turned corporate, tribal owned lands into private property with explicit monetary value. The deliberate policy of capitalization introduced under American guidance was far more damaging to the tribes than the earlier policies of direct military confrontations. One of the top most government priorities in the 1960's was to settle the tribes. Deprived of their traditional pastoral means of subsistance, the tribes rapidly became impovrished and were deliberately converted by the State into labourers to work in the newly founded industries in Iran. In the 1970's the government announced a plan to settle half a million of Iran's nomadic tribes near fifty sugar plants and other industries to provide seasonal labour. The SAVAK was active in suppressing and imprisoning tribal leaders during this period.

Politically and culturally another effort made by the Government to assimilate the tribals, was the creation of a tribal education programme. In this, some prominaent tribal leaders cooperated with the government. At this point there was a reversal of the earlier governmental policy of ruling indirectly through the tribals own leadership. An attempt was made to annihilate the traditional ethnic identity by depriving them of their traditional means of subsistance and culture. The higher Qashqai leaders were banished and executed and the lower ones converted into State functionaries.

The fall of Raza Pahlavis regime in 1978-79 gave an initial gap to the direct or even indirect rule over the tribals. The Khomeini regime at first paid lip service to the sufferings of the tribals under the Shah regime and later adopted equally coercive means to deal with them. They strategically isolated the tribals from their leaders. The Khans were completely destroyed and the State attempted to restore economic prosperity to the people but now the policy was one of assimilation. Through all this till today the Qashqai have managed to retain their identity as an ethnic group. In the 1979, the collapse of the State led to a resurgence of cultural identity which is still held onto.

In the history of various tribes, especially in relation to the white colonialism survival, even demographically, has not been possible. In their greed to control the resources of the world, the European powers in the past one or two centuries have depleted and ravaged indigenous populations. The prime examples of these are Africa, Australia and the United States.

Russia, China and Iran and other such Nation States dealing with their own ethnic minorities have at least idelogically maintained a semblance of ethnic equality. But misguided by their religious theology and scientific tenets of evolutionism and social Darwinism, the European population's interaction and policies regarding the racially different populations of colonised territories has varied from treating them as non-human, sub-humans, inferior humans, irrational humans and so on. And in this a colonial and European science (at least to begin with) like anthropology carries its own burden of ethnocentrism.

Two major interests dominated European colonalism—the politico-economic one of control over resources and the more altruistic one of humanizing the pagans by proselytization—both carried on with equal zeal. The government policies were not directed to socio-cultural upliftment but primarily to strengthen the European empires. "The officially declared objective of extending British interests in East Africa were (a) establishment of political power or so called spheres of influence, (b) the conversion of Africa to christianity (c) the devolopment of trade and commerce for the supply of raw materials to expanding industry in Great Britain."

In their attempts at a totalitarian control over economic resources, White colonists in both East Africa and South Africa evolved a policy of almost total segregation of the races. The Blacks being relegated to the position of virtual serfs and the Whites to dominant positions of control. However, as Barnes has discussed in his (1955) paper, this stage only came after colonial rule had been totally established. He distinguishes four phases in the government's (White) policy towards the natives in South Africa. These are (1) Foreign policy, (2) Frontier phase, (3) Paternalism and (4) Integration.

The first phase of contact had no racial connotation to begin with. The initial aim was to establish trade relations. The White government entered into negotiations with Black States in order to make an entry into their territories. This period lasted till about 1900 but during this time White political control steadily increased. However, British, Portuguese and Dutch interests also played up Blacks against each other. In reality, it was more like a negotation of power between the White colonists themselves using indigeneous political leaders as pawns. The main goal of this game was spelled out in politico-economic terms. "Of greater relevance was the differential control of resources, of which the most important were warriors, land, cattle and guns" (Barnes ; 1955 : 175).

The second phase of frontier is marked by a desire, albeit unachieved on the part of the Whites to raise an impenetrable barrier between Whites and Blacks. What happened in reality was a period of contact in which the Whites gradually assumed supremacy. Dutch and Hottentot contact led to the displacement and depopulation of the latter as well as extensive miscegenation that led to the creation of a new race of mixed breeds. The Bantus suffered a similar fate in Transversal. This period was also marked by widespread slave trading.

In 1889 with the securing of a charter by Rhodes of his British South Africa company the Whites pushed inwards into African territory. The White economic interest was dominated by minerals. The White govenment's attitude was purely economic and paternalistic, looking upon the Blacks in an attitude of tolerance. This was specifically because there was no clash of interests with respect to resources. The mining done by the Europeans had not interested the Blacks and they were inducted only as mining labour. The Whites and Blacks came in conflict where the Whites had interest in the latter's pasture land to convert them into their own farm lands. Here the Whites assumed a racial superiority of rights quite often backed by religious ideology. As Barnes writes, regarding White (Dutch) and Hottentot's competition over land resources in Cape Town, "On the huge farms, which were regarded as the natural birth right of all White men, captured Bushmen children were put to work. The farmers were strongly religious in the calvinistic faith and it was in this period that the doctrine was formulated that the Hottentots were children of Ham, destined by God forever to hew wood and draw water"(10) (Ibid 1955 : 176)

In the last phase which followed, almost total political economic control by the Whites, a system of integration was formulated. This was based on a dotrine of racial compartmentalization which, as pointed out by Leo Kuper (1965) was ideologically the most efficient system of integration that could have been devised. By allotting each race a particular place in the economic and political division of labour and keeping them apart by the policy of strict racial segregation, a system of integration based on inter-dependence could have been achieved had the system been capable of total ideological acceptace as well.

As documented, there was a well organized division of labour in the Public sector. For example in the provincial Architects Department in Natal, the African served as labourers, cleaners and messengers, Indians as gardners, drivers and other semi-skilled work and the apex of administrative posts held by Europeans. The compartmentalization which allotts all priviledged places to Whites and all lowly statuses to Blacks with Indians coming in between is further supported by policies of spatial segregation as well as sexual segregation.

"There are extensive restrictions on the geographical mobility of African and Indian labour, and on the occupational mobility of all non-Whites" (Kuper 1965 : 273). Further, even if some positions can be occupied by members of different races, they are paid differently, as in case of teachers of the three races.

Africans are treated in abstraction as a reserve labour pool. They are put into reservations away from urban, industrial centers from where exact labour resources are drawn wherever necessary, and put back whenever unnecessary. The labour has to be just reproduced and no heed is paid to their quality of life. The 'less than human' ideology prevails here exactly as it prevailed during slave trading.

Behind the strict rules on miscegenation is the same principle of total blockage of racial interaction at a level of equality. "The laws passed since the accession of the national Party Government provide controls for almost every conceivable social situation, involving members of different races—marriage; 'illicit carnal intercourse; promixity between traders and neighbours; inclusion on a common electrol roll; school education for Africans (and now for coloureds); industrial conciliation machinery for Africans; trade unions; reservation of occupations; control of contact in trade; control of contact with Africans in schools, hospitals, clubs, places of entertainment, public assemblies, and churches (under certain conditions); occupation of premises for a substantial period of time; university education; partaking of refreshment; and (pending) all aspects of African life and work" (ibid. 276).

Such a comprehensive policy of segregation is directed towards buttressing an ideology of separation and effectively eliminating all forms of competition between Blacks and Whites. The Whites' control over all strategic resources, including that of human labour is incorporated within this policy.

The unbashed cultural and racial ethnocentrism was, as in cases of both Africa and as we whall see in Australia, a result of historical contact. (Berndt and Berndt: 1965). In the initial phases, the relations of superordination and subordination were not clearly marked off. In the initial period of contact the policies were more cautious and exploratory. The guiding ideology was an equation of human with Christianity and with White culture. In Australia, the first phase treated all natives as British subjects and as such they were expected to behave according to the normative patterns of British citizens. They were treated like errant children who had to be taught to behave.

Not being children, however, the natives did not meekly submit to the policies of "making humans out of them". The punishment for their errant behaviour often amounted to genocide. The ideology of treating natives as "sub-humans" made offences committed against them inculpable offenses. Although officially they were treated as British subjects, no White British subject could be hung for killing an Australian aborigine. In fact no punishment was ever officially pronounced for any kind of offence of violence or rape against them.

In Australia whose aboriginal popualtion was largely unable, either militarily or demographically, to resist the White onslaught, two results of the White and aboriginal contact resulted—(a) The creation of a hybrid race by miscegenation, (b) the total extinction (like of the Tasmanians) or depopulation and cultural and economic pauparization. In South Africa, where the indigenous population was seen as a real threat to the numerically inferior but politically dominant population, a policy of total segregation had been adopted. By the time the Australian aborigines had absorbed the full impact of White contact, there was very little left in them by way of competition.

The Australian Government's major policy at the end of the Nineteenth century was one of the protectionism. This involved herding the remnants of various tribal groups into reservations and providing them with the most essential items of survival, like food and blankets. Here a segregation was made between those natives who were entitled to protection, being the ones who had lost all independent means of survival, and those who were entitled to citizenship and hence treated at par with other British subjects which strictly meant 'non-tribal'. Upto 1957, to be called a British citizen a person had to dissolve all tribal affiliations, only after 1958 was the Native Welfare Act amended. A separate ethnic identity of a mixed population was also evolved.

The creation of the Native was in administrative terms the problem of looking after the people who were incapable of looking after themselves. It was this outlook that justified the use of the special term "aboriginal". In the words of the Hon. Paul Hasluk,(13) "Historically the term "aboriginal" has been kept for those "primitive and weak people whose lands have been overrun and who themselves lapsed into a condition of being subordinate to or excluded from the general body of the community......"

The tribal policy or aboriginal policy of protectionism excluded administratively those who lived close to Europeans and who could be treated as disadvantaged people within the European community. Thus in Australia the terms aborigine obtained a socio-economic connotation rather than a purely racial one. Consequently, there was great variation in different States of Australia as to who was regarded as an aborigine and who was not. In 1953, all people of mixed blood were no longer regarded as aborigine.

The aborigines were viewed as people who were kind of liability on the State in that they were not even capable of taking care of themselves. They were accorded a special legal protection and special laws meant for them which effectively made them totally dependent upon the State, losing whatever identity they had. The aborigines were not regarded as full citizens and had consequently no rights as such. They were reduced to a state of passivity and not deemed social adults in any sense of the term. At this time increasing use was also made of their labour in the growing pastoral and mining industries. The pastoral station owners who employed the aborigines used their labour like that of domesticated animals. They were opposed to payment of wages, to missionary endeavours and education.

By the 1930's and after the Second World War, the administration again changed to a policy of assimilation. By this time as Elkin (1951)[14] has pointed out, the aborigines had developed "intelligent parasitism" and the Whites had, no doubt aided by the anthropologists, developed "intelligent' appreciation" of the native.

The policy of paternalism and isolationism gave way to one of assimilation; with a recognition of the native as a human being like any other. However, the explicit policy was stated as follows, in a conference in Canberra on the 26th and 27th January 1961—"The policy of assimilation means in the view of all Australian governments that all aborigines and part aborigine are expected eventually to attain the *same manner of living as other Australians* and to live as members of a single Australian community enjoying the same rights and privileges, accepting the some responsibilities, *ob-*

serving the same customs and influenced by the same beliefs, hopes and loyalities as other Australians". In other words, such a policy visualised the virtual cultural and ethnic disappearance of the natives into the mainstream of White Australians, or as Vachon points out, to convert "Aboriginal communal labour to wage labour". Whereas the South African whites favoured a complete isolation, the Australians favoured a virtual disappearance of the native. The Australian government in this regard was avowdly non-racist. Under Australian conditions with the vastly depopulated aboriginal population, this seemed a favourable policy. According to the Rev. Hasluck, an administrator, "(The aborigines) is a scattered minority which seems bound to lose gradually year by year any prospect of continuing as a separate and assertive group".

The earlier policy of the Australian government to keep the aboriginals away from the mainsteam and in reservation underwent a natural turnover by the discovery of valuable mining resources on the Aboriginal land. It was no longer deemed feasible that the Whites should altogether keep away from Aboriginal territory converted into reserved stations under earlier policies. But the aborigines did not accept a passive role in the matter. In 1963, in Yirrkala a petition was filed. The government had in 1960 established the Aboriginal Benefits Trust Fund into which royalties from mining resources on Aboriginal territories was to be paid. In 1968, the aborigines in Yirrkala filed a petition to stop mining altogether as it violated their sacred lands. They were told by the law court that they were not legal owners of the land.

26th January, 1972 was the day of announcement of a new Government Policy on the aborigines based on a principle of self-determination but which remained close-lipped on land issues. The aboriginals staged a protest which made it clear that "the aborigines were aliens on their own land" (Peterson: 1982 : 446).

A great deal of political activity both on the Government front which came to be ruled by the Labour Party and on part of the increasing politically conscious aborigines led to the Aboriginal Land Rights Act (1976) which became law on 26th January, 1977 and by 1978 some amount of land was transferred into Aboriginal ownership.

The tussle went on between the large mining companies who were interested in the valuable resources on Aboriginal land such as oil fields, Bauxite and Uranium. The aboriginals wanted all mining to stop as it desecrated their land. The government ultimately conceded that the aborigines could negotiate economic and social conditions of mining.

This economic input from the royalties gave the aborigines the financial back-up to fight their cases. As Peterson points out, "Although most aborigines are still actively opposed to mining, royalties from mining are central to the success of the land-rights legislation. All of the major mines and oil and gas fields in the territory are so far on Aboriginal land. Income from these mines, currently around $ 3 million annually...it is these monies that are financing the land councils and the lawyers to fight the land claims, and which in future will give the aborigines the power to negotiate their place in Territory society on their own terms" (1982 : 454)

Simultaneously there has been a growth of the 'outstation' movement under which the aborigines are increasingly moving away from reservations into their own territories, presumably to carry on their own way of life. The government has been sympathetic towards such decentralization. "In 1976-77, the new Liberal-National Country Party Government granted $ 358, 183 towards the establishment of outstations, and this figure rose to $ 2,645,500 in 1979-80. (Coombs, etal : 1982-430)

The crystallization of the policy visualized an autonomous aboriginal township conducting and managing its own affairs. However, there are wide disparities in federal government and State government policies which, particularly in case of Queensland and Western Australia, remain racist. Further as quoted from Aboriginal Australia,[20] the government grant of land to aborigines has been mainly of those that were useless to Europeans.

The governments' approval of policies of decentralization serves to create perhaps a much desired dichotomy between the Whites and the aborigines but the latter in the process have developed a political consciousness which is bringing them into continuous conflict with the capitalists over questions of resource control. The Whites' claim to land and resources is a hang up of the white man's original ideology of theirs being a natural or birth right over most territories which they had happened to usurp by sheer force.

The history of colonization of America unfolds a similar story. The American Indian and White contacts follows a long bloody line of negotiations and coercion. The aim of every White who landed on the New continent was to wrest its resources from the original inhabitants. In the initial period the military conquests were not effective but a number of treaties totaling upto nearly four hundred were signed with the tribal chiefs and ultimately each was broken to establish a forced domination over land. Even the semblance of some sort of civilized negotiation was discarded after the Civil War.

"Food, clothing and shelter were destroyed, animals were seized and land was devastated, leaving the Indians the option of surrendering or starving....The ecological effects of these wars was devastating. The buffaloe of the Plains, which was essential for Indian survival, was almost totally and deliberately eliminated.

An estimated thirteen million bisons existed on the Plains in 1867, by 1883 were only 200 left"(21) (Burkey : 1978 : 177).

The policy was one of clear extermination and control of resources. It was backed by racist ideology and a nearly "non-human" view of the Indian. "A good Indian is a dead Indian" was a widely held norm. The killing of Indian children on ground that "nits breed lice" was also common. The display of Indian scalps were acts of heroism. The dominant social Darwinism advocated even by intellectuals at that time was that the so called "savage" races were anyway deemed to extinction.

However, the concentrated genocide still left behind some surviving Indian population. The government took the option out by putting them into Reservations of land earmarked only for their use. Such territories were the most unwanted ones. The creation of reservation took away all political decision making activities from these people. They were made totally dependent and subservient on the State. The government, by 1865, negotiated with Protestant missionary societies to educate the Indians in English language, to make them Christians and teach them the agricultural art.

In other words, having completely destroyed their original way of life, an attempt was made to resocialize them as white Amricans. The boarding schools run by Bureau of Indian Affairs forcibly separated Indian children from their families and prohibited them from meeting their parents even for as long as eight to ten years. All things Indian was totally forbidden. The misguided intentions and corruption of government officials soon made it clear that the reservations were inhuman, to say the least.

After 1880, the public opinion became oriented to assimilation of Indians into mainstream American life to make "Yankee farmers" out of them. With this view in mind the Daws Act was formulated in 1887. According to this the reservations land was to be broken up into individual plots, with each head of family given 160 acres, each single person over eighteen years, 80 acres and each person below eighteen, 40 acres. In 1871 there were 30 million acres of land under reservation, by 1934 sixty per cent of this was lost to the Indians as a result of this Act. Sixty million acres were declared surplus and sold to Whites and the Indians sold 27 million acres of their own land. The main problem was that the Indians were not able to manage the lands under the State legislations like land taxes etc. of which they had very little awareness.

Citizenship rights were first granted in 1901 to the five "civilized" tribes of Oklahama and by 1924 extended to all tribes. Till 1940, however, seven States did not grant right of franchise to Indians. A rethinking of government policy led to the Reorganization Act under John Collier, the then commissioner for Indian affairs. "The act called for the return to tribal ownership of all surplus lands not yet leased, the formation of an Indian Civil Service, self-determination of tribal governments on reservations, and the guarantee of the exercise of religious freedom and the use of Indian languages" (Burkey 1978 : 237).

The majority of American Indians viewed this Act as pluralistic and opposed it. The American Indians have been vassalating between assimilation and pluralism. There is a definite movement as among the Australian aborigines to reclaim tribal land and reinforce tribal identity. The Canadian tribes such as the Cree Indians, who have through their traditional mode of subsistance hunting have established on economic viability through the fur trade are stating a claim to the 'back to homeland' movement. Along with this is a concentrated move against government or outside encroachment on indigenous resources. They have successfully opposed the laying of a pipe line through their areas. The government is reluctantly modifying its policies to grant greater autonomy to such groups as are still in a position to claim it. The Red Power Movement composed largely of educated Indians was aimed towards a pluralistic society. Under a successful protest from the American Indian Movement, the government had to concede to the extent of raising the Bureau of Indian Affairs (BIA) budget from $ 20 million to $ 593 million. The success of this event made 150 Indians in war paint take over the village Wounded Knee. The demand was a return of the Dakotas, Mantanas and Nebraska to the Indians. The government put up a resistance and took recourse to military intervention but taking care not to involve a loss of life. However, the government is increasingly becoming conscious of the civil rights movement.

From the above account it becomes clear that the tribal policies have always been conditioned by the tribe/non-tribe contact situation and have changed or modified only according to the changing demands of this equation.

From the non-tribal side, whether they have been White colonists usurping native territories or indigenous ethnic populations forming Nation States, the dominance has always been to establish a control over coveted resources. In this, direct competition at times has been averted because both the groups have not found the same resources desirable. In this, all such populations that were poor and marginal had been largely ignored if they continued quietly on their own ways. Quite often conflict and a necessary domonstration of force has been necessary because the acquisition of coveted resources may clash with the interests of native group, not because both want the some things but because what either party wants is itself impossible to obtain in a complementary fashion. For example, the Australian aborigines protested against the descration of their sacred land by miners and prospectors.

Every time the intrusion has been couched in ideological terms and rarely perceived in a simplified manner of direct predation. The European colonisation with its accompanied brutality accepted European superiority as the natural order of things. In Russia, Russian superiority has been advocated ideologically in the interests of a global spread of Socialism. China and other so called ethically pluralistic societies have perpetuated domination in the name of national interest. Wherever the relationship has been of equality or perceived equality, direct conflict has occurred as in Iran, and in the initial phase of colonisation of Africa, America and Australia.

Once a group has been sufficiently subjugated so as not to pose a threat, the dominating group has developed paternalistic attitudes. In some cases as in Russia the situation may have been initially so. The paternalism has inevitably been in the direction of indoctrination of the subjugated groups in the way of life and ideology of the dominant group. This is accompanied in most cases by a desire to maintain boundaries between groups in social terms while attempting a political integration in a way that the superordinate/subordinate relationship is perpetuated. An extreme of such a policy of division and consequent integration is Africa with its apartheid policy but one that has been followed in all countries with some watering down including the Communist ones. The last phase in historical terms or rather the current phase is an increasing tendency for the dominated groups to reassert themselves. The move is, by and large, to reclaim their lost assets and to come to a relationship of equality with the dominant group. In political terms this would mean that many such populations would want to seccede from the Mother Nation.

Here comes the most crucial aspect—to what extent self-determination by tribal and minority groups endanger the very existence of large Nation States ? Is an equitable global distribution of resources possible with the existing structure of Nations and the capitalist system ? The Nation States themselves think to the contrary. Continuous suppression or regional movements is a testimony to this.

What should be the nature of future policies ? Ethically and morally one stands up for policies of self-determination. Will such policies, if ever effective, change the map of the wold ? Such questions, not easily answered, need pondering.

REFERENCES

1. 1988 *"Aboriginal Australia"* Department of Aboriginal Affairs, Canberra, Rey, Ed.
2. Barnes, John : 1955, 'Race Relations in The Development of Southern Africa' in Andrew Lind (Ed.) *Race Relations In World Perspective.* Hawaii, University of Hawai'
3. Beck, Lois : 1986, *The Qashaqi of Iran* New Haven, Yale University, London.
4. Berndt, Ronald and Catherine Berndt (Ed.) : 1965, *Aboriginal Man In Australia* London: Argus and Robertson.
5. Elkin, P. : 1951, "Reaction and Interaction: A food gathering People and European Settlement in Australia" *American Anthropologist* Vol. 53 pp. 164-86.
6. Burkey, Richard M : 1978, *Ethnic And Racial Groups : The Dynamics of Dominance* Cummings Publishing Co. Inc.
7. Coombs, H.C. Etal : 1982, "The Outstation Movement In Aboriginal Australia" *in Politics and History in Band Societies (Ed.)* Eleanor Leacock and Richard Lee, Cambridge, Cambridge University Press.
8. Dragadze, T. : 1980, "The Place of 'Ethnos' Theory in Soviet Anthropoligy" In Ernest Gellner (Ed.) *Soviet and Western Anthropology,* London, Duckworth.
9. Eickelman, Dale. F, : 1981, *Middle East,* Englewood Cliffe. Prentice Hall Inc.
10. Karklins, Rasma : 1986, *Ethnic Relations In the USSR.* Boston : Alllen and Unwin.
11. Kolarez, Walter. J : 1975, "Race Relations in the Soviet Union" in

Andrew. W, Lind (Ed.) *Race Relations in World Perspective.* Hawaii, University of Hawaii Press.

12. Kiano, J.G : 1966, "Towaards Economic Integration With Special Reference to Racial Tensions' in *'Racial and Communal Tensions in East Africa'* Africa, East Africa Publishing House, Nairobi.
13. Kuper, Leo : 1965, *An African Bourgeosie,* London, Yale University Press
14. Peterson, Nicholas : 1982, 'Aboriginal Land Rights in the Northern Territory' in *Politics and History in Band Societies.*
15. Roy-Burman, B.K : 1983, "Transformation of Tribes and Analogous Social Formations". *Economic and Political Weekly.* XVII. pp. 1172-1174.
16. Vachon, Daniel. A. : 1982, "Political Consciousness and Land Rights Among the Australian Western Deserts People' in *Politics and History in Band Societies* (Ed.) Eleanor Leacock and Richard Lee. Cambridge, Cambridge University Press.

[illegible] Ecology [illegible] Harvard University Press.

17

Evolution of Tribal Policy in India—An Appraisal

Sukant K. Chaudhury

Two aspects deserve attention while discussing tribal policy in India.[1] Firstly, with the advent of the colonial regime, the tribal cultures have gradually and sometimes recklessley been subjected to disintegration. Secondly, the ensuring consequences of disintegration caught the attention of tribal observers, administrators, social workers and also those engaged in launching and carrying forward the freedom struggle.

Although, compared to the vast populace of India, the tribals constituted a minority, in areas of strategic importance and in those which were rich with resources, they played a crucial role. Hence, the administration needed to have a serious look at the tribals. The process of coming to terms with tribal problems started with the British, it continued with intensified efforts in post-independent India. Besides a number of committees and commissions, plans and sub-plans, a separate ministry (with other units) was created in 1985 to look after the tribal problems and devise appropriate methods to solve their pressing needs.

For studying the evolution of tribal policy in India, one has to begin with the British policy towards them. The British administration had two entwined aims. To exercise hegemonic control over the land coupled with exploiting resources that could enrich the development of industries at home. For accomplishing these aims, the British opened up the country by laying down railway lines, increasing the methods of communication, thus freely allowing the migration of people, mainly non-tribals to tribal terrirories. Fearing that one of the consequences of such an opening up would be to accelerate the process of bringing the tribals into the Indian mainstrem, providing further nutritive maintenence to freedom struggle, the British were interested in isolating the tribals and this was achieved by forming excluded and partially excluded areas. And when the anthropolgists also voiced their opinion for isolation, the British ideas of excluding the tribals received academic legitimacy.

Programmes for the development of the tribes needed to take into cognizance some of the aspects of tribal backwardness, that had primarily emerged out of the contact situation. The tribals were widely dispersed and isolated from the general mass as they inhabited the forests or forest clad hilly tracts. Being economically backward, and relying on crude methods of cultivation, they required an all-round economic development. A sense of modern rationality could be inculcated with the programmes of education that would also bring them in modern organisation and occupational structures. All these could speed up the nation building process.

All these above aspects could be attributed to welfare motives. However, there were other aspects of colonial interest which were based on the political economy of that time. It was mainly based on three factors : rule, resources and rationality. The British wanted to exercise their rule on the whole country with a centralised administrative system. This implied a control on the tribals too, for which the Britishers needed to keep a track of those tribals who were relatively isolated. The tribal tracts were rich with mineral and forest resources, which needed to be siphoned off. Consequently roads and other communication network were laid down. Further they wanted to inculcate a sense of rationality through various welfare measures, so that they could gain the sympathy and sanction of the tribals. The aspect of rationality included opening up Christian Missions which through their various welfare activities could alert rationality, in turn legitimizing their administration.

Let us now briefly discuss the situations which led the colonial government to frame policies for the tribals. Before the onset of British rule, the situation was quite different. The tribals were relatively isolated and left undisturbed during the pre-British times. But, the contact situation had already started during the Moghul rule. The Moghuls rulers and the landlords encouraged the settlement of peasant communities in the wild hill tracts, to reclaim land in tribal areas. The trade and strategic routes passing through the forest tracts, though scantily, gained significance during this time. Many tribes such as Bhils, Minas, Kolis and Gonds were regarded by the Muslim rulers as dominant communities. In some cases such as Gonds and Cheros, the chiefs encouraged non-tribal peasant communities such as Kurmis, Koeris and Kunbis to settle in their areas. It could have been because the non-tribal peasants were good agriculturists who succeeded in producing surplus. Compared to them, the tribals had a subsistence economy in which the chances of a huge surplus were largely remote (Singh, 1968).

But with the advent of the British, the situation became completely different. There was total restructuring on the agrarian front. Zamindari/ryotwari system was introduced in full scale. Land owners in the tribal areas were recognised as Zamindars (in Bengal), Malgujars (in Bihar), Ghatwals (in Behar), Bissoyies, Muttadars (in Orissa and South India). The agrarian system of Pre-British era marked by the concentration of land in the hands of tribal chiefs, underwent an institutional change, leading to the creation of a powerful class above types of landowners, who were no more tribals, but in most cases were non-tribals/outsiders. Thus the agrarian system which was having mild traces of feudalism, turned into a well entrenched hierarchial feudal system during the British rule. Trade transations through markets gained momentum. Monetary economy encroached upon the tribal subsistence. Consequently the middleman factor entered the tribal life. All these resulted in wide spread revolt, rebellion and mutiny by the tribals all over the country.

How the British looked at the tribals and their problems is clear from the following case.[2]

The Pahariyas of Raj Mahal Hills are well known as they were the first to come under the control of the British. They violently protested against the externally imposed colonial system. Augustus Clevelend was given the charge to pacify them. Their leaders were paid a fixed sum as pension-which amounted for Rs. 15,000 annually and they continued for about 100 years to report all crimes. Clevelend created a ring fence at the foot of the hills by allotting land for settlement to the disabled/retired soldiers. He asked the Government to withdraw the Raj Mahal Hill tract from the jurisdiction of ordinary courts and instead he constituted a session court known as the Hill Assembly, comprising of the hereditary leaders, which was to meet atleast twice a year to try all offences. Raj Mahal Hill tracts were withdrawn from the jurisdiction of ordinary courts in 1782, and the Hill Assembly started smooth functioning. Cleveland also solved the land encroachment problem : the land was formed into a Government Estate held by Pahariyas directly from the Government, free from any rent. Thus the tract was unified and known as Daman-i-Koh. However, whatever rules were drawn up by the Hill Assembly were made law by Regulation I of 1796, but it was given the status of specially administered area with no interference from outside. It continued till 1827 and after that Regualtion I was repealed and the Pahariyas came again under the jurisdiction of ordinary courts. Why it was repealed in 1827 was not due to a welfare motive, but it was a selfish motive in the sense that it was becoming costly for the Colonial Government as they were not getting any rent and in addition had to pay pension to the tribal leaders. Hence, a charge of suspicion of glaring lawlessness and subsequent inquiry by James Sutherland led to the repealing of Regulation I of 1796 in 1827. Thus the Pahariyas were specially administered till 1827. G.S. Ghurye has aptly named Daman-i-Koh as the precursor and prototype of the non-regulation tracts, the scheduled districts, the Backward Tracts or the Excluded Areas (Ghurye, 1963).

Subsequently many tribes rose in rebellion and gradually all of them came under one or the other policy. After the Kol Mutiny of 1831, the Government put the entire Chota Nagpur area under the charge of an officer, designated as Agent to the Governor-General. A set of rules for criminal justice was specially provided by the Governor-General and it remained in force till the Criminal Procedure Code of 1861. In 1884, again the designation of the province was changed and it was put under the direct control of Lieutnent-Governor of Bengal to be administered as a non-Regulation Province. According to S.C. Roy, in spite of being the specially administered area, ordinary laws enacted in

Bihar, Bengal and Orissa came to be introduced in backward Chota Nagpur one by one.

Similarly the immediate outcome of the outrageous and devastating Santal rebellion of 1858 was that the Santal Parganas including Daman-i-Koh was formed a separate district and declared a non-Regulation area by Regulation XXXVII of 1855. The Scheduled Districts Act XIV of 1874 empowered the local Government to declare in respect of the tract specified in the Act, what enactments were or were not in force, and to notify the application, with modifications or restrictions if necessary, of any enactments in force at the time in any part of British India. By this act all tribal tracts became Scheduled Districts.

The Kondhs revolted against the administration after the custom of human sacrifice was stopped in 1846 and after suppressing it, Angul (where the Kondh tract was placed) was Annexed in 1848. The British had already acquired Goomsar Estate of Ganjam District (near Angul) in 1855. It was made subject to India Act XXIV of 1839, whereby civil and criminal jurisdiction was vested in the Agent and his assistants.

The famous Rampa Rebellion in South India was a result of wide scale exploitation by the feudal lords and it led to framing up of policies for them to curb their exploitation. The Hill Reddies of the erstwhile East Godavari Agency of Madras Presidency rose to rebellion in 1879. They were ruled by a Mansabdar who was non-Reddi. The Mansabdar in fact had given the villages to the sub-ordinate chiefs *(muttadars)* and from whom he received an annual income of Rs. 8,750 each. The oppressive rule by him and particularly the excise regulation forbidding collection of palm wine for domestic consumption and leasing the toddy revenue to the contrators entitled to collect taxes at their own discretion, resulted in widespread protests. To curb this, heavy police force was used. A protective land legislation was passed and enacted only in 1917 to stop transfer of land from tribals to non-tribals. Haimendorf pointed out that the aboriginal tribes, even inherently not of a warlike character, are capable of considerable efforts if driven to extremities (Von Furer-Haimendorf 1982).

To quell the rebellions, the British from time to time had established Agencies to administer them. Famous among them are the one of Bhils (1833). Meriah Tract (1839-65) and Ganjam Agency (1839). The Agencies worked towards pacifying the tribals, settling them, opening communication links and markets (Fuchs, 1992).

Now let us discuss the causes of these uprisings, revolts and rebellion by the tribals. All of them demonstrate a common trait-resistance against the British policies to administer them. It was resistance to a new system, new class of people, taxation, evangelisation, new landlords, money lenders and officials. The erosion of traditional rights over forests, restriction on shifting cultivation, exploitation by local functionaries and high land rents were also the causes of such protests.

The value of rationality, understood in the western sense, was imposed on the tribals through the missionaries. The role of missionaries in the tribal tracts in India is crucial, as they had close links with the colonial government. At the ideal level, however, they had all welfare programmes such as educating the tribals, providing health care facilities to them and so on. But at the back of it was the concept of rationality, which the missionaries were propagating covertly, it was in fact rationalising the colonial policies. The puritanical ethics which was preached by them was not something acceptable to the tribals and it had its disruptive effects on them. Further, the missionaries imposed an ideology of peasant systems in the tribal regions. In some places, they also supported the peasant struggles, for instance in Bengal, they supported the struggle against indigo planters and in Chotanagpur against the zamindars. They also worked for the passing of agrarian laws to curb exploitation against the tribals. But their links with administration weighed more, as they were creating a sense of loyality among the tribals for the colonial government (Singh, op. cit.).

With various local modifications, the British policy for tribals continued till the Govt. of India Act of 1919. In the 1919 Act, special modified administration of various areas, regarded as backward, could be ordered by the Governor-General in Council, thus wholly exempting the people from the said areas from administration under the provisions of the Act. It also provided for the appointment of officers to administer civil and criminal justice, to supervise the settlement and collection of revenues and all matters relating to rent and otherwise to administer the scheduled districts.

In 1919 reforms, the representation of Council of Tribals was one or two out of 76 elected members, which never served the purpose of the tribals. S.C. Roy suggested to the Goverment to form separate province for Chotanagpur and Santal Pargana under one administrator directly under the Govenor General, to form separate provinces for the tribal tracts in Orissa and to constitute the tribal tracts into a sub-province under a major province.

J.P. Mills and G.H. Hutton proposed complete exclusion of tribal areas from constitutional reform so as to keep them under direct control of the British administration. As member of the British Parliament, they proposed it prior to 1935 reforms. The Government declared 4 tracts as excluded areas. The Indian National Congress opposed this idea which was enacted from January, 1937; as it would be easier for the British to exploit the resources and also in suppressing them. Thus the approach of isolation came into being, which received vehement criticism from all sections of the society.

The controversy in the isolation approach is well known; Verrier Elwin is often confused as the propounder of the policy of isolation. In fact it was G.H. Hutton who was the arch exponent of this policy. Elwin's idea of National park which was never implemented fully, was often confused and taken as the policy of isolation. Elwin repeatedly made it clear that he never wanted the tribals to be isolated and put them into zoo. Yes, he favoured a policy of isolation from the debasing and impovershing contact. In his words—"The aboriginal cannot remain as he is, but is it necessary for him to pass through degradation before he emerges as a civilized man in future" (Elwin, 1958).

During the phase of transfer of power also, the British administrators proposed to keep tribal tracts under them as they claimed to be the protectors of them and suggested that to look after their upliftment, officers should be appointed under the direct control of High Commissioner in India. However, finally it did not materialise, and they had to abandon it.

Opposed to the isolation policy, the short-sighted assimilation approach by the social workers and even social scientists like G.S. Ghurye is well known. There were many arguments and counter arguments on the issue for some time, and finally emerged the integration approach which has been hailed by all section of the society and which is still the guiding factor for formulation of any policy towards the tribals. Nehru, the architect of the 'integration policy', intended to integrate the tribals into the mainstream of the country and culture. He first proposed the policy in the foreword to *A Philosophy for NEFA* in 1958 through the Panchsheel (5 principles).

Nehru's policy implied three important aspects : appropriate development programmes for the tribals, participation of the people in both planning and implementation of programmes and empowerment of the people. Whether we have been able to keep up to the Nehruvian ideal needs concern. A plethora of programmes to ameliorate their conditions have been implemented. Different agencies were created-504 tribal development blocks were created. In the fifth five year plan, Tribal sub-plan was implemented, under which 193 Integrated Tribal Development Projects are running in the tribal concentrated areas. Modified Area Development Approach (MADA) scheme is on in the areas of less concentration. Primitive Tribal Group has been created under which 74 minor and small tribes are receiving area specific attention. Large scale Multipurpose Cooperative Societies (LAMPs) have been created in the tribal areas to look after the marketing aspects. Further, 'cluster approach' has also been followed in the 6th five year plan, where tribals are scattered and the above agencies could not work. On the other hand the task of looking after the problem and development of the tribals was given to the Scheduled Caste & Scheduled Tribe Division in the Ministry of Home Affairs, Government of India till 1965, which later shifted to the Department of Social Welfare till early 70's, then came back to the home ministry with an expanded set up, and finally landed up in the newly created Ministry of Welfare in 1985.

The total number of tribes today is 461 (Singh, 1984). The tribal population of the country has increased by 25.67 per cent from 1981 to 1991. They constitute 8 per cent of the country's population numbering 6.7 crores (according to 1991 census). The population is constantly increasing and their problems have also increased manifold. Most of the programmes and the money spent on them, do not reach them. The development programme, as many studies emphasise, are not area specific, culturally rooted and people oriented.[3] Further the target oriented approach of the implementing agencies have made the programmes non-contextual. It is urgently required that development is taken as a seious concern. Most of the ethnic movements, which culminate either in the demand of a district or a state, have surfaced because the development programmes are unable to alleviate the sufferings of the tribals. Integrating the tribals into the mainstream can only be made effective by a drastic reorientation of the policy framework with emphasis on cultural identities and people oriented programmes.

NOTES

1. This is the revised version of the paper presented in the National Seminar on "Tribal Policy Issues and Themes" held on March, 1991 at the Department of Anthropology, Delhi University. I am grateful to Prof. J.S. Bhandari, Delhi University for his useful comments.
2. The cases of Parariya, Santal & Kondh are taken from Ghurye (1963).
3. For a detailed account see Chaudhury (1993).

REFERENCES

Chaudhury, S.K. 1993. *Myopic Development and Cultural Lens,* New Delhi : Inter-India.

Elwin, V. 1957. *A Philosophy for NEFA,* Shillong.

Fuchs, S. 1992. *The Aboriginal Tribes of India,* New Delhi : Inter-India.

Ghurye, G.S. 1963. *Scheduled Tribes,* Bombay : Popular Prakashan.

Sachchidanand, 1992. *Tribal India : Past and Present;* Calcutta : Institute of Social Research & Applied Anthropology.

Singh, K.S. 1968. *Tribal Situation in India,* Shimla : Indian Institute of Advanced Studies.

Singh, K.S. 1994. *The Scheduled Tribes,* New Delhi : Oxford University Press.

Von Furer-Haimendorf, C. 1982. *Tribes of India : The Struggle for Survival.* New Delhi : Oxford University Press.

Conclusion

Tribal India—Past and Future

J.S. Bhandari

Understanding of the contemporary tribal societies requires a basic appreciation of the historical processes that have determined the course of successive changes which have affected the peoples of India, including the tribal societies, which were equally influenced by the forces of change which were economic, socio-cultural, ideological and political in their manifestations. Keeping in mind the vastness of the Indian sub-cultural multitudeness of its people, one can only generalize that the historical experiences would be as variable for different people as their interaction with their environment and the socio-political forces that they might have encountered from time to time. This *time and space* framework is essential to understand the tribal societies in the right perspective.

The history of many tribal societies in India is perhaps longer than that of the non-tribal people. With the development of civilization in India, whose ethos was Hinduism and whose socio-economic structure was provided by the caste system, there was a constant interaction between peripheral autonomous communities and the civilization that surrounded them. Although we have hardly any historiographical evidence of peripheral community civilization interaction during the early periods, it may be inferred that the process of Hinduization might have been the earliest form of transformation and subsequent incorporation of these societies into the folds of dominant civilization, with concomitant changes in their economic relations. This was an adaptive process demanding the least structural modifications. The basic characteristics of the process was of integration with the civilization without losing original identity. It meant participation in social, economic and religious system with a new symbolic boundary but without the loss of cultural identity. However, all such groups which adopted a few facets of Hinduism did not attain any place in the structure of Hindu society, they maintained their social and cultural boundary and subsistence economy. History of tribe-civilization interaction is history of incorporation (in structure); acculturation and of isolation leading to cultural autonomy. The tribal groups that were not fully incorporated lived in relative isolation and were able to resist changes from outside.

However, even the relative isolation was shattered with the establishment of colonialism in India. With imposition of colonial economy, not even the forest dwelling tribes were spared, as is clear from the policy resolution of 1894, which regulated and restricted the unfettered rights of the forest dwelling people over its resources and their utilization. Some tribes in fact rose in rebellion when *jhumming* (shifting cultivation) was restricted amongst them. But the greatest blow to the tribal economy under the colonial rule was in the form of land policy of the colonial administration, as a consequence of which large land holdings in tribal areas were alienated from the tribals by the newly created class of intermediaries, money lenders, land owning peasants. The phenomenon of landlessness is a glaring consequence of the land and forests being taken from the tribesmen's possession; who had always lived off them. Those who escaped total alienation of their land and homes became affected in other ways through the policies of the exploitative system. Their control over forests and cultivable land was curtailed by extraneous factors. The British and European scholars, of the colonial period, however, totally glossed over the evolution of Indian civilization and highlighted the socio-cultural diversity to emphasise the tenuous character of India rather than looking at the intricate web of integrated social system of India. They depicted India in contemporanious perspective and created a static, changeless, stagnant Indian society.

Thus by the time we gained our freedom, the people of India had undergone tremendous structural and cultural changes, the most important one being absolute pauperization of its people. The tribal people were one of the most exploited and the least known segments of the country. With the attainment of Independence, reorganization of Indian economy was the most important challenge that faced the country. In fact the founding fathers of the Constitution of India were fully aware of the magnitude of the disparity and inequality in its vilest form among a very large segment of Indian society who were formally recognized as Scheduled Castes and Scheduled Tribes Communities. For these two segments the Constitution made provisions so that over a period of time they could catch up socially, economically and politically with rest of the people of the country. The Constitutional provisions made for them, in my opinion, are one of the most outstanding features of Indian Constitution which on behalf of the Nation makes amply clear the social injustice and economic exploitation of the tribal and low caste groups at the hands of the more dominant groups throughout the history, and enjoins the Nation to fredeem the situation by giving them protection. For this purpose the Constituent Assembly had set up a sub-committee under the chairmanship of Sri A.V. Thakkar for "excluded" the "partially excluded" areas (other than Assam). It recommended that the "new democratic state had a responsibility towards the tribal people and the development of tribal areas, however remote or unaccessible they may be".

The Constitution is however not a blue-print for ameliorating their condition, it has merely enjoined the states to do it. So the major task before the Government was to devise ways and means to their rapid development. The nation in a way was in search of a policy that would fulfill the Constitutional obligation.

Pt. Jawaharlal Nehru enunciated a policy of tribal transformation which is popularly known as 'Panch Sheel" approach to the tribal societies. Nehru's philosophy has been praised any number of times as the most appropriate approach to tribal development in the country. As a humane approach to ameliorate the condition of the tribal people, no body can find fault with it. Nehru was also fully appreciative of tribal cultural heritage in the form of their myths, songs, dances, dress and language and realized the need to give them respect and protection for the survival of tribal identity. He was opposed to cultural domination of any type. Tribal people in many parts had already forgotten their traditions, after having converted to new faiths. The effect of christian missionaries was quite negative, specially in conversion efforts to erase the past along with its present manifestation from many tribal people. Nehru's policy made it clear that economic development and modernization of tribal societies was the final goal but not at the cost of the loss of identity of any tribal community. The identity of a people is their language, their values, their way of life. In a small way, participation of various tribal people through their songs and dances in the Republic Day Parade was a recognition of their contribution in the rich heritage of India's folk culture. It was symbolic of the growing awareness of nation's unity.

Now let us see what has been done for the tribal people in the last 45 years through democratic planning, and what has been its intended and unintended consequences.

Tribe in India is a generic term which includes a very diverse variety of social formations ranging from the bands of hunter-gatherers to those who have achieved statehoods within the democratic framework of the country. We have 250 scheduled tribes (including another 200 subtribes)* spread throughout the country in various proportions, speaking about 100 languages besides 225 subsidiary languages. They are also variable in their size from a few hundred to 5 million. However, each of the tribal community had its own cultural and social boundary manifesting varied spectrum of economic adaptation,ethnic and cultural diversity. As per the 1991 census the scheduled tribe population numbered 6.7 crore, which was 8% of the total.

The tribal societies in India are not homogeneous culturally, socially, linguistically, politically and economically. Unlike the rural poor in rest of India, we cannot generalize about the tribal societies. The rural people in India, by and large, suffered from the same problems or the causes of their poverty were mainly dependent on similar factors (viz. land tenure system and its concomitant ramification). However, the problems of the tribes were linked to various factors which varied from tribe to tribe. It was therefore imperative that the planned development for the tribal society had

* According to K.S. Singh (1984) their number today is 461.

to tak cognisance of the complex reality of tribal problems in the country.

Planning in India was ushered in 1951. The First Five Year Plan (1951-1956) was mainly meant to reorganize the Indian economy. Many projects were taken up for implementation but there was no integrated approach. In this plan tribal development programmes were allocated Rs. 19.93 crores which was just 1% (one percent) of the total plan outlay. The programmes under the heads of economic, educational and social development of the tribal communities were undertaken. The First Five Year Plan had hardly any impact whatsoever on any tribal community. In 1952 C.D. Programme was launched with a view to initiate integrated rural development. With the same comprehension, keeping in view the locational and institutional problems of the tribal areas, 43 MPTD blocks were started in the country in 1954. But soon the realization was made that it was not possible to cover the tribes in such an intensive and extensive scale. So smaller areas with smaller population were taken up for development. And by the end of Third Plan 2/3rd of the tribal areas were expected to be covered under various development schemes. But the SMPT Blocks covered only about 40% of the tribal population, as areas having less than 2/3 but more than fifty percent were covered by CD Block. The CDP proved a stagnant programme with limited funds and amorphous approach and was phased out. The Third Five Year Plan had a total expenditure of 82.85 crores which was about 1.2 percent of the total.

The developmental strategy was changed during Fourth Five Year Plan which was oriented to specific problem areas (SFDA, DPAD, MFAL). On the pattern of SFDA, six (6) Tribal Development Agencies were created. Such TDA covered a group of TD blocks and their aim was economic and social development though in final analysis their programme got stuck at agriculture and some development in infrastructure like road building etc. This programme never could become viable. Fourth Plan had Rs. 75.00 crores for TD which was only .5% of the total outlay. Experiences gained up to Fourth Plan only provided a new thrust and thinking for Tribal Development in the Fifth Five Year Plan. By the end of the Fourth Five Year Plan, the Government realized that there were many weaknesses in the programmes and their formulation. Among these were (1) lack of adequate funds for some schemes that depended on different allocations, (2) the planners did not comprehend the distinctive features of tribal areas and tribal societies and treated them as if they constitute one single undifferentiated cluster of human group living under the same environmental conditions, and (3) the implementation of such unified approach was totally unsuitable and the plan executors could not but spend money on faulty and unimaginative programmes.

This was nothing short of a very callous attitude of the policy makers towards the tribal development programmes. It was not due to the lack of information about the structure and distribution of tribal people and their various problems. In fact as early as 1959, the Renuka Roy Committee had recommended an integrated approach keeping in mind the needs and possibilities in each tribal area. Besides, there were many other Expert Committee, working group reports and vast anthropological literature available about a large number of tribes. But the planners were more interested in articulating the total plan rather than planning according to the needs of the people and the area. It was only with ushering of the Fifth Five Year Plan, the Government of India decided to seriously take up tribal development by emphasising that each sector must take up development of tribal areas and tribal communities. The emphasis was laid down on area devlopment with focus on development of tribal communities. For this purpose areas of tribal concentration were recognized and other forms of developmental strategy was planned for dispersed tribal groups. Thus in the Fifth Plan the concept of Tribal sub-plan was utilized. The basic aim of the Tribal sub-planners was to keep in focus the basic social, cultural, economic and political milieu of different tribal societies; it was also belatedly realized that there are areas of tribal concentration where 'area approach' could be adopted and the other realization was about what were termed as primitive tribal societies which were still quite isolated and had to be tackled differently and the 'family oriented approach' was most suitable for them. The Tribal sub-plan aims at an all round development with a focus on the individual family. But the most important area were those developmental schemes that would help in productivity levels in various aspects like agriculture, horticulture, animal husbandry and forestry etc. The second importance was given to Education.

It was in the Sixth Five Year Plan that besides the Tribal Sub-Plan approach, poverty alleviation programmes were initiated. They were at the family level, besides developing the infrastructural facilities. The Sixth Plan envisaged a target of 2.3 lakh families to be brought above the poverty line. But the expectation was that about 40 lakh families would be benefitted by this due to 'special efforts' of the implementation. It was realized that the tribal people cannot be developed with an 'amorphous approach' and unless family is taken as a unit not much headway can be made. But as usual, it was only a target oriented scheme and the planners were satisfied with the number of the families thus covered under the programme. What really happened is an entirely different story. There has been many studies of 'poverty alleviation programmes' and they have all shown a glaring difference between the targets achieved and the actual units covered. Even those who did receive the help were seldom in a position to use the schemes to augment/maintain their income at a minimum level of Rs. 3500/- on a continuous basis so as to remain above the poverty line. According to official hand out 41,32,460 tribal families were benefitted upto end of 1985. The targeted achievements continued to be impressive in the subsequent plans as well. If we measure the extent of tribal development in quantitative terms of the amount spent by the Central and state Goverments and the targets achieved by various programmes, we will have to admit that the progress must be tremendous in bringing about a revolutionary change in the economic condition of the Scheduled Tribes in the country. However, the situation is not so rosy. The crossing of the poverty line is expected to accrue with an investment of Rs. 10,000/- per family. As per the planning commission's own estimate, 15 lakh families including 3 lakh added during the sixth plan are already above the poverty line and 85 lakh still left to be economically assisted to cross the poverty line. For the 7th Five Year Plan about Rs. 5000 crore were envisaged to bring the rest of the families above the poverty line.

The progammes under 'family-oriented anti-poverty schemes' and 'family oriented schemes of economic assistance' have suffered badly at the hands of officials who were responsible for their implementation. The aim of the schemes was two fold-first, to provide financial and necessary help and second to make the family utilize them to become economically viable and maintain the family income above the poverty line. Neither of the two could be achieved in majority of the cases due to rampant corruption among the officials who siphoned off the money but officially fulfilled the targets. Another major reason for the non-viability of these income generation schemes was a lack of fit between the capabilities and aptitude of the beneficiary and the emphsis on commodity production. Basically 'income generation' meant commodity production except in case of wage employment or self employment. Thus, for instance, the programme for distributing milch cattle could never get off in most of the areas, because of no marketability of the commodity, or lack of expertise in dealing with it. Similarly other schemes of introducing industry, tracing of artisans etc. have been useful only in those areas that are exposed to towns and markets. Many other programmes are being gradually introduced. They are based on more realistic appraisal of the tribal people, and their locational stituation. Agriculture based schemes, forest based schemes, are such thrusts. Our purpose here is not to go into all aspects of planning, but to see the major thrusts of planning for the tribal development in the last 40 years. It clearly emerges from the perusal of the plans that there has been a slow perception of the tribal situation in the country and each Five Year Plan has led to changing strategy in the next one. It is only in Fifth Five Year Plan that a major thrust was launched and has been continued since then. For the first 25 years, planning for tribal development was amorphous and sectoral. Although each plan or study team began with the prologemna discussing the varied and heterogenous characteristics of Indian tribes, yet it was realized only after spending crores of rupees and years of time that the tribes need to have an integrated and differential pattern of development, keeping in view their ecological, economic, and socio-cultural diversity. It was also not concealed from the Government that the two most important contributory factors to the misery of most of tribal people are land alienation and restrictive forest policies. Yet they were not given serious attention either in legislation to rectify them or in their implementation by the bureaucracy. Both remain still the most important problems either by way of wholesale dispossession of the land for 'public enterprises' or 'restrictive use of forest and its products.'

In the last 45 years, however, there has been a sea change in tribal India, both due to developmental activities, as well as democratic processes. Today the tribal people are politically conscious and have an articulate leadership. They are capable of judging for themselves their place in the community of the people in the country. This has led to consciousness of their own subdued existence and is now manifesting itself in the form of 'trans-tribal ethnic formation'. The basic reason for such development is ultimately due to realization of economic disparities and deprivations through which they have gone through in the past and are still experiencing in the present. Today, the tribal people are not merely talking in terms of economic development but see it through political idiom, which in other words provides them the opportunity of taking decisions by themselves and for themselves. The reorganisation of some of the states of the North-East India is a tribute to the tribal people of India as well as to democratic framework of our country that has been consolidated greatly by Nehru's policies. The tribal societies will never be the same with the incorporation of new institutions. But one thing is clear : with the growing consciousness of ethnicity, the tribal communities are likely to maintain their identity and cultural autonomy even while participating in political and economic culture of the country by the adaptive processes of integration.

automatic dispossession of the land for public purposes, the restrictive use of forest and its products.

INDEX